ATTENTION DEFICIT DEMOCRACY

ATTENTION DEFICIT DEMOCRACY

The Paradox of Civic Engagement

BEN BERGER

PRINCETON UNIVERSITY PRESS

PRINCETON AND OXFORD

Published by Princeton University Press, 41 William Street,
Princeton, New Jersey 08540
In the United Kingdom: Princeton University Press, 6 Oxford Street,
Woodstock, Oxfordshire OX20 1TW
press.princeton.edu

Library of Congress Cataloging-in-Publication Data

Berger, Ben, 1968–
    Attention deficit democracy : the paradox of civic engagement / Ben Berger.
        p.   cm.
    Includes bibliographical references and index.
    ISBN 978-0-691-14468-9 (hardcover : alk. paper)   1. Political participation—United
States.   2. Democracy.   I. Title.
    JK1764.B465 2011
    323'.0420973—dc23   2011018236

British Library Cataloging-in-Publication Data is available

This book has been composed in Sabon
Printed on acid-free paper. ∞
Printed in the United States of America

10 9 8 6 5 4 3 2 1

CONTENTS

PREFACE

JUDITH SHKLAR NAMED Montaigne the "hero" of *Ordinary Vices* because "in spirit he is on every one of its pages, even when his name does not appear."[1] Alexis de Tocqueville is the hero here. Tocqueville, author of the justly famous *Democracy in America*, approached democracy as a well-wisher who felt compelled to illustrate its potential excesses and deficiencies, not for the sake of undermining its credibility but for the sake of promoting its success. Tocqueville's continuing relevance and resonance owe not only to his praise of democratic governance but also to his nuanced view of its limitations. He saw that democracy may require different institutions and practices in different periods and contexts, but that at root it must keep its citizens' attention and energies focused on collective affairs—not always political, but collective—enough to avoid despotism, anarchy, or gross injustice. Yet while he understood that democracy's citizens require collective action to protect their freedom from encroachment, he also grasped the pull and validity of self-interest and privatism. He grasped a central paradox of democratic freedom: citizens may freely choose disengagement, in opposition to their own long-term interests, but attempts to coerce their compliance generally fail. Tocqueville's "new political science" promoted institutions and practices that might instruct and persuade citizens about the importance of collective action. But for democracy to succeed in the long run, citizens must want what they need.

I share Tocqueville's commitments, and I approach democratic *scholarship* and *theory* in a similar manner: as a well-wisher illuminating certain foibles not for the sake of undermining democratic scholarship's credibility but for the sake of promoting its success. Democratic scholarship has fallen in love with civic engagement, an evocative and appealing term representing community, political participation, social connectedness, trust, and moral virtue that has nonetheless caused more confusion than clarity. I criticize *civic engagement* (the term, not the goals it represents) and even call for its demise, but only so it can be reborn as the constituent parts—political, social, and moral engagement—that can help us to think and talk more clearly about modern democracy. I unpack "engagement" to reveal its primary components, attention, and energy, which have been recognized as political staples since Aristotle but which have proved fickle and elusive for just as long. Thinking critically about civic engagement leads us to think critically about attention and energy. Thinking critically

[1] Shklar (1984: 1–2).

about attention and energy leads us to follow Tocqueville's example in courting those resources for essential affairs without coercing them illiberally and ineffectually.

But while this book parses *civic* engagement into *political, social,* and *moral* varieties, it focuses primarily on the political. Social engagement has been analyzed extensively already, especially in the work of Robert Putnam (under the name of civic engagement).[2] I reserve moral engagement for a separate book-length treatment. The main question in this book remains: from the perspective of political theory and political science, how good is political engagement and how far must we go to promote it? Some participatory democrats fall into a trap of assuming that we need as much political engagement as we can get, without adequately considering how much citizens want or how much it will cost. But as Tocqueville does, we too should honor the "democratic" part of democratic theory. In that spirit, I aspire not to tell citizens what they ought to want and what they must do but help them to consider their goals' hidden costs and then achieve their considered goals more effectively. I remain committed to political engagement personally, and I oppose its restriction from any citizens who desire it. But because promoting political engagement will require costly outreach, innovation, and institutional reform, we must do a better job of assessing its value and of considering whom political disengagement harms most. In particular, we must resist romantic notions of politics' intrinsic worth that at best defy demonstration and at worst court paternalism. Political engagement does matter, and democracy requires it, but how much and from whom? By doing more with our existing political attention and energy—eliciting more attention and energy to politics through suasion, education, and other voluntary means—and by reaching out to those citizens most likely to be hurt by political disengagement, we can get what we want and need from democratic government while preserving the freedom to do *without* politics for those who choose it.

Not long ago many observers feared that almost everyone would choose the latter freedom, and democracy would dissolve into what Tocqueville had called "license or tyranny."[3] In the year 2000, Putnam's chronicle of forty years' declining social capital and civic engagement resonated widely with scholars and citizens alike.[4] In 2008 Sheldon Wolin criticized the surface appearance, or "myth," of democracy that gilds a more sinister phenomenon of foreclosed public discourse and

[2] Putnam (1995, 1996, 2000).
[3] Tocqueville (1969: 735). Hereafter *DA*.
[4] Putnam (2000).

"inverted totalitarianism."[5] But while Putnam was pointing out valid, discouraging, long-term trends, Carmen Sirianni and Lewis Friedland were tracking a decade-long movement of "civic renewal" and a potentially rosier future for participatory democracy.[6] And while Wolin was lamenting the end of public discourse, Barack Obama was electrifying citizens—not only via television but in town hall meetings and mobilization efforts modeled on grassroots organizing—and ultimately winning a historic, and historically participatory, national election. Myriad newspaper stories, magazine articles, and weblogs praised Obama's message of hope and change, some claiming that his extensive outreach (and use of the Internet) had redeemed the promise of participatory democracy.[7]

Thus we see democracy portrayed simultaneously as on the ropes and on the rebound. Both portrayals have their appeals. When we look closely at engagement and pay attention to its constituent parts, we see that democracies throughout history—not just in the United States, but dating back to ancient Greece—have almost always struggled to focus their attention and energies on political affairs. When fully free to prioritize commerce, luxuries, leisure, entertainment, or family life over politics, citizens often do. Democracy can suffer. But American democracy has also featured more resilience than critics have anticipated. We citizens, free to opt out of politics, have evolved forms of engagement that may serve as functional substitutes for a time. More importantly, at intervals we have refocused our attention and energies on politics to foment for causes of deep concern.[8] James Fallows characterizes our repeated political valleys and peaks, and our repeated expressions of despair and hope, as a uniquely American "cycle of crisis and renewal."[9] Indeed, from a fever pitch in 2008 even the so-called Obama revolution has flagged, with rough-and-tumble politics replacing campaign enthusiasm, an economic recession continuing unabated, and complex, partisan policy debates tiring all but the most ardent political junkies.[10] Yet while political engagement on the left faded, a more populist and libertarian Tea Party

[5] Wolin (2008). For a similarly timed protest against "monocratic" government that has subverted true democracy while citizens turn the other way, see Meyers (2008).

[6] Sirianni and Friedland (2001).

[7] On the opposing side, many Republicans were mobilized by Sarah Palin's personal charisma and some by opposition to Obama.

[8] According to Samuel Huntington, American politics have been characterized by "an overall pattern of political continuity and equilibrium, occasionally interrupted"—every three or four decades—"by the intrusion of passion, moralism, intensified conflict, reform, and realignment." Huntington (1983: 130).

[9] Fallows (2010).

[10] Kennedy-Shaffer (2009).

movement mobilized around opposition to governmental activism.[11] In contrast to the 2008 general elections, marked by Democratic energy, the 2010 midterm elections evinced an "unprecedented level of political engagement by Republicans."[12]

I mention these cycles to suggest that from the perspective of achieving our participatory potential we are neither so imminently endangered as the most dystopic writers fear nor so newly enhanced as Obama's most ardent admirers had hoped. Democracy's attention deficit, which has persevered on and off from ancient times to the present, probably cannot be cured but certainly can be treated. (By "attention deficit" I refer to the reality that most citizens enduringly pay much less attention to political issues and action than most theorists' ideals have prescribed.) Understanding that limitation might chasten those who are tempted to increase political engagement by coercing it, abandoning liberalism, and might bolster those who are tempted to throw up their hands, abandoning democracy. The purpose here is to diagnose our limitations for the sake of progress that is both liberal and democratic.

•   •   •   •   •

This book's roots date back to the late 1990s, when I was a graduate student at Harvard University. I served as one of many assistants for Robert Putnam's landmark study, *Bowling Alone* (2000); his intellectual creativity and amazingly broad scope of inquiry inspired my own investigations. It was around that time when I began conceptualizing democracy—not just the American variety, but extending back to ancient Greece—as *attention deficit* democracy, a form of government that almost always makes observers wish that its constituents would attend to politics more closely and that almost always disappoints the critics' desires. At the 1999 Midwest Political Science Association conference I presented a paper on Alexis de Tocqueville's anticipation of "attention deficit democracy," although the concept was still inchoate in my mind. At the same time, while studying democracy's ups and downs I saw how closely linked the term *civic engagement* had become with conceptions of democracy's well-being, and yet how few people could agree on its

[11]The Tea Party" movement represents a uniquely American phenomenon: political activism aimed at quelling political activism (or, at any rate, governmental activism). As opposed to some Obama activists who hoped that the 2008 election would increase political engagement broadly and enduringly, Tea Party participants evince a more circumscribed aim. Their activism seems to accord with Hibbing and Theiss-Morse's (2002: 2, 130) findings that many Americans do not want more political influence or political engagement but "just do not want decision makers to be able to take advantage of them," and will occasionally mobilize simply to enforce the "most intense desire" not to be treated as "suckers."

[12]Silver (2010).

definition. Through the intervening years I continued to marvel at civic engagement's growth, influence, and fuzziness. As this book developed I linked the concerns about (1) democracy's continuing struggles with attention, and (2) civic engagement's continuing struggles with clarity, even among those who studied and promoted it.

Several years ago I was chatting with the executive officer of a prominent nonprofit organization dedicated to promoting responsible citizenship on college campuses. The executive reflected on the organization's recent success at "introducing college students to civic engagement." She paused and then added, "whatever that means." As we laughed together I knew that the time for my book had arrived.

Many friends and colleagues have given valuable aid at various stages of this project's development: Rob Mickey, Jennifer Pitts, Sankar Muthu, Patchen Markell, Michaele Ferguson, Sharon Krause, Bryan Garsten, Tamara Metz, Seth Green, Russ Muirhead, Michael Sandel, Harvey Mansfield, Robert Putnam, and Peter Berkowitz, among others. Andy Sabl and Sandy Green deserve special thanks for the countless hours they spent talking through ideas and interpretations, reading drafts, and lending moral support. Ian Malcolm at Princeton University Press has been the platonic ideal of a scholarly editor, as all who have worked with him already know.

Swarthmore's Lang Center for Civic and Social Responsibility has generously funded me as I developed my community-based learning courses, which have broadened my understanding of democracy's promises and challenges and improved this book in the process. Thanks also go to Project Pericles and to Swarthmore College for supporting my teaching and my scholarship, which have always enriched each other.

I am grateful to my family, on both the Berger and the Morton side, for helping to keep me grounded, and to my children, Harry, Arnie, and Tess—all born during the period that I worked on this book—for sweetening my life even as they contributed to my own attention deficit. Finally, I extend great love and gratitude to my wife, Debra Morton, a talented filmmaker, exceptional mother, and affectionate partner whose patience knows few bounds.

ATTENTION DEFICIT DEMOCRACY

Chapter 1

INTRODUCTION

Pay attention to matters of importance.
  —Diogenes Laërtius, *The Life of Solon*

Habitual inattention must be reckoned the great vice of
the democratic spirit.
  —Alexis de Tocqueville, *Democracy in America*

THIS BOOK ABOUT what Americans do and think begins by analyzing how we talk and write. The premise is that language matters; our choice of words may reflect or even affect our frames of
mind. To borrow from Max Weber, humans are "suspended in webs of
significance that [we ourselves have] spun," ensnared in the logic that our
choice of words dictates.[1] Such is the case with civic engagement. Born of
a movement to analyze, promote, and possibly save democracy, nurtured
with the best of intentions, the term *civic engagement* has grown out of
control and has outlived its purpose, sowing more confusion than clarity. However, this book not only exposes the confusion but also turns it
to our advantage. Acknowledging the problems with civic engagement
terminology prompts us to examine it more closely, and a closer look can
yield fresh insight into the unarticulated values and anxieties that have
contributed to the term's popularity. Through that exercise we can recognize more clearly the resources—especially attention and energy—that
frequently flee from the public sphere and civil society but that must be
protected and promoted for democracy's sake. Thus we can learn from
civic engagement even as we bid it goodbye.

Indeed, civic engagement as we know it is ready for retirement. That
judgment might surprise the scholars, journalists, educators, and community leaders for whom civic engagement has become a household word.
Since Robert Putnam first popularized the term in his 1993 political science classic, *Making Democracy Work*, it has spread through the pages of
newspapers, Internet sites, academic books and journals, and mainstream

---

[1] Clifford Geertz attributed this widely cited line of thinking to Weber. Geertz interprets
the self-spun web to denote culture, but language and rhetoric fit the metaphor just as aptly.
Geertz (1973: 5).

political discourse.[2] Politicians praise it; foundations fund its study and implementation; educational institutions encourage their students to undertake it.[3] Nongovernmental organizations (NGOs) promote it in developing democracies. But like other buzzwords civic engagement means so many things to so many people that it clarifies almost nothing. Thus I come to bury civic engagement, not to praise it.

Scholars use civic engagement to describe activities ranging from bowling in leagues to watching political television shows, writing checks to political advocacy groups, and participating in political rallies and marches.[4] For many journalists, public officials, and political activists civic engagement can mean everything from charitable giving to associational membership, political participation, artistic expression, or community service.[5] Some maintain that civic engagement has declined in the United States and other liberal democracies over the past forty years. Others disagree, contending that civic engagement has simply changed its shapes and forms.[6] We cannot easily judge these disputes because their advocates employ such disparate standards, using civic engagement to describe entirely different things. The conflicting parties do agree on one point: whatever civic engagement is, we need as much as we can get.[7] But they are confused about its meaning and wrong about its value.

To be clear, no particular individual or group bears the blame for our terminological confusion. Despite the best of intentions we have inadvertently fallen into a linguistic trap by choosing flexible, broad terminology. Different thinkers have stretched the popular terms in their own desired directions, none of them violating rules of logic or grammar in the process. But the result has been many concerned friends of democracy talking past one another. Rather than blame those who have been trapped by civic engagement—which means all of us involved with its study and scholarship—we should disarm the trap and start afresh.

In that spirit this book advocates the end of civic engagement. Not the end of political participation, social connectedness, associational

[2] Among political theorists see, for example, Barber (1984 and 1998); Cohen and Arato (1992); Sandel (1996); Fishkin (1997); and Gastil and Levine (2005). Among political scientists see Putnam, Leonardi, and Nanetti (1993); Putnam (2000); and Skocpol and Fiorina (1999). Among sociologists and historians see Oldenburg (2001) and Ehrenhalt (1995).

[3] In January of 2002 an Internet search for the term *civic engagement* using the Google search engine returned approximately 15,000 results. By January of 2011 the number exceeded 3.9 million.

[4] Putnam (1995: 65–78); Schudson (1996: 17–27); Ladd (1999a); Barber (1998: 47–53).

[5] Connolly (2006); Tillotson (2006); McGann and Johnstone (2006).

[6] See, for example, Schudson (1998) and Ladd (1999a) for arguments that civic engagement has not declined but has been overlooked and misidentified.

[7] As one among many examples of tremendously broad endorsements: "Civic engagement is one of the most important instruments in democracy." Maiello, Oser, and Biedermann (2003: 384).

membership, voluntarism, community spirit, or cooperative and tolerant moral norms but rather the umbrella term, *civic engagement*, used to encompass all of those topics while clarifying none. Civic engagement as it is currently used includes political, social, and moral components, or the entire "kitchen sink" of public and private goods. It exemplifies Giovanni Sartori's concern about "conceptual stretching," or "the distortion that occurs when a concept, applied to new cases, does not fit the new cases."[8] The stakes go beyond mere semantics. Words frame our debates, shape our research agendas, and affect the ways in which we view the world. When our words yield "vague, amorphous conceptualizations" rather than widely accessible concepts—concepts that mean something similar for most people most of the time—we cannot easily study, operationalize, or discuss the social and political phenomena that surround us.[9] In conversations about "making democracy work"—the subject of Putnam's landmark work and also this book's overarching theme—civic engagement confuses more than it illuminates, and hence it must go.

Yet only half of the term merits early retirement. We should put *civic* to rest while coming to grips with *engagement*. Civic simply means that a subject pertains to citizenship or a city, so it can easily be subsumed under the rubric of *political* without any loss of conceptual clarity.[10] In fact, clarity prevails when we stop stretching civic to mean sociable, helpful, or trusting, as so often happens in civic engagement scholarship. But *engagement* possesses untapped potential, and part of my purpose is to tap it. Engagement is a uniquely appropriate term for discussing ways of making democracy work, but only if we understand its full significance. At present we do not. Literally, engagement entails a combination of attention and energy (or activity), the two primary components of political governance or any intensely interactive relationship.[11] And while civic engagement is this book's nominal subject, attention and energy are its informal stars. When we worry about declining engagement, which we have done at increasing rates over the past fifteen years, we are worrying about the elusiveness of our attention and energy—and well we might.[12] Since the era

---

[8] Sartori (1970: 1034); Collier and Mahon Jr. (1993: 848). Democracy, for example, connotes widely divergent attributes in different scenarios, but scholars continue to use that single, stretched concept to describe divergent phenomena, and hence they talk past one another.

[9] Sartori (1970: 1034).

[10] Civic. Definitions 1a and 2a. *Oxford English Dictionary*, 2nd ed., 1989.

[11] Engagement can also denote an act or a condition, the act of engaging or the condition of being engaged. This presents difficulties for political science and political theory analyses, as I will discuss later in this book.

[12] Throughout this book I use the terms *energy* and *activity* interchangeably because activity is an actualization of our potential energy. They are not perfect synonyms, of course, but many other writers—ranging from contemporary scholars to canonical political theorists—use energy in precisely this sense: as an individual power (*dunamis*, in Aristotle's

of ancient Greece, democracies have struggled to maintain these same resources. Attention involves selectively focusing one's wits on subjects that generate special interest or demand redress; activity involves following through on the subjects attended to, investing energy in their maintenance or resolution.[13] Democracy's citizens must indeed be engaged, which is to say attentive and active. But attentive to what? Active in which ways? That vague designation, "civic," gives us little indication.

When sociologists laud civic engagement they commonly mean what I call *social* or *moral* engagement, people's attention and energies invested in social groups and networks or focused on moral reasoning and follow-through. When political theorists and political scientists laud civic engagement they often focus on what I call *political* engagement, people's attention to and activity in political issues and processes. These issues and processes require interaction with organs of the polity at any level of government. But democracy may flourish with only middling levels of political engagement if it is rich in social and moral engagement. That possibility goes against the belief, common among participatory democrats, that we need as much political attention and activity as we can get. Rather than disparage political engagement, we should recognize the costs as well as the benefits of promoting it and should remember that democracy requires a variety of dispositions, values, and behaviors.[14] We should be asking which kinds of engagement—political, social, or moral—make democracy work, and how they might be promoted. Civic engagement (should be) dead; long live political, social, and moral engagement.[15]

The concern with making democracy work spans the history of political theory and political science, from ancient Greece to the present day. Aristotle, Rousseau, Madison, and Tocqueville all stress the importance of an attentive and energetically active citizenry. But (as I also advocate) they distinguish among different kinds of attention and activity; they understand that not all engagement is political, that social and moral engagement are equally vital to democracy's health, and that the three may

---

terminology) to be actualized in dynamic activity (*energeia*, in Aristotle). Aristotle, *De Anima* (1988: 412a22-8) and *Nicomachean Ethics* (1985: 1153a10).

[13] James (1890: 404). For a more contemporary account see Cohen and Magen (2005).

[14] The costs to which I refer include the sheer monetary cost of increasing political participation among a reluctant citizenry, whether through revitalized citizenship education, paid holidays for public deliberation (Ackerman and Fishkin 2004), or other forms of outreach, which I discuss in chapter 6. They also include the costs to individual freedom incurred by attempts to coerce political engagement through such initiatives as mandatory public service or compulsory voting (Lijphart 1997).

[15] Others have recognized that civic engagement is too broad, and one set of scholars takes the promising but incomplete step of distinguishing between *civic* and *political* engagement. Zukin et al. (2006). However, for reasons discussed below their distinction does not resolve the difficulties it sets out to remedy.

stand in tension with one another. Too many present-day scholars, politicians, educators, and community activists ignore this critical approach and wrongly assume that participation in political processes and institutions, participation in social dynamics and networks, and participation in tolerant, responsible, moral agency always go together—lumped conveniently under the umbrella term *civic engagement*—and that to promote any of them is to promote all three.

But in fact they are distinct. Political engagement means activity and attention relating to the political processes and political institutions of local, regional, or national government. It can include voting, seeking or holding public office, attending town hall meetings, circulating a petition—any engagement whose purpose is to influence state actors and political outcomes.[16] Social engagement means activity and attention relating to social groups, dynamics, and norms. It can include myriad involvements ranging from Putnam's bowling leagues to parenting groups to friendship circles, all of which are often categorized as civic engagement although they have no obvious connection to citizenship or the polis. Moral engagement means attention and activity relating to moral reasoning and moral agency.[17] And while these different kinds of engagement can accompany one another—political engagement can involve social and moral components, for example—they need not do so.[18]

Political and social engagement can coexist with an absence of moral engagement—what the political theorist Hannah Arendt calls "thoughtlessness," or a failure to "think what we are doing"—as in the cases of nationalist extremism, religiously inspired terrorism, and racial supremacists' hate groups.[19] Conversely, tolerant, charitable, and socially engaged

---

[16] Here I draw upon Weber's definition of the state as "a human community that (successfully) claims the monopoly of the legitimate use of physical force within a given territory," and politics as "striving to share power or striving to influence the distribution of power either among states or among groups within a state." Max Weber, "Politics as a Vocation," in Weber (2007: 78). Power itself comprises a controversial subject, but an all-encompassing definition is not necessary for present purposes.

[17] These definitions raise more questions than they answer; I will address some of the relevant questions in chapter 2.

[18] Social engagement always involves at least some kind of moral engagement, an underlying consciousness of the appropriate norms of behavior. Most political engagement involves at least some kind of moral engagement, as well, an underlying consciousness of the appropriate goals to pursue through political action. But my category of moral engagement involves a more demanding kind of moral attention and energetic follow-through, in which moral reasoning is brought to the forefront. Further, some moral codes and moral reasoning are more appropriate for liberal democracies than others. Hitler's inner circle may have been morally engaged but with a kind of moral reasoning incompatible with liberal democracy.

[19] Arendt (1963). Technically, Arendt's "thoughtlessness" describes total disengagement from moral reasoning. But as noted above, virtually everyone engaged in political or social dynamics participates in some moral code and exercises moral agency, although the moral

individuals may eschew political participation but still contribute to democracy's success. And very high levels of political engagement, in the absence of essential democratic ingredients such as responsive political institutions, can engender violent instability and jeopardize public safety.[20] Civic engagement enthusiasts often overlook these vital nuances.

My goal is to make democracy work better rather than make it work ideally. This book inquires into democracy's core requirements—those conditions that it must have (or avoid) in order to work at all—before positing its ideal features.[21] Citizens might disagree about the latter because reasonable people hold divergent ideals, but we can probably agree upon the phenomena that make democracy fail: for example, rampant lawlessness, weak or unresponsive political institutions, capture of government by unrepresentative factions, or citizens widely unable to communicate, cooperate, or compromise.[22] Grounding ourselves in "guarding against the worst" lets us ground ourselves with a measure of consensus.[23] But beginning with the worst does not mean dwelling on it exclusively. It leaves ample room for a chastened idealism that strives to achieve not the best but a variety of goods—not a single, greatest good that fits everyone equally but a framework in which individuals and communities can pursue pluralistic goals and values, including the values of individualism and communal cohesion.[24]

---

codes with which they engage may not be compatible with liberal democracy. Further, Arendt's activity of "thinking," a kind of moral reasoning, involves temporary withdrawal from the world of action. Chapter 2 of this book discusses these matters further.

[20] See, for example, Bermeo (2003) and Armony (2004) for detailed chronicles of democracies or democratizing nations in which high and widespread political engagement accompanied instability, violence, and, at times, the end of democracy.

[21] For an excellent explanation of this core/ideal distinction, applied to liberal virtues, see Sabl (2005b: 207–35). See also Shklar, "The Liberalism of Fear" in Shklar and Hoffmann (1998: 3–21).

[22] Like Shklar I "begin with what must be avoided," but I broaden the scope of ills to include not only "the worst" but also the very bad. We must avoid totalitarianism, slavery, organized cruelty, and constant fear of the preceding—which are awful but not terribly likely in most Western democracies—and also radical atomization, enforced marginalization, and systematic unfairness (denying certain people or groups a reasonable chance of achieving goals their fellow citizens take for granted). The latter type of deprivation pales in comparison with the former but would be shunned by any who take liberal democratic values seriously. See Allen (2004) for a vivid account of twentieth-century forced marginalization in the southern United States and its incompatibility with democratic ideals.

[23] Rosenblum (1998b: 48). Robert Dahl posits a similar aim and rationale: "Because it is easier to discover ways of reducing inequality than ways of achieving perfect equality (whatever that might mean), an advanced democratic country would focus on the reduction of the remediable causes of gross political inequalities." Dahl (1989: 323).

[24] Martin Krygier proposes "Hobbesian idealism" that begins with the worst but then "thinks simultaneously about avoiding evil and about pursuing good; about threat, about promise, and about their interplay." Krygier (2005: 148).

This book advocates clear terms and discourse, and to follow those standards I must clarify what I mean by democracy. Just as civic engagement has been stretched to the point where it means almost anything to anyone, so too democracy carries numerous connotations. This book analyzes engagement in modern, representative democracies as opposed to face-to-face direct democracy, possible only in small communities. Modern, representative democracies are also liberal democracies, polities committed to individual rights and dignity as well as to any perceived public good. We must specify liberalism because democracy by itself— majority rule—can involve illiberal coercion, excessive paternalism, or stultifying social conformity unless citizens and officials uphold legal and constitutional protections vigilantly. Liberal democrats value autonomy and choice, but that very autonomy means that citizens may disengage politically if they choose.[25] What are the stakes? How should democracy respond?

Democracy would not be democracy, rule of the people, without at least a modicum of political attention and activity from its citizens. But beyond the core requirement of avoiding radical disengagement, what value does political engagement promise to individuals and communities and how much of it does liberal democracy require? Scholars commonly assume that we need as much political engagement as we can get, that more politically engaged democracies are healthier than others, and that modest declines in political engagement should give us cause for grave concern. Some of the most common arguments in this vein either disregard empirical evidence or otherwise fail to convince. Political engagement may still hold great value, but we must do a better job of defining and defending it.[26]

Viewing political engagement as a combination of attention and energetic activity helps us to understand its value as well as the reasons why democracies often struggle with deficits. Attention and energy are essential to intensive, cooperative undertakings yet are difficult to attract and sustain. That dilemma gives rise to the other half of this book's title. Some scholars assume that citizens would pay close attention to politics were it not for assorted, confounding influences—the baffling complexity

---

[25] By granting citizens the freedom to reject the very practices that led to liberalism's success, "liberalism itself . . . bears no small responsibility for the stiff challenge it now faces." Berkowitz (1999: 174).

[26] Others have argued convincingly that normative theory cannot dispense with empirical evidence. See, for example, Dennis Thompson (1970). Thompson criticizes the trend toward "prescriptivism," which attempts to construct normative democratic theory without input from empirical social science. He also criticizes the opposite extreme, "descriptivism," which assumes that empirical evidence can simply "disprove" any normative claim or ideal. My stance resembles Thompson's.

of modern politics or the pressures of time and money, for example.[27] According to this line of thinking, as the sociologist Robert Bellah has written, "democracy means paying attention."[28] That view is mistaken. Democracy means, and in practice has always meant, citizens struggling to pay attention and invest energy politically.[29] In other words, to say democracy is to say attention deficit—at least, a deficit between theorists' ideals of political attentiveness and activity, and citizens' actual priorities and practices. Unlike its modern-day association, "attention deficit disorder," attention deficit democracy is simply a diagnosis rather than a malady. The diagnosis need not be a counsel of despair, but if it goes unacknowledged our political theories will be at odds with our choices and capacities.

Democracy's attention deficit is certainly nothing new. Even ancient Athens, widely regarded as a paragon of participatory democracy, saw its political pretensions skewered by the comic poet Aristophanes: "Here, on one of the Assembly days—broad day, too!—not a soul is in place! They're gossiping in the market, shifting here and there to dodge the long rope's red paint smear."[30]

Athenians so often preferred gossip to deliberative politics that the city's soldiers employed "red-dyed ropes . . . to chase citizens from the Agora [marketplace] towards the half-filled assembly."[31] Being roped meant entanglement and also embarrassment; the telltale red stains invited ridicule and a fine. In subsequent years Athenians began paying a daily stipend for political participation, and in Aristophanes' later play, *Ekklesiazousai*, soldiers used the same red-dyed ropes to keep citizens out of the overflowing assembly.[32] That stipend apparently compensated for any boredom.[33] But neither scenario—neither the gossiping derelicts

[27] See, for example, Dewey (1935).

[28] Bellah et al. (1992: 255).

[29] Not only modern, liberal democracies but also ancient, direct democracies have struggled with this problem.

[30] *Acharnians*, in Aristophanes (1927: 19–23). The play dates to 425 BC.

[31] Hansen (1987: 18). Scholars estimate the average attendance level of an Athenian assembly (*ekklesia*) at between 20 percent and 40 percent of the total citizenry, but some interpret this range as indicating fairly high interest in politics given the relative frequency of the assemblies (nearly one per week). See Ober (1991: 132).

[32] *Ekklesiazousai*, in Aristophanes (1927). The play dates to 392 or 393 BC. "Without this stipend, poorer men would have found it hard to leave their regular work to serve in these time-consuming positions." Martin (2000: 113).

[33] "The poorest of the citizens—the old, handicapped, unlucky and unskilled—might well attend the Assembly regularly as a way to collect money not otherwise available to them." Ober (1991: 136). Note that not all citizens who participated were motivated by the money, and the stipend may well attest to Athens's egalitarian commitments rather than a concession to low attendance. Martin (2000).

nor the mercenary attendees—suggests the presence of an independently attentive demos.

More than two thousand years later democracy had changed locations but not its ability to focus. Alexis de Tocqueville, now widely (but wrongly) regarded as an unqualified enthusiast for American civic engagement, observed a potential problem with New World democracy. He remarked that the average American citizen "does everything in a hurry . . . he hardly has the time, and he soon loses the taste, for going deeply into anything."[34] Absent the distractions of a high-tech environment or the pressures of a heavily industrialized economy, Tocqueville still witnessed a "habitual preoccupation" with private affairs that left each individual "concerned with several aims at the same time." He considered ancient as well as modern democracies and concluded that "habitual inattention must be reckoned the great vice of the democratic spirit."[35]

In the early twentieth century attention and energy once again took center stage in the still-influential Dewey-Lippmann debate. American philosopher John Dewey argued that universal education, a civically educational media, and thoroughgoing economic reform could promote awareness of mutual interests, direct attention toward public affairs, and "release human energy for pursuit of higher values."[36] As a result "the average individual would rise to undreamed of heights of social and political intelligence," and citizens could collectively direct their governments and destinies.[37] Public intellectual Walter Lippmann countered that modern society presents a bafflingly complex political environment and criticized Dewey for promoting a "myth" of the "omnicompetent citizen."[38] In spite of any educational reforms, most citizens "even if they had genius, would give only a little time and attention to public affairs."[39] Lippmann proposed much more modest goals for democratic politics, offering "a theory which economizes the attention of men as members of the public, and . . . confines the effort of men, when they are a public, to

---

[34] Tocqueville (1969: 611).

[35] Ibid. Dana Villa (2008) has pointed out that Tocqueville did not witness and could not fully grasp the possibility of corporate and global capitalism, which may have done more toward crowding out the role of citizens than even big government has done. Even with that point granted, however, Tocqueville did notice Americans' frequent inattention to politics, especially outside of the tiny New England area that he praised so highly. He also bemoaned the increasing influence of economic power and commercialism on American culture and politics. See Craiutu and Jennings (2004: 398). More on these points in chapter 4.

[36] Dewey (1935: 90).

[37] Ibid., 70.

[38] Lippmann (1925: 21). Although Dewey wrote *Liberalism and Social Action* after Lippmann's *Phantom Public*, the quotes presented here are illustrative of the two theorists' long-standing debate. See also Lippmann (1929) and Dewey (1927).

[39] Lippmann (1925: 127).

a part they might fulfill." The appropriate part for citizens would involve action "only when there is a crisis of maladjustment," and even then it would simply entail choosing among competing elites.[40]

Present-day scholars tend to endorse one of these two arguments while ignoring the rich terrain in between. To generalize broadly, Dewey has won the day in educational studies and political theory and among those who advocate a "participatory" model of democracy. Lippmann holds more currency among economists, political scientists who study voting behavior, and those who advocate an elite model of democracy.[41] In analyzing what causes political disengagement and whether greater participation is desirable or possible, I steer a middle course between Dewey's excessive optimism and Lippmann's undue pessimism, between the participatory and elite models of democracy, while confronting similar problems of limited political attention and energy.

To be fair, empirical political scientists have done a better job than normative political theorists of acknowledging citizens' limited political attention. But political scientists focus almost exclusively on limited attention's implications for voting behavior and public opinion, which constitute only a small bit of what political theorists consider the meat of democratic political engagement.[42] This book attempts to combine some of each camp's strengths: a clear-eyed acknowledgment of citizens' limited political attention and the implications for democratic politics, extended to include the many varieties of political engagement beyond episodic voting and political awareness.

Thus far I have focused primarily on attention, but citizens' energies are equally important. Much has been written about democracies' need for so-called social capital, which denotes "features of social organization, such as trust, norms, and networks, that can improve the efficiency of society by facilitating coordinated actions."[43] When we participate in voluntary associations and other cooperative endeavors—when we are socially engaged—we can develop interpersonal relationships that fa-

---

[40] Ibid., 199.

[41] The participatory (or deliberative) model insists that for democracy to merit its name, well-informed citizens must actively participate in political deliberation and decision-making. The elite (or pragmatic) model envisions modern politics as the province of well-trained elites who are periodically checked by competitive elections. For more on the debate between the participatory and elite models, see Posner (2003). For prominent arguments of the former type, see Pateman (1970); Gutmann (1987); Fishkin (1991); and Leib (2005). For prominent arguments in the latter group, see Converse (1964); Zaller (1992); Somin (1998); and Caplan (2007).

[42] Political scientists considering limited attention generally ask whether a politically inattentive citizenry can comprise a rational and self-governing public. Converse (1964), Somin (1998), and Kuklinski and Quirk (2000) consider evidence to the contrary, whereas Popkin (1994) and Lupia and McCubbins (1998) present more optimistic arguments.

[43] Putnam (1993: 167).

cilitate further cooperation.[44] We can draw upon social capital as well, just as we draw upon financial capital, to help us achieve individual or collective goals; we can channel social capital into political outlets and institutions, thus facilitating specifically political goals.[45] But we cannot generate social capital in the first place without moving beyond passive attention to invest our energies in cooperative endeavors and thus forge useful relationships, bonds, and reciprocal norms.

I will advance an original argument about the relationship among attention, energy, and citizens' tastes. Attention generally precedes energetic activity; if a topic does not capture our attention it will not enduringly attract our energy. So to attract our energy and form social or political capital, a subject must first attract and hold our attention. Attention, in turn, is shaped by many factors, including ideology, habituation, culture, and perceived threats or dangers. But it is also strongly influenced by individual taste, and as the old saying goes there is no accounting for that. So to a greater extent than many scholars acknowledge, attention follows tastes and energy follows attention.

Tastes → Attention → Energy → Social and Political Capital

Perceived self-efficacy—one's ability to succeed at a given endeavor and make a meaningful impact—can also affect tastes and attention, as Tocqueville recognized. More on that in chapter 4.[46] We pay attention to things that we like, sometimes at the expense of our own long-term interests. All of us know hobbyists, sports fans, or even video game enthusiasts who focus raptly on trivialities (and invest substantial energy) while ignoring policy debates that could vitally affect their futures.

In other words, having an interest does not always mean taking an interest. Having a stake in an outcome does not mean that we attend to it.

[44] Social capital represents a potentially useful but confusing construct, because it refers not only to the norms—such as trust and reciprocity—already present in social organizations or movements but also to the relationships that people can build when they join social organizations or movements. The first kind of social capital helps people to build the second kind, but the second kind also helps to build the first kind. Which one comes first? That question has been examined in other studies and lies beyond the scope of the present analysis.

[45] "Like other forms of capital, social capital is productive, making possible the achievement of certain ends that would not be attainable in its absence. . . . For example, a group whose members manifest trustworthiness and place extensive trust in one another will be able to accomplish much more than a comparable group lacking that trustworthiness and trust. . . . In a farming community . . . where one farmer got his hay baled by another and where farm tools are extensively borrowed and lent, the social capital allows each farmer to get his work done with less physical capital in the form of tools and equipment." Coleman, *Foundations of Social Theory* (1990: 302, 304, 307), cited in Putnam (1993).

[46] For social psychological research in perceived self-efficacy and engagement, see Bandura (1977 and 1997). For efficacy and students' attention and engagement, see Linnenbrink and Pintrich (2003).

When democratic citizens can do as they like, politics seldom fares well in the taste test. Not only now but also in most previous eras political affairs have attracted citizens' enduring attention only when faced with few and boring competitors.[47] Nonetheless, understanding our capacities and proclivities equips us to think about effective responses to disengagement. That is exactly what this book aims to do: diagnose democracy's tendencies and limitations and then prescribe pragmatic means of making democracy work better.

Thus the diagnosis of attention deficit democracy also entails a kind of public philosophy, a set of beliefs that "specify general directions for public policy within a basic understanding of how the world works."[48] In other words, the diagnosis plus the prescriptive directions that follow from it—which I will detail in chapter 6—comprise the public philosophy of attention deficit democracy. Some public philosophies are formulated from the top down, meaning that they are held by politically active intellectuals who hope to guide the public's practices and institutions.[49] Examples include the worthy political theories of deliberative democracy and civic republicanism. Self-described deliberative democrats, giving priority to political equality and democratic legitimacy, generally insist upon widespread participation in deliberative political forums, with procedures that prioritize reason over narrow interests and conditions that guarantee all an equal voice.[50] Self-described civic republicans, for the sake of meaningful political liberty and self-governance, tend to stress an ideal of active citizenship and civic virtue more than reason-based deliberation. They insist upon greater citizen control over "the forces that govern our lives" and greater participation in timely moral and political debates.[51] Other theorists concerned with public freedom exhort citizens to assert themselves, exercise their full prerogatives as citizens, and hold governments as well as corporations fully accountable for their actions.[52] But as William Galston reasonably cautions, "given most Americans' ambivalence about

---

[47] "Men may be frustrated in their primary activities [involving work, play, love, family, friendship and the like] without ever turning to politics for solutions . . . since the primary activities are voracious in their demands for time, political activity must enter into competition with them. For most people it is evidently a weak competitor." Dahl (1961: 180).

[48] Galston (1998: 64).

[49] Ibid.

[50] Fishkin (1997); Weeks (2000); Gabardi (2001); Ackerman and Fishkin (2004).

[51] Sandel (1996); Barber (1998). Not all civic republicans emphasize participation and moral deliberation; see, for example, Pettit (1997). Here I am concerned with the more participatory version. For more on the varieties of civic republicanism, see Honohan (2002) and Berger (2010).

[52] Villa (2008: 25) writes that "the only way of combating this bogus inevitability [of overreaching, emergency-power governments doing whatever they like] is to reclaim our capacity for action as citizens, rather than as members of single-issue focused interest groups." Meyers (2008: 264–66) insists that a renewed dedication to active citizenship remains our only means of resisting overly ambitious and possibly malicious governments.

the place of political activities in their lives, it remains to be seen whether ideals of a more engaged and demanding citizenship can gain public support and become the basis of an effective new public philosophy."[53] Top-down public philosophies can play a valuable role in our political discourse, proffering ideals and goals toward which we might strive. As political theories they may have much to recommend them; they prescribe what Dennis Thompson has called "reconstructive ideals," without which political philosophy would lack imagination or vision.[54] However, such reconstructive theories rely upon a majority of citizens adopting practices and commitments that most have tended to regard with distaste when regarding them at all. So for the foreseeable future these public philosophies are far more philosophical than public.

Attention deficit democracy, conversely, points to an accessible public philosophy, a set of ideas about the public that is embraced by the public as well.[55] It summarizes the belief that marshaling continual, widespread political attention and energy is nearly impossible, but that we can and should do more with our collective resources than we have in recent years. Rather than implying cynical resignation, attention deficit democracy entails an enlightened and chastened idealism that pragmatically battles democracy's ever-present tendencies toward privatism. It prescribes what Thompson calls "constructive ideals," or improvements that could be implemented without foundationally restructuring society or the citizenry.[56] It eschews utopian plans not out of pessimism but rather to focus on the concrete steps by which we can fight the costs of preventable disengagement.

A surprising number of canonical political theorists agree with my empirical diagnosis. For example, Jean-Jacques Rousseau, Alexis de Tocqueville, John Dewey, and Hannah Arendt, all commonly perceived as participatory enthusiasts, recognize that free societies will struggle to muster and maintain political attention and activity. But they do not develop the implications of their observations, so their uneasiness generally goes unnoticed even by the scholars who celebrate their work. Recovering this aspect of our philosophical tradition—philosophers' underappreciated unease about the challenges of sustaining political attention and energetic

---

[53] Galston (1998: 79). Galston here addresses deliberative democracy but his comment could just as easily apply to civic republicanism.

[54] Thompson (1970).

[55] John R. Hibbing and Elizabeth Theiss-Morse (2002: 183) find that "in contrast to theorists' speculations," a vast amount of survey data indicates that "people's dislike of politics runs deep and is unlikely to be eliminated if they would only get involved with other people in political procedures." However, subjects also acknowledged that problems could arise from too much disengagement.

[56] Thompson (1970).

activity—helps us to view our current predicament as part of an age-old struggle rather than as a new and uniquely frightening development.

My empirical diagnosis should prove relevant and useful even to those who disagree with my prescriptions. To ignore the diagnosis entirely would be to practice what Robert Nozick ironically calls normative sociology, or "the study of what the causes of problems *ought* to be."[57] Incomplete diagnoses invite misleading prescriptions. For example, some social and political theorists in the communitarian or civic republican schools lament a perceived decline in political and social engagement and prescribe increased political participation to remedy democracy's alleged malaise.[58] Some of them blame the impersonal forces of an unfettered free market or an unresponsive "big government" for dampening public discourse and political engagement.[59] Others criticize an ethos of excessive individualism that undermines our commitments to one another and to the public interest.[60] Those diagnoses arise from sound observations and thus have struck a responsive note with many citizens. But sometimes they overlook equally sound observations that complicate any prescriptive advice. While market forces and bureaucratic government may be partly responsible for subduing political engagement, we citizens also play a significant role. Thus, while I do not deny that global, economic, and governmental forces can stifle political engagement I choose to focus here on voluntary disengagement, not only because others have extensively indicted those larger, impersonal forces but also because citizen inattention has plagued democracy for as long as democracies have existed, long predating big business, big government, and modern mass media.

Indeed, despite our concerns about political and social engagement most citizens shrink from changes and commitments that might counter the perceived trends. We may value a sense of community, but we also value economic opportunity, privacy, and mobility, which helps to explain why we relocate frequently, spend considerable time alone or with intimates, and find it difficult to feel rooted in any particular place.[61] We

[57] Nozick (1974: 247).

[58] Michael Walzer claims that some communitarians "prescribe citizenship as an antidote" to modern isolation and atomization. Walzer (1992: 90). Bellah et al. (1992) and Barber (1984) belong to that camp.

[59] Pateman (1970); Barber (1996); Wolin (2008). Dana Villa acknowledges some self-incurred aspects of citizen disengagement but places more blame on an arrogant, arrogating executive branch for ignoring popular dissent and creating an "atmosphere of generalized fear," as well as the "tyranny of public relations and advertising," not to mention "robustly global competition," because "far more than government, the marketplace throws us back upon ourselves." Villa (2008: 5–9).

[60] Bellah et al. (1992: 270).

[61] According to the U.S. Census Bureau, 43 million Americans (approximately 16 percent of persons one year old and over) changed their residences during the one-year period between March of 1999 and March of 2000. Of these 43 million, 39 percent were considered "long distance mov-

rue low rates of voter participation and generally intend to vote, but often fail to follow through.[62] We value political participation, but not participation that is compelled. Cherishing our individualism, we are loath to allow our peers, let alone our government, tell us (without invitation) how to live, what to think, or how to spend our time. In other words, we Americans value community and political engagement but hold other values that make them difficult to sustain, and we do not want to be forced to resolve the discrepancy. Thus we wrestle with political antinomy, an opposition between equally reasonable principles. Such tensions are neither rare nor incoherent; in almost every society "the themes of common sense . . . pull in contrary directions," and the ensuing struggles can elicit fruitful moral debates.[63] Attention deficit democracy's diagnosis acknowledges the fact of our reasonable antinomies, and its prescriptions try to accommodate our conflicting values.

This book assumes from the outset that our own choices may lead to undesired outcomes. I draw upon classic works of political theory to illuminate those outcomes: how they arise, why they are undesirable, how bad they are compared with available alternatives, and what can we do to effect a change. Our response must be tempered by a sobering question. If preservation of democratic freedom is one of our animating concerns, can we reverse trends of voluntary disengagement without coercing citizens illiberally and hence compromising the very ideals that we had hoped to serve?

Jürgen Habermas, articulating a common theme of democratic theory, maintains that democracies should establish a public sphere in which all citizens can participate equally in rational deliberation, a situation that he calls the "ideal speech situation."[64] Indeed, the public realm could and should be more inclusive, welcoming, and fair. Nonetheless, if my argument is correct then even Habermas's "ideal speech situation"—itself a distant if not unrealizable goal—might not be enough to counteract voluntary political disengagement. That daunting realization should not dampen but only redirect our aspirations from an exclusive focus on political supply—the opportunities for citizens to engage on equal footing—to the less commonly appreciated problem of political demand.

---

ers," having changed residence across counties or states. A fairly normal annual relocation rate is 16 percent; in the mid-1980s as many as 20 percent of Americans moved in a single year.

[62] According to the Pew Research Center for the People and the Press, in late October of 2000, 97 percent of registered voters said that they planned to vote in the November elections, whereas 67.5 percent actually turned out to vote. Voter turnout was substantially higher in 2004 but still far lower than the level of those who expressed an intention to vote.

[63] Billig (1995: 64–81; and 1996: 238). As an example of reasonable antinomy, "patience is a virtue" and "he who hesitates is lost" each represent sound advice in the appropriate context.

[64] Habermas (1984a and 1984b).

The motivation to engage involves many complex factors, including citizens' levels of social connectedness, educational attainment, and economic status. Providing an "ideal speech situation" without addressing widespread deficiencies in these socioeconomic resources will not yield widespread political reengagement, as Habermas acknowledges.[65] But wealth and education do not guarantee political engagement, either; political attention and energy wander even among the well educated and well heeled.[66] The public philosophy of attention deficit democracy focuses on stimulating our demand for political engagement through liberal democratic means.

Four possibilities for pragmatic reform follow immediately from my diagnosis, and I will develop them more fully in later chapters. First, citizens and their representatives can strive to make local and national politics more appealing to widespread tastes. Second, we can look to habituation and early education to make our tastes more political. Third, we can reform our political institutions so that they channel existing political attention and energy more efficiently. Fourth, we can target the attention (and energy) of constituencies most prone to disengagement. Aside from working with tastes, we can strive to make political institutions more welcoming—to give citizens a meaningful sense of political efficacy. That aspiration points us toward local political institutions and engagement, where any individual citizen might hope to make an impact.

Chapter 2 shows how and why the term *civic engagement* quickly rose to prominence, illustrating the term's meteoric rise and the confusion that accompanies its widespread use. Civic engagement has remained popular, influential, and ultimately misleading for a number of reasons. The second half of the term, engagement, is one of those reasons. *Engage* entails a combination of activity and attention, an investment of energy and a consciousness of purpose. At some level that has registered with the public; during the very same years of civic engagement's meteoric rise, public discourse showed an accelerated concern with attention, distraction, and the difficulties of engaging with the pace of modern life.

But not all engagement is political, although the term *civic engagement* lumps league bowling together with town hall meetings. Nor is political engagement necessarily moral; consider the Ku Klux Klan or other violent hate groups. Thus chapter 2 distinguishes among political, social, and moral engagement—distinctions usually elided in civic engagement scholarship—and sketches examples of each type. It further differentiates among engagement undertaken at the local, national, and international level, each of which entails unique challenges, commitments, and

---

[65] Held (1980: 396).
[66] See, for example, Putnam (1995 and 2000).

rewards. I consider the somewhat striking and unpopular possibility that liberal democracies may require social and a certain kind of moral engagement (stressing toleration, reciprocity, and law-abidingness) more or less continuously, but political engagement only episodically.

That claim brings up the question of whether political engagement is really as valuable as most of us seem to think. Advocates of political engagement either take its worth for granted or make one of two kinds of claims on its behalf. They assert that political engagement is an instrumental good for citizens of representative democracies or an intrinsic good for human beings.[67] Intrinsic arguments differ from instrumental arguments in that the former praise political life not for what it can elicit but because of what it is. Political participation, in the intrinsic view, is excellent or strongly choice worthy simply for what it represents, and it carries a dignity all its own.

Chapters 3 and 4 turn to Hannah Arendt and Alexis de Tocqueville for representative versions of the intrinsic and instrumental defenses of political engagement, respectively; these two views still strongly influence contemporary debates. Tocqueville and Arendt share an intellectual link—Arendt acknowledges a debt to Tocqueville's work—and a common focus.[68] Both are anxious friends of democracy who worry that withdrawal from public life, whether voluntary or involuntary, may undermine the foundations of democratic freedom. At the beginning of *Democracy in America* Tocqueville promises to address the question, "where . . . are we going?"[69] At the beginning of *The Human Condition* Arendt proposes to "think what we are doing."[70] Both Tocqueville and Arendt hope to improve their readers' vision or, as Tocqueville puts it, to help readers "see not differently but further."[71] They offer long-term perspective to citizens who can be too closely immersed in day-to-day activities to realize that their choices may jeopardize their interests.

Both Arendt and Tocqueville associate political engagement[72] with a motivating force or dynamism that inheres in all individuals but finds its fullest expression when exercised in concert. Tocqueville calls both the individual and the collective capacity by the single name, "energy"

[67] For similar distinctions between intrinsic and instrumental goods, see Parfit (1997: 203–21). See as well Aristotle's *Nichomachean Ethics* (1985: 1096b15). Additionally, David Miller (1995: 194) distinguishes between liberals and "nationalists" according to their instrumental and intrinsic valuation of politics, respectively.

[68] On the point of Arendt's acknowledged debt to Tocqueville, see Lloyd (1995) and Benhabib (1990).

[69] Tocqueville (1969: 12).

[70] Arendt (1959: 5).

[71] Tocqueville (1969: 20).

[72] Neither Arendt nor Tocqueville uses the term *political engagement*, but both are concerned with active, attentive involvement in community and political affairs.

(*énergie*). Arendt calls the individual capacity "action" and the collective phenomenon "power." For Arendt and Tocqueville, the societal environment—institutional arrangements as well as political, social, and moral norms—strongly influences whether energy or power will flourish or fade. Tocqueville goes one step further, focusing on citizens' attention as well as their energy. A close reading shows that in Tocqueville's eyes, political energy fades when citizens' political attention wanders, which in democratic societies will probably be the norm. (That claim might not in itself seem revolutionary, but previous scholarship has not emphasized the vital link between attention and energy in Tocqueville's thought, and the possible means of countering their dissipation.) For Arendt and Tocqueville, the problem of sustaining political engagement might be conceptualized as the problem of generating political energy or power.

Arendt, one of the twentieth century's most influential philosophers, is often cited by those who promote the participatory democratic theories sometimes known as civic humanism, civic republicanism, or communitarianism because she champions political engagement for its own sake and lauds the dignity and joy of spontaneous, unfettered political action.[73] But Arendt's arguments exemplify the difficulties of defending political engagement for its intrinsic merits. I will propose a new reading of her work suggesting that her praise of political engagement and action should be interpreted as intentional overstatement. If interpreted literally it either lapses into internal contradiction or else into elitism, neither of which seem likely from a thinker of Arendt's stature and egalitarian commitments. Arendt is ultimately more successful at expanding our understanding of the evils that we must avoid at all costs, which include political, social, and moral disengagement, than at teaching us about the goods that we must pursue together.

In recent years Tocqueville's star has burned even more brightly than Arendt's. A great number of books and articles in the civic engagement literature cite Tocqueville approvingly to illustrate how citizens can learn about democracy through engagement with local associations and

---

[73] Maurizio Passerin d'Entrèves (1993: 2) writes, "Arendt's conception of politics, with its stress on civic engagement and unconstrained political deliberation, is clearly indebted to [classical civic republicanism]," and certain strains of modern-day civic republicanism in turn owe a debt to Arendt.

Participatory civic republicanism, sometimes termed *civic humanism* and tracing a lineage to ancient Athens, comprises the strain of modern civic republicanism associated with Arendt. But other forms of civic republicanism, such as the *institutional* version—which traces its lineage to ancient Rome and is espoused by contemporary theorists such as Philip Pettit and Quentin Skinner—do not stress participation as an intrinsic good and have no particular affinity with Arendt. For more on the participatory and institutional strains of republicanism, see Berger (2010).

government and then steer society meaningfully.[74] But too often scholars celebrate him for the wrong reasons. Many of them cite the same
few passages from Tocqueville's voluminous works and pass over the
many observations that contradict their assumptions. Even the recent
term, neo-Tocquevillean—occasionally used as an epithet to characterize scholars who overvalue civic engagement as the sole or primary ingredient for making democracy work—reflects an imperfect grasp of his
teachings and insights, demeaning Tocqueville along with the alleged
neo-Tocquevilleans.[75] To be sure, Tocqueville stresses the importance of
voluntary associations and political participation, but he also stresses
the need for institutional design that can channel citizens' collective energy into useful political outlets and connect local energy with regional
and national politics. Further, political scientists commonly misinterpret
Tocqueville as an optimistic champion of American democracy, ignoring his suspicions that Jacksonian America's high political engagement
could not endure.[76] This book provides insights into the ways in which
Tocqueville and Arendt should, and should not, be drawn upon when we
theorize about democracy in America and elsewhere.

For all of their similarities Arendt and Tocqueville ultimately value political engagement for different reasons. Arendt defends participation in
public life as an intrinsic good, one of the most valuable experiences of
human existence, the essence of human freedom, and an end in itself.
Tocqueville values political engagement instrumentally, doubting that it
directly constitutes the good life for most people. In truth, each thinker
shares ground with the other. Arendt understands politics' instrumental
benefits and Tocqueville grasps that exceptional individuals might cherish political life for its own sake. But Tocqueville alone stresses political
engagement's instrumental value as the primary reason why democracy
cannot do without at least some of it, and Tocqueville alone implies practical prescriptions for regenerating some of that value even as the world
changes in ways that threaten social and political engagement. After mining Arendt's and Tocqueville's work for underappreciated insights into
our relationship with political, social, and moral engagement, chapter

[74] Among political scientists, Putnam, Skocpol, and Fiorina all cite Tocqueville in introducing their works on civic engagement. The *American Prospect* chose the name "The
Tocqueville Files" for its multipart, multiauthor debate on civic engagement. In the po-
litical theory compilation *Freedom of Association* (1998), Amy Gutmann, George Kateb,
Sam Fleischacker, Daniel A. Bell, Alan Ryan, Nancy Rosenblum, and Yael Tamir all cite
Tocqueville to contextualize their claims about the importance of association in liberal
democracies. Gutmann and Tamir, in fact, open their essays with quotes from Tocqueville's
Democracy in America.

[75] See Berman (1997).

[76] This point might surprise Tocqueville dilettantes but not specialists such as Craiutu and
Jennings (2004) and Villa (2008).

4 finds Tocqueville's instrumental defense of political engagement more persuasive.

None of the scholars who defend widespread political engagement, including Tocqueville, makes a fully convincing case that democracy always (or even usually) requires such engagement from all or most of its citizens, all or most of the time. Chapter 5 catalogs the most prominent arguments for political engagement's importance and shows that each, individually, presents circumstantial evidence: suggestive and perhaps plausible but ultimately inconclusive. But in political theory as in courtroom trials, circumstantial evidence can prove decisive if compiled in quantity and assembled coherently. From the available evidence I build a case for political engagement's importance that can stand up to critical scrutiny where others, individually, fall short. The case suggests that political engagement is likely to bring at least some of a wide range of benefits to at least some of liberal democracy's citizens at least some of the time. Thus we cannot be indifferent to political engagement, as some theorists of "elite" democracy hold.[77] But neither can we regard it as the grand solution to what ails us.[78] Liberal democracy cannot do without political engagement but does not necessarily need high and widespread levels either. In fact, in the area of political engagement liberal democracies' top priority should be preventing radical *disengagement*, which threatens a variety of undesirable consequences, and also to promote political attention and activity among those segments of the population most likely to suffer when disengaged.[79]

That proposal accords with my general approach to democratic reform. We are hard-pressed to establish the exact conditions required for liberal democracy's health, but we can discern those conditions that will almost certainly undermine it. They include not only radical political disengagement but also balkanized social engagement, very low levels of liberal-democratic moral engagement, and weak or unresponsive political institutions. Before embarking on potentially coercive and paternalistic

---

[77] Schumpeter (1942); Somin (1998).

[78] Meyers (2008: 191–93).

[79] In chapter 3 and 4 I describe some of the harms that can accompany radical disengagement. Regarding those groups most likely to be harmed by political disengagement, Verba, Schlozman, and Brady (1995: 178) demonstrate a robust correlation between income and education levels, on one hand, and political engagement on the other. They also demonstrate the presence of "participatory distortion." Distortion refers to "the circumstance in which political activists do not reflect accurately the larger population from which they come with respect to some politically relevant characteristic," and it occurs much more significantly among poor and poorly educated segments than the rest of the population. Those with fewer economic and educational resources are less likely to engage politically and more likely to be misrepresented when disengaged. Bartels (2009) and Rosenstone and Hansen (1993) also provide extensive data on the disproportionate participation and representation of white, wealthy, and well-educated citizens.

campaigns to increase political engagement nationwide, liberal democracies should promote a number of conditions that are not yet well established. Specifically, they should take care to ensure responsive political institutions, generalized social engagement, generalized liberal-democratic moral engagement, episodic political engagement, and what we might call political attention monitors—nongovernmental, independent actors and institutions (including partisan watchdog organizations, newspapers, television shows, weblogs, and community activists) that pay attention to political developments and can attract citizens' attention (and mobilize their energy) when exceptional circumstances demand it.

Chapter 6 closes with some modest proposals intended not to cure democracy's attention deficit but to keep its worst effects enduringly in check. As mentioned above democratic citizens can elect to alter their tastes through political education and habituation; can change the tenor of political discussions, debates, and media coverage so that politics appeal more effectively to existing tastes; and can alter political institutions so that they utilize and channel existing political attention and energy more efficaciously. I am least sanguine about the first option and most sanguine about the third, but the second is of special interest because—as I will explain in chapter 4—it follows from Tocqueville's teachings yet is almost totally ignored in today's political engagement scholarship.

In addition to prescriptions directed at all citizens equally, checking the worst effects of democracy's political attention deficit means focusing on certain groups' disengagement more than others. Promoting political engagement among the upper middle class or among college students at elite institutions—who already tend to participate at much higher rates than the rest of the population—is unlikely to improve democratic representation, fairness, or legitimacy commensurate with its cost. The poorest and least educated citizens are most likely to be disengaged both politically and socially and least likely to be accurately represented by politicians or activists.[80] Engaging these marginalized citizens would improve their prospects and serve the broader polity as well by promoting the widely shared goals of fairness and democratic legitimacy.[81] By the same token promoting political engagement at the local rather than national level speaks to a broad range of democratic values and goals and can pave the way for national-level engagement.[82]

The preceding issues affect not only political theorists but also a broad range of citizens, so this book addresses multiple constituencies. To political scientists it promises that clarifying our discourse and specifying our terms can improve the study of democratic politics. By distinguishing

---

[80] Verba et al. (1995: 463–508). Also see Strolovitch (2007).

[81] Lijphart (1997: 1).

[82] Cf. Fung (2006); Sirianni and Friedland (2001); Sabl (2002b).

among political, social, and moral engagement, which do not always co-incide, it encourages political scientists to specify the attentive activities most essential for democratic societies rather than lumping them all into one "civic" category. By highlighting attention and energy as the fundamental concerns shared by almost all scholars using the infelicitous term *civic engagement*, it encourages future studies to consider means of attracting, sustaining, and harnessing those resources more effectively. This book also encourages political scientists to extend their study of limited attention's political implications beyond the realm of periodic voting. Limited attention can affect all forms of political engagement and can affect social and moral engagement as well, all of which matter greatly in projecting democracy's success.

To political theorists this book recommends a more earnest engagement with the empirical evidence of human beings' limited attention and of citizens' tastes, values, and choices regarding political and political participation.[83] Tocqueville shows us the way with his "new political science," dictating philosophical inquiry based on empirical observations. But some political theorists overlook the evidence of our limited political attention and participatory ambivalence, projecting their own taste for political engagement onto the public.[84] Theorists must acknowledge contemporary empirical data and also the diagnoses of wandering political attention that recur throughout the philosophical canon, and they must grapple with the means of accepting, rejecting, or overcoming those assessments.

To scholars in other academic fields—psychologists, sociologists, and any researchers interested in the capacities and limitations of attention, energy, and tastes—this book recommends an interdisciplinary dialogue that benefits from diverse expertise. Political scientists and theorists tend to focus on what I call *political engagement* (even when we mistakenly call it *civic*); sociologists focus on what I call *social engagement*; social and cognitive psychologists focus on *moral engagement* and *disengagement*. But we should be talking to one another instead of working by ourselves.

We should be talking to ordinary citizens as well. This book gives an account of political engagement, social engagement, and moral engagement—their meaning, value, and challenges—in which we citizens can

[83] To be sure, many political theorists take a close account of empirical evidence regarding political participation. Cf. Thompson (1970); Pateman (1970); Mansbridge (1999); Fung (2006). But many more do not, especially regarding attention and tastes.

[84] Democratic theorists seldom cite studies chronicling American citizens' dislike for political engagement, such as Hibbing and Theiss-Morse (2002) or suggesting that "people whose political networks involve greater political disagreement are less likely to participate in politics. Hibbing and Theiss-Morse (2002: 183–208). See also Mutz (2002 and 2006).

recognize ourselves and our experiences. The public philosophy of attention deficit democracy is currently on the tips of our tongues, capable of invigorating public debate once articulated. Because it speaks to widely held commitments, values, and doubts, it complements rather than supplants top-down theories such as civic republicanism and deliberative democracy. Any public philosophy that prescribes worthy but controversial changes in our policies and practices, such as deliberation guided only by neutral reason or greatly increased political participation, should try to persuade the public to its point of view by engaging citizens on their own terms, respecting their current values, tastes, and goals.

This book's commitment to addressing a broad audience follows from Immanuel Kant's insistence that scholars employ their reason before "the entire reading public."[85] Citizens are the core element of democratic politics, so political theorists who take democratic politics seriously must take citizens seriously as well. When we citizens begin to understand why political engagement is esteemed yet frequently deserted we can begin to consider realistic solutions. I present attention deficit democracy not as a cynical last word on our plight but as the beginning of a hopeful public conversation.

[85] "What Is Enlightenment?" in *Kant: Political Writings* (1991: 55). For Kant the "entire reading public" meant a much smaller group than it does now, so in a sense my aims are even more democratic.

Chapter 2

THE RULES OF ENGAGEMENT

> We are left to swim in a sea of empirical and theoretical messiness.
> Intolerably blunted conceptual tools are conducive, on the one hand, to
> wasteful if not misleading research, and, on the other hand, to a meaning-
> less togetherness based on pseudo-equivalences.
> —Giovanni Sartori, "Concept Misformation in Comparative Politics"

I HAVE ALREADY BEGUN the case against civic engagement. In this chapter I introduce further evidence that consigns the term to exile or obsolescence, including an overview of its short but mischievous life. I will also expound on my proposed replacements. We need a richer vocabulary to help us think and talk about the various kinds of attention and activity that help to make democracy work.

Some might doubt whether we can or should distinguish among political, social, and moral engagements. Not only can we, but Hannah Arendt correctly asserts that we ignore those distinctions at our peril. To Arendt, politics comprises the space of human freedom and "the social" must not infect its domain.[1] Arendt's "social" denotes a realm of human life marked by necessity that opposes freedom.[2] Her category of the "social" thus includes economics, which must be barred from consideration in the free political realm. Politics, conversely, involves people coming together freely to strive greatly, act boldly, and—in the shining light generated by free individuals acting cooperatively—reveal their distinctiveness and find meaning in their lives. I demur from Arendt's idiosyncratic characterizations of the political and the social but I agree with her overarching point: politics loses all meaning if anything and everything can fall within its purview.[3]

Arendt also stresses the vital importance of judgment and "thinking what we are doing," traits and orientations that resemble what I call moral engagement.[4] In the absence of judgment—in the presence of

---

[1] Cf. Pitkin (1998).

[2] Arendt (1959: 37, 51; 1963: 96–97; 1973: 329).

[3] Mark E. Warren also distinguishes between "politically (power) oriented associations" and "socially oriented associations." See Mark E. Warren (2001: 122).

[4] Arendt (1959: 5).

thoughtlessness—people can condone or perform egregious actions, with Adolf Eichmann representing the thoughtless individual par excellence.[5] Thoughtless individuals still possess cognition, of course, which Arendt describes as mere "instrumental reason" divorced from courage, conviction, or moral sense. She implies that in an era of scientific breakthroughs and nuclear capabilities, unless citizens and officials muster the moral resolution to "think what we are doing"—unless we pay attention to, and act in accordance with, legitimate moral principles—we may end the world with a bang, not a whimper.[6]

Tocqueville, writing more than a century before Arendt, also distinguishes social and moral from political involvements, but with a more traditional understanding of "the political." Tocqueville defines political associations as groups "by which men seek to defend themselves against the despotic action of the majority or the encroachments of . . . power." He distinguishes these from social groups or "civil associations," groups in civil society "which have no political object."[7] To put Tocqueville's insights in my terms, not all social engagement is political. Tocqueville further recognizes that neither political nor social or civil associations will always promote moral virtues such as generalized tolerance or mutual respect; in other words, not all political and social engagement involves meaningful moral engagement. Political associations can encourage moral disengagement because, as Tocqueville witnessed in France, "by the single act of uniting" citizens can make "a complete sacrifice of their judgment and free will," which "greatly diminishes their moral strength."[8]

My purpose in distinguishing among political, social, and moral engagement is not to stake out an essentialist claim about the nature of any particular attentive activity. One trend in contemporary political theory has moved in the opposite direction, as scholars have challenged traditional boundaries between political and apolitical in order to expand the former significantly. Feminist theorists such as Carole Pateman insist on "making the personal political" because traditional public/private distinctions have rendered certain issues, of great importance for social justice, ineligible for political intervention or reform.[9] Václav Havel suggests

[5] Of Eichmann, Arendt writes: "There was no sign in him of firm ideological convictions or of specific evil motives . . . it was not stupidity but *thoughtlessness*." Arendt (1978: 4). Later, in volume 1, Arendt writes that "wickedness may be caused by absence of thought." Ibid., 13.

[6] Arendt (1959: 5, 262). Hanna Pitkin (1998: 79) points out that Arendt presents bureaucracy, "'the most social [and hence apolitical] form of government,' as "an abdication of human initiative and judgment."

[7] Tocqueville (1969: 513). By "political objects" Tocqueville means goals that require the action of governmental institutions or processes. In his view many (or even most) associative involvements have nothing to do with such institutions or processes. See also Stolle and Rochon (1998).

[8] Tocqueville (1969: 195).

[9] Pateman (1988).

that apparently private decisions and actions can connect with and influence political outcomes.[10] Michael Schudson summarizes a decades-long trend of expanding the commonplace definitions of politics: "A woman physician or accountant can feel that she is doing politics—providing a role model and fighting for recognition of women's equality with men—every time she goes to work. The same is true for African American bank executives or gay and lesbian military officers. . . . Wearing a 'Thank you for not smoking' button is political."[11]

I do not contest these claims' underlying logic. The personal or private can indeed be political, if and when citizens seek to express personal decisions or influence previously "private" issues through the polity's organs: political processes and institutions. Until then their pursuits are either apolitical or prepolitical.[12] They might be of intense interest to political scientists and political theorists, but we should not conflate them with attentive activity that directly engages political processes and institutions if we care about establishing a coherent, far-reaching dialogue across academic disciplines.

That conjunction, *if*, contextualizes my attempt to parse the various engagements. I do so with a particular purpose in mind: to help us think and talk more clearly about making democracy work. Conceptual clarity and agreement affect our ability to diagnose problems and prescribe solutions cooperatively. What kinds of orientations, activities, and relationships should friends of democracy be concerned to promote? When our language does not permit us to distinguish between political and apolitical (or prepolitical) engagements—and when we cannot even be certain what "engagement" entails—we build an academic Tower of Babel one essay at a time.[13] Civic engagement has become just such a tower, with countless scholars at work on its scaffolding sans mutual appreciation or cooperation.

As stated earlier, I do not intend to blame any scholar or group for our confusion or to condescend to the many who take civic engagement as their nominal subject. I share many of their goals. The concept of civic engagement has jump-started many productive research agendas, in part due to its breadth, ambiguity, and positive connotations, but we must

[10] Havel, "The Power of the Powerless," in *Open Letters* (1991).

[11] Schudson (1996: 18).

[12] Hibbing and Theiss-Morse similarly insist on distinguishing between social and political involvements: "In advocating more group membership activity, Mathews (1994: chap. 7) refers to it as 'politics that is not called politics,' but it is clear . . . that the reason it is not called politics is because it isn't." Hibbing and Theiss-Morse (2002: 189).

[13] Verba, Schlozman, and Brady (1995: 40) agree that while "the boundary between political and non-political activity is by no means clear," coherent analysis requires that we nonetheless attempt to make such distinctions.

recognize the confusion that it has sown and the difficulty, if not impossibility, of simply cleaning up the term. A range of theorists and practitioners, apparently reacting to the confusion that I have documented, have recently tried to do just that. But their attempts, while often well executed individually, conflict with one another and only reaffirm that the term *civic* means too many things to too many people to be of much use for social science analysis.

As one example among many, Clifford Zukin and his colleagues have dedicated an entire book (*A New Engagement?*) to rethinking and clarifying civic engagement.[14] They conceptualize civic engagement "in contrast to political engagement," defining the former as "organized voluntary activity focused on problem solving and helping others."[15] (When actually measuring civic engagement they include membership in *any* kind of group or organization, which would include Putnam's bowling leagues or choral societies—engagements not necessarily connected to problem solving or moral engagement.) Defining civic engagement thusly allows them to rate politically disengaged but communally or socially active young people as reasonably good citizens.

Peter Levine's *The Future of Democracy* takes up a similar, clarifying project but heads in exactly the opposite direction. Levine defines civic engagement as follows: "any action that affects legitimately public matters (even if it is selfishly motivated) as long as the actor pays appropriate attention to the consequences of his behavior for the underlying political system."[16] Thus, while Zukin and colleagues attempt to rethink and clarify civic engagement by stressing its social and moral components to the exclusion of any political components, Levine undertakes the same kind of project and stresses civic engagement's political components to the exclusion of most social and moral components.

In short, none of the attempts at clarification have succeeded. Going forward, some scholars writing about civic engagement might choose one of the conflicting reconceptualizations, such as those offered by Zukin and Levine; most will probably continue to draw upon whichever political, social, and moral elements of civic engagement most appeal to them or seem easiest to measure. Neither outcome bodes well for students of democracy. That concern, rather than a desire to blame civic engagement researchers, leads to my conclusion that we would be better served by using different terms altogether than by continuing to utilize such a contested and confusing one.

To grasp civic engagement's grave shortcomings, consider John Gerring's eight criteria for evaluating conceptual "goodness" (see table 2.1).

[14] Zukin et al. (2006).
[15] Ibid., 7.
[16] Levine (2007: 13).

Gerring's standards bolster the case that common sense initiates: civic engagement lacks conceptual coherence, parsimony, depth, differentiation, and utility.

Civic engagement evinces familiarity and resonance, the first two of Gerring's criteria. But the concept lacks parsimony; its list of defining attributes exhausts memory and patience. It also lacks coherence. What thread could coherently link bowling in leagues, voting alone, writing checks to political candidates or interest groups, attending dinner parties, creating politically conscious artwork, volunteering at soup kitchens, attending church, and watching politically relevant television programs, all of which have been counted as forms of civic engagement?

Nor is civic engagement differentiated or easy to operationalize.[17] One would be hard pressed to distinguish its attributes from those of similar concepts such as social networking and social capital, political participation, civic virtue, and even friendship. Operationalizing civic engagement becomes as difficult as operationalizing any kitchen sink concept, because it means measuring a vast array of phenomena and attributes. Civic engagement fares just as poorly on the criterion of conceptual depth. Only surface similarities link the instances grouped under its umbrella. Some phenomena labeled *civic engagement* involve attention but little activity; some involve activity but little attention; some involve a political component while lacking a social component; others involve a social component while lacking a political component; and some involve a strong, liberal-democratic moral component while others do not.[18]

The work of Sidney Verba, Kay Schlozman, and Henry Brady generally embodies great scholarly care and precision but still can yield to the conceptual stretching that civic engagement invites. In *Voice and Equality* (1995) Verba, Schlozman, and Brady attempt to distinguish between political and social activity, focusing primarily on the former.[19] But in "Civic Participation and the Equality Problem" (in Theda Skocpol and Morris Fiorina's *Civic Engagement in American Democracy*) the authors, adopting the civic engagement rubric, group together both nonpolitical voluntary activities—which are primarily social in nature—and also explicitly political activities that have no social component, such as "writing letters to public officials" and "making political contributions."[20] My intention is not to impugn the authors (who were, after all, contributing

[17] Operationalization involves defining a concept or variable so that it can be measured quantitatively.

[18] For civic engagement as attention without activity—in these cases, television viewing as civic engagement—see Schudson (1996) and Jones (2005). For civic engagement as activity without attention, see Ladd (1999a), which construes political donations as forms of civic engagement.

[19] Verba, Schlozman, and Brady (1995: 19, 40).

[20] Verba, Schlozman, and Brady, in Skocpol and Fiorina (1999: 428–29).

TABLE 2.1.
Criteria of Conceptual Goodness

1. Familiarity	How familiar is the concept (to a lay or academic audience)?
2. Resonance	Does the chosen term ring (resonate)?
3. Parsimony	How short is a) the term and b) its list of defining attributes (the intension)?
4. Coherence	How internally consistent (logically related) are the instances and attributes?
5. Differentiation	How differentiated are the instances and the attributes (from other most-similar concepts)? How bounded, how operationalizable, is the concept?
6. Depth	How many accompanying properties are shared by the instances under definition?
7. Theoretical utility	How useful is the concept within a wider field of inferences?
8. Field utility	How useful is the concept within a field of related instances and attributes?

Source: Gerring (1999: 367)

to an edited volume with "civic engagement" in the title) but to show how civic engagement invites an erosion of conceptual and categorical clarity even among those dedicated to pursue the latter.

Civic engagement also disappoints in the area of theoretical utility. The modifier *civic* has such broad connotations that no one is quite sure what it means. It allows anyone who invokes it to evoke something of special interest to that party—social connectedness, political participation, sociable norms, and so on. Finally, for some of the same reasons that civic engagement lacks conceptual depth it also lacks field utility for those within political science and sociology who address pressing questions about making democracy work. Some use civic engagement to measure political activity, some to measure social connectedness, and some to gauge citizens' commitment to their communities.[21] The result is that

[21] For civic engagement as political activity, see Nicholson (2003: 403); for civic engagement as social connectedness, see Putnam et al. (1993) and Putnam (2000); for civic engagement as moral commitment to community, see Sandel (1996). For civic engagement used interchangeably with political engagement, see Bowler et al. (2003: 1118) and Smith (2009).

rather than giving these scholars a common vocabulary, civic engagement leaves them talking past one another.[22]

While civic engagement fares poorly with all but two of Gerring's criteria—familiarity and resonance—my proposed replacements of political, social, and moral engagement satisfy far more of the same criteria without ceding ground on the criterion of resonance. Civic engagement rings, or resonates, with contemporary sensibilities, but my proposed replacements do not sound alien. Civic engagement retains only one advantage over its political, social, and moral cousins: greater familiarity, stemming from its media saturation. But by the end of this chapter its familiarity may breed contempt.

Some concepts achieve familiarity through long-standing use. Not so with civic engagement, which originated quite recently. Civic engagement struck a chord from the outset, and its resonance among scholars and ordinary citizens accounts for part of its meteoric rise to prominence and familiarity. But part of the term's appeal lay in its ambiguity. From its inception civic engagement meant different things in different situations, and its early elasticity invited a slew of further stretching. Unlike terms and concepts whose origins are shrouded in the distant past, civic engagement is of such recent birth that we can glimpse some of the factors, present from the beginning, that invited both widespread use and confusion.[23]

Prior to 1993 civic engagement appeared only rarely in scholarly discourse and almost never in American political discourse or popular media.[24] On rare occasions it was used in a manner totally unlike its current usages, with *civic* adhering to its dictionary definition, "of or pertaining to the city," and *engagement* denoting an appointment or meeting. Accordingly, one Australian writer praised his city's conscientious mayor for spending her birthday amid city hall meetings, "with her first civic engagement at 10 a.m."[25] An American university chancellor reminisced about her tenure, in which she was "privileged to find

---

[22] Ladd's (1999a) critique of Putnam constitutes perhaps the most glaring example of scholars talking past one another due to conceptual ambiguity. Ladd criticizes Putnam for having missed "new" trends in civic engagement, such as the replacement of PTAs (parent-teacher associations) by PTOs (parent-teacher organizations), and the development of mailing-list associations that occasionally draw members into face-to-face meetings. However, in the process Ladd fails to consider whether the "new" types of civic engagement might involve lower levels of attention and activity than the more "traditional" types, and whether they might therefore represent some sort of diminution.

[23] As Tocqueville wrote of individuals and nations, the same holds for words and concepts: they "always bear some marks of their origin. Circumstances of birth and growth affect all the rest of their careers." Tocqueville (1969: 31).

[24] In peer-reviewed journals, the term's only mention prior to Putnam's book appeared in Gans (1992).

[25] Partridge (1985).

rewarding professional responsibilities, fulfilling civic engagements, and numerous kindred spirits."[26] But apart from those occasional usages, civic engagement played no significant role in public discourse about democracy's health.

One landmark book changed the rhetorical landscape. Robert Putnam's *Making Democracy Work* (1993) emphasized "civic engagement" and "social capital" in comparing northern Italy's economic and political successes with southern Italy's relative shortcomings. In that study *civic* acquired an extraordinary breadth, encompassing social connectedness, sociability, and interpersonal trust as well as issues relating to politics and citizenship. Engagement came to mean involvement of any kind, whether passive (paying attention to social and political affairs) or more active (investing energy in social or political affairs). Putnam found that northern Italy's rich "civic engagement"—its citizens' participation in voluntary associations, diverse friendship circles, and formal political processes—corresponded with much higher levels of trust and reciprocal norms, and far greater political and economic efficiency, than in the "civically disengaged" regions to the south. Northern Italy's vibrant array of social and political groups contributed toward what Putnam called a "civic community." Southern Italy's relative dearth of associational life contributed to an "uncivic" community, rife with political corruption, economic stagnation, and "feelings of exploitation, dependency, and frustration."[27] In other words, high civic engagement accompanied desirable political, economic, and moral results; low civic engagement accompanied the opposite. Scholars began to take note, and civic engagement entered their discourse and research.[28]

But while Putnam's outstanding analysis set the agenda for an entire new field of useful research in political and social science, it inadvertently gave rise to a seminal confusion by conflating "civic engagement" and "social capital." In *Making Democracy Work* "social capital" means "features of social organization, such as trust, norms, and networks, that can improve the efficiency of society by facilitating coordinated actions" (167). What kinds of norms and networks did Putnam have in mind? Norms and networks of *civic engagement*, which, in turn comprised "an essential *form* of social capital.[29] To be fair, Putnam probably intended civic engagement not as a form but as a source of social capital. According to his analysis civic engagement meant those associative

---

[26] Dr. Blenda J. Wilson, quoted in PR Newswire, May 20, 1992.

[27] Putnam et al. (1993: 111). Further citations noted by page number in the text.

[28] Chrislip (1994: 25); Gough (1994: 35–36).

[29] Putnam et al. (1993: 173; stress added). As many as eighteen times throughout the book, Putnam refers specifically to "the norms and networks of civic engagement." (1993: 15, 16, 115, 116, 129, 152, 161, 167, 171, 173, 174, 176, 177, 178, 180, 181, 183, 184).

involvements—whether political or not—that enmesh individuals in "networks and norms" of trust and reciprocity and hence generate social capital.[30] Rather than picking and choosing social and political components willy-nilly, Putnam carefully selected those indicators that correlated most closely with the performance of public institutions.[31] Thus in *Making Democracy Work* Putnam's civic engagement encompassed participation in mass political parties as well as neighborhood associations, choral societies, sports clubs, guilds, unions, and literary societies.[32] It also involved a moral component—norms of trust and reciprocity—along with its political and social elements.[33]

Two years after publishing his Italian study, Putnam introduced civic engagement to a broader audience by focusing on twentieth-century U.S. history. In a series of influential articles he argued that Americans' civic engagement, now defined as "involvement with the lives of our communities," had steadily declined over several decades' time. Civic engagement continued to encompass political participation, associational memberships, informal socializing, citizens' trust in government, and interpersonal trust, and Putnam found all five to be trending sharply downward.[34] His data seemed to affirm many citizens' generalized complaint, or gut feeling, that America's social life and political life were not what they had once been.[35] And since in Putnam's Italian study low civic engagement correlated with very poor economic and political outcomes, his findings in the United States seemed cause for alarm. In short order civic engagement became a cause célèbre.

Soon, federally funded research initiatives began measuring the "Nation's Index of Civic Engagement," as well as "How Civic Disengagement Weakens America and What We Can Do About It."[36] Nongovernmental organizations (NGOs) won grants to promote civic engagement

[30] Ibid., 170. In Putnam's portrayal all civic engagement produces social capital, but not all social capital is produced by civic engagement. Close friendships and family relations, for example, can produce social capital without falling under the rubric of civic engagement.

[31] For a further methodological explanation, see Putnam, "Community-Based Social Capital and Educational Performance," in Ravitch and Vaterri (2001).

[32] Putnam at al. (1993: 173, 181).

[33] Note that norms of trust and reciprocity would not by themselves constitute what I call *moral engagement* unless people take corresponding action to actualize that trust. But Putnam uses the term "civic *dis*engagement" to encompass all three of what I distinguish as political, social, and moral disengagement. Putnam et al. (1993: 15). Eric Uslaner writes extensively on the moral component of trust, and the connections between trust and moral behavior or action. See, for example, Uslaner (1999).

[34] Putnam (1995).

[35] Ladd (1999a).

[36] National Commission on Civic Renewal (1997); National Commission on Philanthropy and Civic Renewal (1998).

in emerging democracies.[37] In the academic world, Harvard's Theda Skocpol formed an interdisciplinary Civic Engagement Project to study American political development. High school and college educators augmented traditional classroom offerings with civic engagement internships and created campus centers to encourage students' extracurricular civic engagement. At UCLA civic engagement became an academic subject in its own right, a concentration in which students could minor.[38]

The term caught on outside of the policy and academic communities as well. In 1995 the national weekly *People* magazine devoted a three-page spread to Putnam's civic engagement thesis, remarkable coverage for a scholarly project.[39] Writers in regional and national newspapers increasingly discussed the apparent spread of civic disengagement and potential solutions, such as a hip-hop artist's "message of civic engagement" for urban youth.[40] By the time Putnam published his 2000 book, *Bowling Alone*, which summarized and expanded upon his earlier findings, regional and national newspapers were regularly chronicling perceived trends of civic disengagement and urging citizens and officials to stem the tide.

Not everyone agreed with Putnam's U.S. assessment. But even the dissenting voices generally disagreed only on the question of civic engagement's alleged decline rather than on its meaning or value. Some critics maintained that civic engagement still thrived but had changed shapes and locations.[41] According to their line of thought, involvement with little league baseball might have shrunk but youth soccer leagues had taken its place. Nationally networked Parent-Teacher Associations (PTAs) might have diminished, but independent Parent-Teacher Organizations (PTOs) had filled the void. And while venerable fraternal and sororal organizations such as the Elks, Rotary, and DAR might have lost many members, small self-help groups provided outlets for those who sought to connect and engage civically—although no one thought to specify what that meant.[42]

Figures 2.1 and 2.2 illustrate civic engagement's remarkably rapid ascension from obscurity to commonplace topic in scholarly articles and U.S. newspapers. In each medium, civic engagement began attracting notice around or after 1993, the year of Putnam's first book on the subject.

[37] Levinger and Mulroy (2003).
[38] Shumer (1997).
[39] Day (1995: 125–27).
[40] Melvin (1996); Rosenblatt (2004).
[41] See especially Ladd (1999a).
[42] Ladd (1999a); Wuthnow (1996).

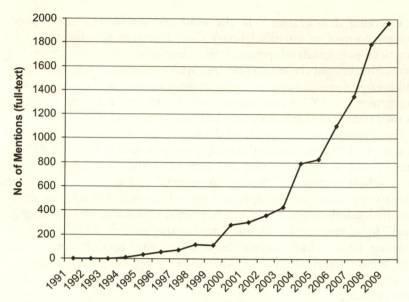

Figure 2.1. Civic engagement in U.S. newspapers and wires (full text). *Source*: LexisNexis Academic.

Why did civic engagement catch on so quickly and widely in the late twentieth century? Its subject matter was certainly nothing new. Following the eighteenth and nineteenth centuries' industrial revolutions, theorists such as Tocqueville, Marx, Durkheim, and Tönnies worried about the dispersal of rooted agrarians into masses of urban laborers. They lamented a perceived decline in social connectedness, traditional values, and political solidarity. Other intellectuals expressed similar worries amid the early twentieth-century's social and economic upheavals, which included the growth of vast cities, the vicissitudes of economic depression, and the travail of world wars. Yet none of the words coined to discuss those concerns—isolation, atomization, alienation, and anomie, for example—captured the popular and scholarly imaginations as broadly or quickly as civic engagement and disengagement, which are used in ways that encompass all of the others.[43] In Gerring's terms, civic engagement resonated with scholars and with the general public, and its deep resonance led to widespread familiarity. But its resonance and familiarity, in the absence of conceptual parsimony and differentiation, encouraged

[43]Tocqueville (1969); Arendt (1959); Tönnies (2002); Durkheim (1951); Marx, "The Economic and Philosophical Manuscripts of 1844," in Marx and Engels (1978); Kornhauser (1959); and Sennett (1977). Nancy Rosenblum concludes one essay by warning that "the critical dilemma for liberal democracy in the United States today is . . . isolation . . . [and] . . . genuine anomie." Rosenblum (1998a: 102).

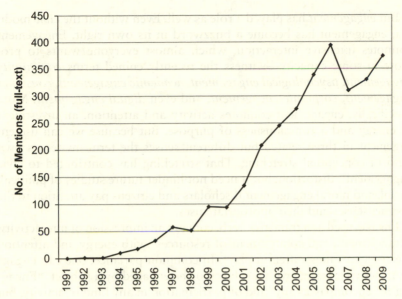

Figure 2.2. Civic engagement in peer-reviewed articles (full text).
Source: ProQuest.

so many people to adopt civic engagement for such a wide range of purposes that it soon lost conceptual coherence. Yet the term's widespread use increased its familiarity, which encouraged further usage and watered down conceptual coherence all the more.

One likely reason for the term's easy resonance resides in the word *civic* itself. Literally, civic means "of, pertaining, or proper to *citizens*," or to "*citizenship*," or to "a *city*, borough, or municipality." But it has come to connote a variety of other subjects as well, almost all of them having positive associations: sociability, public spiritedness, and cooperative norms, for example.[44] And while few people agree on the word's exact meaning, most seem to agree about what civic opposes: narrow individualism, isolationism, or an exclusive focus on oneself or one's intimates. (Note that I am not referring to the antonyms of civic, which might be something like *rural* or *alien*, but to the concepts excluded or opposed by civic's connotations.) The word's combination of benevolence and ambiguity contributed to civic engagement's broad appeal yet also contributed to our current confusion.

[44] Gabriel Almond and Sidney Verba (1989) treat "civic" as a *subset* of "political," with civic connoting a particular kind of cooperative and participatory *orientation* toward fellow citizens and the political system. Journalist Neal Pierce, reviewing the book *The Humane Metropolis*, groups "civic" along with a host of other desirable qualities: "The key words seem to be green, healthy, sociable, civic, and inclusive." Pierce (2007: 2).

But *engagement* has played a role as well. Even without the *civic* modifier, engagement has become a buzzword in its own right. Engagement connotes intensive interaction, which almost everyone wants to promote in some capacity—witness the recently coined terms *community engagement, psychological engagement, academic engagement, consumer engagement, corporate engagement,* and even *digital engagement.* More specifically, engagement connotes activity and attention, an investment of energy and a consciousness of purpose. But because we can use engagement in three related but different senses the term invites its own kind of conceptual stretching. That stretching has contributed to civic engagement's distortion, but it need not hinder future studies of political, social, and moral engagement if scholars and citizens pay attention to the distinct senses and their appropriate uses.

Engage, used as a transitive verb, conveys an impression of interactivity, entanglement, and commitment of resources (with energy and attention the resources most often in play). In common parlance, one can engage in an activity, engage with a subject, or be engaged by a subject. "Engaging *in*" encompasses any kind of participation in any kind of activity, but not necessarily attentive activity. Engaging in an activity can mean rote repetition or perfunctory performance; one can engage in paper pushing, ditch digging, or idle gossip. Conversely, the passive sense of "engaged *by*" implies attention or interest without accompanying activity.[45] One can be engaged by a painting, a television show, or a charismatic speaker. "Engaged *by*" is the verb form for spectators. Finally, "engaging *with*" tells us not only that an activity is being undertaken but undertaken attentively, as one engages *with* an interlocutor, a team member, or an intellectual or moral dilemma.

In summary, and as illustrated in table 2.2, the sense of *engage in* implies activity without attention, the sense of *engaged by* implies attention without activity, and the sense of *engage with* implies activity as well as attention.

Too often, writers contemplating civic (or other forms of) engagement invoke these three senses interchangeably.[46] Scholars who consider politicized television viewing as a form of civic or political engagement are drawing upon the passive sense of being engaged *by* a subject.[47] Television programs with political content might draw viewers' attention to political affairs, but watching television entails little if any political activ-

[45] See, for example, the Earl of Shaftesbury's use in the year 1711: "He admires, he contemplates; but is not yet ingag'd or interested." Shaftesbury (1999: i.III.351).

[46] All of these senses—engage in, engaged by, and engage with—represent legitimate uses of the verb *engage.* However, my concern with the civic engagement literature involves the clarity of terminology rather than its legitimate use.

[47] Schudson (1996: 18–27); Jones (2005: 15–19).

TABLE 2.2.
Senses of "Engage"

Sense of Engage	Involves Activity	Involves Attention?
Engage *in*	Yes	No
Engaged *by*	No	Yes
Engage *with*	Yes	Yes

ity.[48] Verba, Schlozman, and Brady intentionally use the term "political engagement" to denote the attention-only sense of being "engaged by": "interest in politics or concern with public issues."[49]

Conversely, those scholars who count political donations as a measure of civic or political engagement draw upon the sense of "engage in." Donating money via check or online payment involves a brief investment of the donor's energy and very little attention to political affairs.[50] In fact, contributions to advocacy groups are generally a delegation of attention, payment to a third party who will attend to one's concerns.[51] Finally, holding or running for office, attending town hall meetings, or participating in political rallies represent political engagement in the sense of "engaging with" political affairs, a combination of political attention and activity.

Thus scholars who use engagement to denote a particular activity to be counted or measured often underspecify what it comprises: is it attention alone, activity alone, or both activity and attention? Hence they risk missing each other's meaning; one person might claim that political engagement (meaning passive attention) is up while another claims that political engagement (meaning active participation) is down. That apparent difficulty could be overcome if we simply recognize that attention and activity undergird all of our concerns with engagement and take pains to indicate which resources are at stake in a given instance of political engagement. Scholars could still refer to television watching as a form of political engagement but should also specify which of the two essential resources, attention and activity, are at play. The goal would be for professors and practitioners to recognize the resources that underlie the

---

[48] Gathering political information by oneself might be considered preparation for acting as a citizen but does not comprise political activity. As an activity one might call it prepolitical, in the sense in which Judith Shklar (1984) calls her arguments "pre-philosophical."

[49] Verba, Schlozman, and Brady (1995: 16). Verba, Schlozman, and Brady use "political engagement in the sense of "psychological engagement with politics," which includes both political interest and a sense of efficacy (1995: 334).

[50] Cf. Ladd (1999a and 1999b); Foot et al. (2003).

[51] See Verba, Schlozman, and Brady (1995: 176–77).

buzzword *engagement* and to orient their studies toward measuring activity and attention.

But engagement can be stretched conceptually for another reason as well. Engagement can refer to a particular action or to a generalized condition,[52] yet scholars seldom specify which sense they intend (and sometimes oscillate between them). When describing a particular episode or action, engagement can mean activity alone, attention alone, or a combination of the two. But as a generalized condition engagement always means a combination of activity and attention. In other words, engagement as a particular action can utilize the senses of engage *in*, engaged *by*, and engage *with*, but engagement as a general condition only utilizes the sense of engage *with*.[53] A politically engaged populace must be attentive to and active in political affairs, processes, and institutions. No one would call a citizenry politically engaged—meaning a generalized condition of political engagement—if citizens only paid attention to political affairs, processes, and policies but never took action to influence matters or raise their voices in support or protest. The same objection holds for a citizenry in which people participate perfunctorily, voting out of obligation, habit, or fear, yet pay no attention to political affairs and processes and hence have no idea of what their activities mean or express. Activity without attention is something like rote activity, or going through the motions. A bored schoolchild grudgingly completing an assignment may be academically active but is certainly not engaged with her studies.[54] In political life activity without attention might describe the perfunctory voting of a nineteenth-century Tammany Hall supporter, who casts a ballot for the prescribed city candidate in return for a Christmas ham. It also might describe Benjamin Rush's vain exhortation that eighteenth-century America mold its citizens into "republican machines" or "unquestioning paragons of cooperation and self-sacrifice."[55] The perfunctory voter and the republican machine are both politically engaged in a manner of speaking, investing energy in

---

[52]"1.) The action of engaging; the state, condition, or fact of being engaged." *Oxford English Dictionary* online.

[53]Verba, Schlozman, and Brady (1995: 41) focus their study on political activity and not attention, "with doing politics, rather than with being attentive to politics." Studies of citizen competence and political knowledge usually focus on political attention more than political activity.

[54]UCLA's Higher Education Research Institute recently published a study chronicling apathy and alienation among a wide sampling of high school students. The study refers to this phenomenon as "academic disengagement." Levinson (2000).

[55]Benjamin Rush, "Thoughts upon the Mode of Education Proper in a Republic," (1786), cited in Sandel (1996: 129). In the philosophical tradition, René Descartes' "disengaged reason" is disengaged from the physical, sensory world insofar as its focus is diverted from sensory input: "assuré que je ne puis avoir aucune connaissance de ce qui est hors de moi, que par l'entremise des idées que j'ai eu en moi." [Descartes is "certain that I can have

political activities. But we would worry if everyone undertook political activities perfunctorily, acting from force of habit without thinking for themselves. Perfunctory participation has no obvious connection to those political capacities involving critical judgment.[56]

Passive attention and judgment have limits of their own. To be sure, widespread attention to political affairs without accompanying political activity might advance the goal of democratic legitimacy, if one were to construe the viewers' silence as tacit consent. But passive viewers, even if they engage in internal debate, remain on the outside. As if in agreement the National Commission on Civic Renewal calls its final report on civic disengagement "A Nation of Spectators," and Rick Valelly characterizes Putnam's America as "Couch Potato Democracy."[57] Martin Luther King Jr. summarizes the distinction between passive attention and engaged citizenship as manifested in the civil rights movement: "When legal contests were the sole form of activity, the ordinary Negro was involved as a passive spectator. His interest was stirred, but his energies were unemployed. Mass marches transformed the common man into the star performer."[58] Were political engagement as a general condition to comprise only passive attention to political affairs, unaccompanied by political activity, many of democracy's most cherished goals would go unfulfilled. Political spectatorship by itself has no obvious connection to the goals of legitimacy, fair representation, and citizen vigilance against governmental or factional abuses. Attention and activity both matter when we speak and write about the condition of engagement. Indeed, when we focus our attention on attention and activity we can ensure that our studies of politically, socially, or morally engaged populations actually measure the relevant characteristics.

[margin handwritten note: Engagement with not by or in]

Political Engagement

As should be apparent by now, political engagement refers to attentive activity directly involving the polity—whether at the local, state, or national level—or any "activity that is intended to or has the consequences

---

no knowledge of what is outside me except by means of the ideas I have within me."] René Descartes, Letter to Gibieuf, January 19, 1642. Cited in Taylor (1989: 143).

[56] Villa (2001: 299) critiques prevailing conceptions of citizenship that focus on energy invested without accompanying attention to principles and morality: "[So-called] 'good citizens' channel their energy into loyal service to their company, church, schools, and political associations. That the ends pursued and means employed by these groups and organizations are at times morally questionable is something that rarely, if ever, engages their attention."

[57] Valelly (1996: 17–27).

[58] Martin Luther King Jr., *Where Do We Go from Here: Chaos or Community?* Cited in Sandel (1996: 348–49).

of affecting, either directly or indirectly, government action."[59] Thus political engagement encompasses most of the activities that we normally associate with political participation or citizenship: voting, contacting representatives, contributing financially to representatives or interest groups, following political issues (via any media format), associating with groups intended to influence political outcomes, attending rallies or demonstrations intended to influence political outcomes, or running for (or holding) political office. Political engagement as a particular episode could involve only political attention, only political activity, or both of them together, but political engagement as a generalized state must represent attention to political affairs and processes as well as activity aimed at actualization.

Political engagement subsumes civic engagement, because if civic is construed as relating to the city, then the polity subsumes the city. And if civic is construed as relating to citizenship, then the political encompasses issues relating to citizenship as well.[60] While political engagement subsumes civic engagement, it differs from social engagement; political actions and involvements do not always require multiple parties. Many regard solitary voting as the paradigmatic political act.[61] Not only voting but also donating to political candidates or causes, writing letters or e-mails to elected officials or op-ed pages, and following politics via mass media: all of these activities can be undertaken by oneself.[62] Even Aristotle, widely cited by civic republican enthusiasts, does not hold politics to be intrinsically social. In *The Politics* he describes kingship as a "true" form of political rule, yet the ruling activity of one virtuous individual does not involve collective, political deliberation.[63]

Political engagement encompasses all of the attentive activities that citizens' duties require, without the difficulties civic engagement encounters. Consider the case of political activism undertaken by noncitizens. On May 1 of 2006 thousands of primarily Latino workers staged El Gran Paro Estadounidense, the Great American Strike or Boycott, hoping to shape American immigration policy. How could we call their efforts "civic engagement" when many of them were not citizens in the first

[59] Verba, Schlozman, and Brady (1995: 9).

[60] *Oxford English Dictionary*.

[61] The solitary nature of modern voting may make it politically unsatisfying to a civic republican such as Arendt: "The booth in which we deposit our ballots is unquestionably too small, for this booth has room for only one." Arendt, "On Violence" in (1972: 232). But Arendt's point, which follows from her well-known insistence that politics must be "plural" or associative to be authentic, is more of an assertion than a reasoned argument.

[62] Verba, Schlozman, and Brady (1995) count solitary voting, letter writing, and contributing money as acts of "political engagement."

[63] Aristotle (1984: 1284b35–1288b5).

place? Nor were they attempting simply to influence their local city but rather to capture national attention and influence national policy. If we switch political with civic engagement we lose the conceptual problems altogether, because citizens and noncitizens alike can try to influence political processes and outcomes.

Often, political scientists and theorists treat voting rates as a proxy for political engagement because of the easy access to voting data, but voting represents only the tip of the political iceberg. Many forms of political engagement—community organizing, volunteering for a political campaign, attending town council meetings—may involve far more energy and attention than voting, although some—signing petitions, for example—may involve less. When we conceptualize political engagement only as periodic voting we miss the richness and dynamic potential of democratic citizenship. Consider the "elite" school of democracy, represented most famously by Joseph Schumpeter and Walter Lippmann. Those two advocate for less rather than more political engagement because they focus only on national-level elections featuring complex policy questions, and they rightly acknowledge that most citizens—even the most highly educated—will always lack the insider perspective required to master the relevant issues. They fear that asking citizens to do too much, when citizens can understand and attend to so little, is to court either disillusionment or unhelpful meddling or both. But democracy means much more than complex policy decisions undertaken by government specialists, and ordinary citizens can find many opportunities outside the ballot box to affect local, statewide, and national political outcomes in which they take a special interest.

Social Engagement

Social engagement encompasses all manner of associational involvements. It means attentive activity in what Tocqueville calls "those associations in civil life which have no political object," as well as informal socializing and personal friendships.[64] Thus social engagement is conceptually distinct from political engagement, although as discussed above the two can be combined. But social engagement occurs more commonly without a political component; most of our everyday social engagements are apolitical. Repeated social engagement may produce what Putnam and others call "social capital," or relationships of trust and reciprocity, and social capital tends to correlate with political engagement.[65] Thus while social

[64]Tocqueville (1969: 513).
[65]Putnam (2000).

engagement may not be political in itself, it certainly can be prepolitical; it can be a resource that fosters or facilitates political engagement.[66]

Tocqueville's *Old Regime and the Revolution* provides a cogent distinction between the political engagement of citizens and the social engagement of associational members. Tocqueville contrasts the voluntary associations predominant in sixteenth-century France with those found in eighteenth-century France, and finds that only the earlier era's groups evinced political orientations. Associational members in the sixteenth century, "after having taken care of the business of their own associations among themselves, constantly met with all the other inhabitants to deliberate together about the general interests of the city." But by the eighteenth century, members of French voluntary associations "had almost entirely withdrawn into themselves, for the acts of municipal life had become rare, and were always executed by individuals."[67] Any coincidence between social and political engagement was circumstantial rather than logically necessary.

In *Democracy in America* Tocqueville worries about the tendency for democracy to foster individualism, a self-absorbed withdrawal from public concerns and political engagement. But in *The Old Regime* he finds "no individuals who did not belong to a group and who could consider themselves absolutely alone," yet nonetheless "each one of the thousand little groups of which French society was composed thought only of itself" and of "matters which directly affected it." Thus eighteenth-century France was rife with social engagement but also with what Tocqueville calls "collective individualism," and a notable absence of political attention or cooperation.[68] Some modern scholars have criticized neo-Tocquevilleans for idealizing civil associations and assuming that membership always produces public-spirited virtue.[69] But Tocqueville recognized that nonpolitical associations could work to democracy's benefit or detriment, depending upon the exclusivity of members' attachments and the degree to which the state involved them in discourse or simply left them alone.

Sheri Berman describes a similar phenomenon in Weimar Germany, where a flourishing civil society worked at cross-purposes with public-spirited political citizenship. As with Tocqueville's France and its "thousand little groups," Weimar Germany's many voluntary associations "served to hive their memberships off from each other and contribute to the formation of what one observer called 'ferociously jealous small

---

[66] Engagement with social networks can greatly facilitate political recruitment and mobilization. See Rosenstone and Hansen (1993).

[67] Tocqueville (1998: 163).

[68] Ibid., 162–63.

[69] Daniel A. Bell, "Civil Society versus Civic Virtue," in Gutmann (1998: 242–46). Bell singles out residential community associations as insular, self-centered groups whose members prioritize selfish interests against the common good. Tocqueville foresees this very possibility.

republics.'"[70] Berman, like Tocqueville, describes pernicious effects that may ensue when widespread social engagement is divorced from state-sanctioned political processes and institutions: "Germans threw themselves into their clubs, voluntary associations, and professional organizations out of frustration with the failures of the national government and political parties, thereby helping to undermine the Weimar Republic and facilitate Hitler's rise to power."

Only when we distinguish between political and social engagements rather than compressing them under a single civic engagement banner can we draw helpful lessons from the French and German experiences. Those records suggest that widespread social engagement combined with radical political disengagement—in other words, the generation of social capital among people who either cannot or will not translate their energies into political voice and action—can imperil democratic stability. Further, neither social nor political engagement is itself sufficient for political stability; democracies require responsive political institutions through which citizen engagement can be channeled, lest pent-up demand for redress explode into violence or chaos.

Moral Engagement

The category of moral engagement waits in the wings, involved with some but not all political and social engagement. Moral engagement encompasses attention to, and activity in support of, a particular moral code, moral reasoning, or moral principles. This category is the most subtle and difficult to define, but it represents a crucial distinction nonetheless. We should first note that like social and political engagement, moral engagement can represent either a particular episode or a general condition. As the representation of a particular episode, moral engagement can mean either attention to a moral code or activity relating to a moral code or both. As the representation of a general condition, moral engagement means a combination of attention, and activity relating to, moral codes or moral reasoning. At the societal level scholars will care about the widespread condition of moral engagement, but that might be gauged by measuring many different instances of episodic moral engagement (whether attention, activity, or both).[71]

---

[70] Berman (1997: 30).

[71] Hannah Arendt, whose concepts of "thinking" and "thoughtlessness" have informed my construction of moral engagement and disengagement, separates action from reflection in an unorthodox manner. For Arendt, "thinking—much more than mere cogitation but rather a kind of moral reflection—involves withdrawal from the world of appearances and the world of action." But she does not mean to divorce action from reflection enduringly;

As a general condition, moral engagement involves not only an orientation or state of character but also moral activity or follow-through. A morally engaged individual possesses a disposition to act on his or her moral principles; she possesses virtues of character in addition to any intellectual virtues. As Aristotle writes of moral actions, moral engagement involves doing the right thing while being committed to the reasons that justify for the action:

> But for actions expressing virtue to be done temperately or justly [and hence well] it does not suffice that they are themselves in the right state. Rather, the agent must also be in the right state when he does them. First, he must know [that he is doing virtuous actions]; second, he must decide on them, and decide on them for themselves; and third, he must also do them from a firm and unchanging state.[72]

In Aristotle's account incontinent individuals lack virtue because they either fail to perform moral actions or they "go through the motions" without cognizance of the moral justification. In my terms, they either lack moral activity or moral attention. Even if one acts rightly, "saying the words that come from knowledge is no sign [of fully having it]. . . . Hence we must suppose that incontinents say the [moral] words in the way that actors do . . . [merely] saying the words, as the drunk says the words of Empedocles."[73]

To restate, moral engagement as a condition means more than simply going through the moral motions. Friends of liberal democracy cannot relish the prospect of a citizenry habitually undertaking morally laudable activities without any attention to the underlying moral justification or rationale. In the absence of moral reasoning, nothing guarantees that citizens' future actions will be morally desirable. Such citizens would be morally docile, in George Kateb's terms, available for mobilization into any activity without the intermediary of moral judgment regarding its ultimate worth.[74] Yet attention to moral principles without acting to actualize them would be a kind of moral spectatorship, a refusal to act on one's own moral dictates. In his *Letter from a Birmingham Jail* Martin Luther King Jr. condemns this kind of moral passivity: "We will have to repent in this generation not merely for the hateful words and actions of the bad people but for the appalling silence of the good people."[75]

---

the "enlarged mentality" made possible by disengaged thinking and judging undergirds morally responsible action. Arendt (1961: 241). Also see Arendt (1978).

[72] Aristotle (1985: 1105a30-b1).

[73] Ibid., 1147a20-b10.

[74] Kateb (1992: 124).

[75] King (1963). Similarly, Aristotle criticizes those who want to be virtuous people without doing virtuous actions: "they are like a sick person who listens attentively to the doctor,

Of course, even moral engagement conceptualized as attention and activity does not ensure morally desirable outcomes. Good intentions and morally defensible reasoning and actions can still lead to unintended consequences.[76] And if moral engagement with defensible moral codes can end badly, all the more so for moral engagement with indefensible moral codes. In Aristotle's *Politics* the good citizen in an unjust regime undertakes activities morally sanctioned by his fellows yet nonetheless commits injustice because he engages with faulty principles.[77] Extremists of many backgrounds have practiced religious, racial, or ethnic oppression while motivated by, and closely attentive to, a set of moral dictates—illiberal moral dictates, but moral dictates nonetheless.[78] Thus we might claim that stable liberal democracies require a certain kind of moral engagement from its citizens, attention and activity relating to moral principles such as toleration, reciprocity, and law-abidingness.[79] The exact content of democratic moral engagement is a matter for extensive debate that lies outside this book's scope.[80] Because widespread democratic moral engagement is more of an aspiration than an imminent reality, and also because even liberal-democratic moral engagement is subject to misapplication, liberal democracies require stable and responsive political institutions and an established rule of law not only to encourage moral engagement among the citizenry and representatives but also to prevent the damaging consequences that could result from misguided, oppressive, and pernicious moral engagement.

Most important, moral engagement does not equal political or social engagement, because not all moral engagement has a political or social component. Moral engagement certainly can accompany social

---

but acts on none of his instructions. Such a course of treatment will not improve the state of his body; any more than will the man's way of doing philosophy improve the state of their souls." Aristotle (1985: 1105b15).

[76] Good intentions might not pave the road to hell but, as Kant reminds us, we cannot always control their outcome. Kant (1993: 8 §394).

[77] Aristotle (1984: 1276b30).

[78] Thoroughgoing moral disengagement probably occurs but rarely, as in the case of sociopaths who do not attend to any moral code whatsoever. As mentioned previously, less extreme but still dangerous versions include what Arendt calls "thoughtlessness," or a refusal to "think what we are doing." Arendt (1959: 5, 262). Arendt's "thoughtlessness" refers to episodic moral disengagement, a capable moral agent turning her attention from moral principles and reasoning.

[79] For comprehensive historical analyses of liberalism's relationship to virtue, see Berkowitz (1999) and Macedo (1990). Dagger (1997) describes a moderate version of "republican liberalism" that respects autonomy as well as civic virtue. See also Sabl (2005b).

[80] The desire to promote a minimal set of moral dispositions and virtues motivates Chambers and Kopstein's insistence (2001: 839) that associational membership promote the value of reciprocity, and also Rosenblum's admission (1998b: 350) that liberal democracy requires certain moral dispositions including "treating people identically and with easy spontaneity" and "speaking out against ordinary injustices."

or political engagement; religious communities and close friendships combine attention and activity relating to social dynamics and moral principles, and civil rights marches bring together political, social, and moral elements. But often they part company. Jewish tradition values the practice of anonymous charity in which neither the recipient nor the benefactor knows the other's identity.[81] Tocqueville's *Memoir on Pauperism* provides a further example. Tocqueville distinguishes between "two kinds of welfare," one of which is "produced and regulated by society," conceived and administered by people in their collective capacity, involving moral and social engagement. But the second kind of welfare "is a private virtue" that "escapes social action" and "leads each individual, according to his means, to alleviate the evils he sees around him." In other words, the second kind of welfare involves moral engagement without social or political engagement.[82]

When Nancy Rosenblum criticizes the tendency toward "liberal expectancy" among participatory theorists, she means to chide those who assume (without basis) that social engagement will always produce desirable moral engagement.[83] Diverse other scholars make similar points.[84] History provides many examples of politically or socially engaged individuals tragically lacking in moral engagement, from Ku Klux Klan members to Adolf Eichmann (Nazi Germany's model citizen but Hannah Arendt's primary example of one who did not "think what he was doing").[85] To conflate political or social engagement with moral engagement is to ascribe more to political and social involvement than they can sustain, conceptually or historically.

Of course, all social engagement includes at least a modicum of moral engagement among associates. League bowlers must subscribe to minimal, shared norms of behavior among one another. But subscribing to relevant norms of group behavior comprises a very thin kind of morality indeed, not just a quantitative but also a qualitative difference from moral engagement as I have described it. In addition to being thin, the minimal moral engagement among some group members can also be narrow; it can extend no further than the relevant group, and thus can be of questionable utility for democratic politics. Putnam captures this nuance by distinguishing between "*bridging* (or inclusive) and *bonding* (or exclusive)" social capital.[86] The former denotes "networks [that] are

[81] Maimonides (1962: 10:7–12).

[82] This first kind of welfare "leads society to concern itself with the misfortunes of its members and is ready systematically to alleviate their sufferings." Tocqueville (1997: 51).

[83] Rosenblum (1998b: 8–10, 15–17).

[84] Mark R. Warren (2001); Gutmann (1998).

[85] Arendt (1964: 287 and 32–33).

[86] Putnam (2000: 22–23).

outward looking and encompass people across diverse social cleavages," and can promote tolerant norms toward a broad range of people. The latter denotes associations or networks that "are, by choice or necessity, inward looking and tend to reinforce exclusive identities and homogenous groups"; these are useful "for undergirding specific reciprocity and mobilizing solidarity." He means that social engagement does not always entail generalizable moral engagement, precisely the point that Plato taught two thousand years earlier when he reminded us that even pirates or thieves require a modicum of justice among themselves, although they do not extend their code to ill-fated outsiders.[87]

Civil Engagement

For the sake of conceptual clarity we must identify instances in which political, social, and moral engagements occur independently, but in practice they often coincide. One combination merits a separate discussion and perhaps its own category: the social-moral engagement of public-spirited, cooperative problem solving, which I propose to call civil engagement. Not only does that term resonate with the commonplace concept of civil society—the cooperative space between governmental and purely private affairs—but it also meshes with Alexis de Tocqueville's typology. Tocqueville uses civil to describe associations that, while not concerned with political processes or institutions, pursue their members' common ends cooperatively. He maintains that only citizen action, rather than political force, can "[refresh] the circulation of feelings and ideas among a great people." Tocqueville's Americans engage civilly when they "have conceived a sentiment or an idea that they want to produce before the world," such as the "one hundred thousand men [who] had publicly promised never to drink alcoholic liquor" in an effort to influence their fellow citizens by collective example rather than governmental coercion.[88] J.G.A. Pocock supports this distinction between civil, meaning social-moral, and civic or political engagement. Pocock depicts eighteenth-century Edinburgh as experiencing a "proliferation of Spectatorial clubs and societies, practicing the virtues of polite conversation and enlightened taste while discussing the economic, cultural and even . . . the moral improvement of Scottish life," which represented a change from the more explicitly political engagement of an earlier era. In Pocock's terms, "the locus of virtue shifted decisively from the *political* and *military* to that blend of the economic, cultural and moral"; in

---

[87] Plato (1991: 351c–d).
[88] Tocqueville (1969: 516).

other words, the locus of virtue shifted "from the *civic* to the *civil*."[89] And Mark E. Warren calls the virtues promoted by certain associations "'pre-civic' [meaning prepolitical] or simply 'civil' virtues," because they are not immediately (or merely) political but might support some democratic processes.[90]

Civil engagement as I have conceptualized it represents the kind of social-moral engagement that Tocqueville and many contemporary scholars feel to be particularly important for democracies' flourishing. It possesses familiarity and resonance because of its association with the vast civil society literature, and it lacks the pitfalls that have accompanied previous attempts to distinguish cooperative voluntarism from political engagement.[91] As mentioned in chapter 1, Zukin and colleagues call cooperative voluntarism "civic engagement" and political involvement "political engagement," but their terminology invites as much confusion as it resolves.[92] In addition to the linguistic confusion involved with contrasting civic and political when the two terms overlap so enticingly, Zukin's civic engagement includes any kind of associational membership or social engagement in addition to explicitly moral, community-oriented involvements. In other words, it includes involvement in bowling leagues as well as in soup kitchens. Thus the authors inadvertently reconstitute Putnam's original difficulty of conflating concepts. At one pole, their civic engagement may confuse scholars and citizens because we so commonly associate civic with political. At the other pole, their civic engagement blends indistinguishably into the social. Civil engagement lacks these problems and promotes clear discourse.[93]

[89] Pocock, "Cambridge Paradigms and Scotch Philosophers," in Hont and Ignatieff (1983: 240; stress added).

[90] Mark R. Warren (2001: 75).

[91] As one example among many, see Cohen and Arato (1992). Tocqueville's praise 'for Americans' "art of associating" in civil associations has impressed and influenced several generations of political scientists. Tocqueville (1969: 489–96). In Tocqueville's account, those "associations that are formed in civil life and which have an object that is in no way political" often promote intellectual and moral development: "sentiments and ideas renew themselves, the heart is enlarged, and the human mind is developed only by the reciprocal action of men upon one another." Tocqueville (1969: 491). When citizens come together in civil engagement they may develop a sense of efficacy and interpersonal bonds, which is why "civil associations thus facilitate political associations." Contemporary scholars such as Verba, Schlozman, and Brady draw similar conclusions. See Verba, Schlozman, and Brady (1995: 79).

[92] Zukin et al. (2006).

[93] Hibbing and Theiss-Morse (2002: 209) question whether what I call civil engagement actually improves political engagement and effectiveness: "Regardless of how much the theorists muse and yearn, the empirical evidence consistently indicates that involvement either in volunteer groups or in rich, real deliberative settings does nothing to help people appreciate and deal successfully with the challenges of democratic governance."

Some readers might object that I oppose civic engagement because it combines too many distinct components, yet I propose civil engagement, which itself combines several components. But conceptual clarification is not an either/or proposition, with our only choices being to maintain a rigid separation of political, social, and moral engagement categories or else to abandon the clarifying project altogether. Were the situation so stark, we would face a choice between being useful and being right. The reason for reincarnating civic engagement into political, social, and moral engagement is not that the constituent parts never travel together, but that the term *civic engagement* generates such diverse connotations that it has resisted good-faith efforts at clarification. Civic engagement stands on tainted ground. If its use continues unabated we will most likely see continued conflation of political, social, and moral engagement, a conflation that is both counterproductive to good research and conceptually mistaken.

Conclusion

Replacing civic engagement with political, social, and moral varieties (and augmenting them with civil engagement as well) helps us to think and talk more clearly about making democracy work. At present many scholars associate high civic engagement with a range of desirable outcomes, often implying that the former somehow promotes the latter, but they wrongly give the same credit to political attention and activity as to social and moral engagement.[94] But those engagements are distinct, as are their advantages and disadvantages. Chapter 5 further develops those distinctions.

Political engagement still has many things to recommend it, and democracy would not be democracy unless citizens devoted at least some attention and activity to politics. Further, the worthy ideals of political legitimacy and fair representation would be much better served by higher political participation and turnout among groups that traditionally have been less active and vocal.[95] But promoting political engagement will

[94] To confuse matters even more, one scholar recently defined social capital as a measure of "civic group involvement, social and racial trust, and political engagement," thus making social capital dependent upon civic and political engagement instead of the other way around. Brooks (2005: 15).

[95] In particular, citizens at the lower end of the income and educational spectrums have tended to vote at lower than average rates and, when inactive, to have their interests less well represented by self-styled advocates than citizens at higher ends of those spectrums. Verba, Schlozman, and Brady (1995).

require money, time, and other scarce resources. And because many people freely choose political disengagement, promoting widespread change
might also require legal coercion, which liberal democracies cannot undertake lightly.[96]

Coercion comes in many varieties, some more obvious than others.
Ethan Leib, a deliberative democrat, favors the establishment of "deliberative juries" in which citizens would spend days discussing salient political issues and ultimately advise Congress. In Leib's proposal, "service
is mandatory and may be coerced."[97] Arend Lijphart leads the ranks of
compulsory voting supporters (although compulsory voting in Australia
has not materially enhanced citizens' attention to, or knowledge of, politics).[98] Iseult Honohan, under the banner of civic republicanism, defends
compulsory political participation as long as it will elicit "genuine deliberation."[99] And participatory theorists such as Carole Pateman, C. B.
MacPherson, and Nicos Poulantzas endorse widespread, compulsory,
collective action (including the democratization not only of the workplace but also of many other associative bodies) that would necessitate
extensive, invasive, and coercive government action.[100]

While the majority of participatory and deliberative democrats do not
call for coercion, they must explain which methods other than coercion
will overcome the overwhelming difficulties of generating widespread,
voluntary, and sustained political attention and energy. Bruce Ackerman
and James Fishkin suggest paying citizens to deliberate, which would represent an enormous cost for uncertain returns.[101] They also acknowledge
that their proposal would face extremely long odds against adoption.
Thus if deliberative and participatory democrats earnestly wish to mobilize high and widespread political engagement, yet recognize that leaving

[96] By "legal coercion," I mean the kind of policies that compel desired responses, whether
in the form of action or inaction, through the threat of nondraconian penalties. Even political liberals accept legal coercion as legitimate when they are undertaken to prevent harm
or offense to other people. See Feinberg (1990). If radical political disengagement can be
shown to cause the public interest serious harm, then even political liberals might countenance policies that require political engagement.

[97] Leib (2005: 92).

[98] Lijphart (1997). See also Wattenberg (2007). For the critique of Australian compulsory
voting, see McAllister (1998).

[99] Honohan (2002: 246).

[100] "In the participatory state, derived from the likes of Pateman, MacPherson and Poulantzas, compulsory collective action—and therefore the domain of politics—extends to a
great number of social institutions, ranging from the workplace to local, regional, national
and (in theory at least) international communities." Holliday (1994: 242).

[101] As Andrew Sabl wryly notes, Ackerman and Fishkin's proposal to pay citizens 50 percent
more than the minimum wage is "a welcome acknowledgement that most people would rather
stay at home alone than deliberate about politics," as well as "an (unintentional) admission that
deliberation is, for most, half again as unpleasant as their jobs." Sabl (2005a: 150n14).

the matter to personal choice will probably fail to produce the desired results and that to paying high stipends is politically infeasible—the specter of coercion will always lurk in the background.

For those reasons, anyone advocating very high political engagement for all citizens must explain not only what it is but also why liberal democracies must have it in spades. Thus far I have addressed the first question; we should understand political engagement as a combination of attention to and activity in political affairs—affairs that require or demand interaction with political organs or institutions—that can (but need not) be combined with social and/or moral engagement. It remains to inquire into the relative values of these kinds of attentive activity. Is political engagement intrinsically valuable for human beings, constitutive of human flourishing, as certain civic republican theorists maintain?[102] Is it instrumentally valuable for citizens of democracy, conducive to a range of goals such as stability, fairness, political legitimacy, and efficiency, as some political scientists have suggested? Must citizens be politically engaged all the time or only episodically? Perhaps liberal democracies can flourish with relatively low levels of political engagement if they also feature continuously high social and moral engagement—which can be channeled into political engagement should the circumstances warrant—and political institutions able to process that episodic engagement and respond satisfactorily. Perhaps liberal democracies do require high and widespread political engagement for the sake of fair representation and political legitimacy. The following chapters consider these questions, more as an invitation for further scholarly inquiry and discussion than as an attempt at a definitive answer. But we cannot begin our discussions if we do not know how to pose the questions. Clarity issues a simple demand: that civic give way to political, social, and moral engagement.

[102] Cf. Arendt (1961) and (1963). Regardless of whether Arendt fully believed in her words—that politics is praiseworthy in and of itself—she is interpreted by others as a civic republican theorist and cited in support of politics' intrinsic value. Cf. Barber (1984), Sandel (1996). For a non-Arendtian claim of politics' intrinsic value, see Miller (1995).

Chapter 3

POLITICAL ENGAGEMENT AS INTRINSIC GOOD

ARENDT AND COMPANY

> The basic assumption of the ward system, whether Jefferson knew it or not, was that no one could be happy without his share in public happiness, that no one could be called free without his experience in public freedom, and that no one could be called either happy or free without participating, and having a share, in public power.
> —Hannah Arendt, *On Revolution*

I HAVE SUGGESTED THAT we let civic engagement die a noble death, to be reborn as its constituent parts: political, social, and moral engagement, concepts that are better equipped to clarify and enhance our discourse about making democracy work. From this point forward I will focus primarily on political engagement, reserving moral engagement for a separate book-length treatment. Many democrats, ranging from scholars to pundits to community leaders, praise political engagement uncritically, as if we always need as much as we can get. But since American democracy has generally run short of political attention and energy, the task of eliciting high and widespread political engagement might require extreme measures. Liberal democrats cannot countenance coercion or paternalism without first knowing just how valuable political engagement is. How much do we need, and to what lengths should we go to get it?

Those questions loom large, yet too many political theorists and political scientists overlook them and take political engagement's worth for granted. Those who bother to justify their advocacy generally take one of two tacks, arguing that we should care about political engagement—and promote it wherever possible—because it is intrinsically valuable for human beings or because it is instrumentally valuable for democratic polities. The intrinsic defense values political engagement as an end in itself, "an essential part of the good life for an individual," although not necessarily the highest end for human beings.[1] The instrumental defense values political engagement as a means to other, desirable ends but not necessarily as a particularly choice-worthy end in itself.[2]

Intrinsic defenses sometimes appeal to those who appreciate a particular practice or good or state of mind but lack hard evidence that might definitively persuade the uncommitted. The argument often goes as follows, with the variable X representing anything from art to religious faith to romantic love:

> X's goodness is self-evident. X is an end in itself, without reference to other goods or goals. To be human is to enjoy or benefit from X. X elicits our highest capacities. To justify X instrumentally would be to denigrate its goodness or otherwise risk corrupting it.[3]

In other words, intrinsic defenses often resort to declaration rather than disputation. Their validity depends on something like a gut feeling, aesthetic judgment, or pure faith, none of which can be authoritatively proven or disproven. To many readers, arguing thusly for the value of art, love, god, or friendship might make perfect sense at a visceral level. Far fewer people feel similarly about political engagement, but some political theorists and philosophers continue to invoke its intrinsic worth.[4]

In the absence of compelling proof, those who defend a subject's intrinsic worth may cite like-minded authorities to establish their argument's legitimacy. Unfortunately, the like-minded authorities themselves often assert rather than prove the subject's intrinsic worth, so the apparently bolstered arguments recur to a bare declaration after all. Aristotle represents the ancient theorist most commonly cited toward this end. Generations of political theorists have invoked Aristotle's conception of the human being as a *zōon politikon* (ζῷον πολιτικόν, or political animal) to support what Stephen Salkever calls "the politics-as-intrinsic-good argument."[5] According to Salkever, the argument "suggests that Aristotle is

[1] Christiano (1997: 245).

[2] Note that while many philosophers treat intrinsic and instrumental valuation as directly opposite measures, not all do. Christine Korsgaard argues that the concept of intrinsic value measures where something's value resides—inside the thing itself—and so should be contrasted with extrinsic value, "the value a thing gets from some other source." Korsgaard, "Two Distinctions in Goodness," in Korsgaard (1996: 249–74). But present purposes do not require a definitive answer. The goal here is to canvass the most common arguments for political engagement's worth, and political theorists commonly draw upon intrinsic/ instrumental language as if it described a true dichotomy.

[3] Kant describes the intrinsic valuation of art as follows: "taste . . . teaches us to find, even in sensuous objects, a free delight apart from any charm of sense." Kant (1952: 225). Stephen Guest (2002: 307–8) chronicles Kant's influence among other theorists of intrinsic value.

[4] Christiano (1996).

[5] J.G.A. Pocock, one of the most influential scholars in the so-called republican revival movement, writes of "the ancient ideal of *homo politicus* (the *zōon politikon* of Aristotle),

defending the intrinsic value of political life against those who would see it as having only instrumental value." Unfortunately, "this reading runs afoul of Aristotle's apparent derogation of the political life to a rank below the theoretical life in the concluding books of both *The Politics* and the *Nicomachean Ethics*."[6] Bernard Yack similarly resists the use of Aristotle to justify politics intrinsically.[7] But leaving aside Aristotle's exact intent regarding the claim about *zōon politikon*, even he primarily asserts rather than demonstrates the point conclusively. As Yack and Salkever have addressed the misuses of Aristotle's apparent intrinsic defense of political engagement, I turn now to the most commonly invoked modern source: Hannah Arendt.

Arendt draws heavily on Aristotle in *The Human Condition*, connecting "the 'good life,' as Aristotle called the life of the citizen," with a mastery of "sheer life" and transcendence of "the biological life process."[8] Arendt's reading of Aristotle and her intrinsic valuation of politics enjoy wide scholarly influence. Iseult Honohan allocates an entire chapter of *Civic Republicanism* to Arendt's foundational role in the "republican revival" that began in the 1960s, emphasizing (and also criticizing) her intrinsic defense of politics' worth.[9] J.G.A. Pocock, one of the republican revival's leading figures, self-consciously employs "terms borrowed from or suggested by the language of Hannah Arendt" and Arendt's reading of Aristotle to characterize politics as an intrinsic good, influencing a generation of like-minded scholars.[10] In fact Salkever characterizes Arendt as "the modern founder of this reading of Aristotle."[11]

Yack explains "the widespread acceptance of [Arendt's] image of Aristotelian political philosophy"—an image stressing politics as the highest activity, which Yack finds completely "foreign to Aristotle's conceptual vocabulary"—by suggesting that "her claims are read within the context of . . . the debates that have grown up around communitarian critiques of liberal individualism."[12] Michael Sandel acknowledges Arendt's respected status among "the communitarian, or republican alternatives" to rights-

---

who affirms his being and his virtue by the medium of political action." Pocock (1975: 550) cited in Salkever (2005: 38).

[6] Salkever (2005: 38).

[7] Yack (1993).

[8] Arendt, *The Human Condition* (1959: 36–37). Hereafter *HC*.

[9] Honohan (2002: 111–44). Honohan also critiques Arendt's theory of politics' "intrinsic (indeed ultimate) value" (2002: 131). Honohan links Arendt with the participatory versions of the civic republican revival, sometimes called *civic humanism*, as opposed to more institutionally oriented versions of republicanism. Cf. Berger (2010).

[10] Pocock (1975: 550).

[11] Salkever (2005: 59).

[12] This reaction and modern liberalism "inclines modern scholars to exaggerate the nobility and harmony of Aristotelian politics." Yack (1993: 13).

based liberalism, alternatives that often praise politics and membership as ends in themselves.[13] The result has been a boon for those communitarians, civic republicans, and participatory democrats who wish to justify political engagement for its own sake and its inherent dignity.[14]

To be clear, Arendt herself delves into ancient and modern politics much more deeply than many of the readings perpetrated in her name. A nuanced and multifaceted thinker, Arendt does not esteem political engagement simply for its intrinsic worth; she acknowledges certain instrumental benefits of politics as well. But contemporary political theorists who draw support from Arendt's defense of political action more commonly focus on her intrinsic than her instrumental defense, which is why I focus on it here. She represents the single most prominent and influential modern theorist who stands for (or is taken to stand for) political engagement's intrinsic valuation, yet those aspects of her work do not stand up to critical scrutiny.[15] That revelation portends badly for the intrinsic defense more generally, because (as I imply here and will argue in chapter 5) other influential versions of the intrinsic defense fare little better than Arendt's.

Arendt depicts the political realm as the sole space in which freedom can appear—a space marked by the presence of spontaneous, competitive, noninstrumentally oriented human action and by the absence of all matters relating to necessity.[16] Economics, bodily needs, the pursuit of coercive power, and even emotions such as compassion, love, and pity are "out."[17] Courage, creativity, desire for distinction, and identity-revealing performances are "in." Politics thus conceptualized generates a "brilliant light" of freedom and fulfillment for its participants.[18] How should we approach these standards for thinking and talking about politics, which

[13] Sandel (1984: 7 and 1996: 355). Sandel himself does not take a position on political engagement's intrinsic worth. Philip Pettit also acknowledges the common association of Arendt with communitarianism. Pettit (1997: 8). And John Maynor represents yet another republican theorist who associates Arendt with an intrinsic defense of the "meaningful" "flourishing" of political participation. Maynor (2002: 86).

[14] Shiraz Dossa (1989: 139) declares admiringly that "as a political theorist, Arendt's greatest achievement was to recover and restore the ancient conception of the public realm," which represents "the highest form of human association." Steven Ascheim (2001: 10) more dispassionately acknowledges "Arendt's emphasis on the primacy of the political realm and the intrinsic value of plurality."

[15] For more on Arendt's intrinsic valuation of politics, see Villa (1996).

[16] For the political realm as the space of freedom, see "What Is Freedom?" in Arendt, *Between Past and Future* (1961: 146). Hereafter *BPF*. For the role of action in the political realm: "Action, to be free, must be free from motive on one side, from its intended goal as a predictable effect on the other." *BPF*: 151.

[17] Wolin (1983) comments on this exclusion as well.

[18] My analysis here is limited to those aspects of Arendt's voluminous writings concerned with political action and the public realm.

seem impractically restrictive at best and elitist or exclusionary at worst? Existing scholarly interpretations generally fall into one of two broad groups, the literal and figurative readings of Arendt's political ideals.[19]

Some literal readers interpret Arendt's characterizations of politics in the tradition of civic republican theory, with its praise for active citizenship and emphasis on civic duty. They accept at face value Arendt's depiction of political participation as constitutive of freedom and the "good life."[20] Scholars who are inclined toward civic republican ideals may enlist Arendt's claims in support of their commitments.[21] Other literal readers object to the practical implications of Arendt's political prescriptions. Barring economics from the political realm might conserve the economic status quo and exclude those whose primary interests involve competition for scarce resources.[22] Barring bodily concerns might exclude, among others, a range of feminist voices and issues from political discussion. Prioritizing virtues such as courage and competitiveness might make politics the domain of a talented elite.[23] But in spite of such criticisms, most of the literal readers find more in Arendt's work to praise than to reject.[24]

Among those who read Arendt's ideals figuratively, some point to instances in which she demonstrates a fairly traditional understanding of political practices—including the resolution of economic concerns through the use of state power—as evidence that her idealized political characterizations are not intended literally.[25] Perhaps her political rhetoric was simply intentional overstatement aimed at "restoring a sense of balance" when "applied to the era's prejudices, so sated with subtle sociology and finely tuned economics."[26] Other figurative readers place her

[19] I use "literal" not in the sense of "word for word" but "the sense expressed by the actual wording of a passage," which contrasts with "figurative" or "metaphorical" (*Oxford English Dictionary*). When I write of interpretations that are almost completely literal I mean interpretations that take at face value Arendt's claims about politics, not interpretations that treat every single metaphor as fact. Arendt invites both literal and figurative interpretations because she mixes literal and figurative language throughout her writings. Cf. Kateb (1983: 162).

[20] Arendt writes glowingly of Thomas Jefferson's proposed ward system and its "basic assumption . . . that no one could be called either happy or free without participating, and having a share, in public power." Arendt, *On Revolution* (1963: 255). Hereafter *OR*.

[21] Barber (1984). Although Barber does not there endorse all aspects of Arendt's republicanism, elsewhere he groups himself and Arendt as theorists who use strong rhetoric and grand theory in praise of political engagement. Cf. Barber (2000). Also see Pocock (1975).

[22] Pitkin (1981). See also Zaretsky (1997).

[23] Pitkin (1981); Wolin (1983); and Benhabib (1990). For a dissenting view on Arendt as a Greek idealizer, see Tsao (2002).

[24] For example, Mark Reinhart agrees with some of Wolin's and Pitkin's criticisms but proposes to enlist Arendt's insights in his project while "resisting her impulse to purify." Reinhart (1997: 143–49).

[25] Isaac (1992).

[26] Miller (1979: 183, 202).

political ideals in the service of a larger project, seeing them, for example, as "an attempt to conjure a magnificent transfiguring illusion, a *via gloriosa*, and so rehabilitate what she called 'the empty space' to which humanity had withdrawn after Auschwitz."[27]

I propose a reading of Arendt that clarifies her attitude toward political and moral engagement while denying her suitability for the role in which some civic republican and communitarian theorists have cast her. My interpretation incorporates elements of both the literal and figurative readings because neither type can satisfy completely on its own. Figurative readings that explain Arendt's politics as rhetorical overstatement have difficulty accounting for the dichotomous, metaphorical pattern that I will describe in this chapter. That pattern shows a strong connection between the description of authentic politics and freedom that Arendt praises and the fearsome dangers against which she warns—warnings that we cannot help but take literally. Strictly literal interpretation encounters difficulties as well; Arendt probably intended her ideals not as a blueprint for political reform but as a tribute to human potentials that have been overlooked or threatened.[28] But even that recognition does not free Arendt from criticism. She is responsible for having warned against fearful conditions but having proposed political ideals that offer little help in "guarding against the worst."[29] And if her stylized ideals are not intended literally then she purchased subtlety at the price of clarity and is accountable for the ample confusion surrounding her texts.[30]

My critique proceeds from a conviction that Arendt's political writings, properly clarified, can be fruitfully applied to the study of political and moral engagement. Arendt's work is so rich and provocative that we can learn from her missteps as well as her best insights.[31] I begin with her well-known practice of using binary oppositions to draw conceptual distinctions, for example, her stark contrast between the public and the private, the political and the social, and freedom and necessity. I move beyond those oppositions to identify a dichotomous pattern of lesser-known but equally important and integrally connected concepts and metaphors that appears throughout Arendt's works: plurality and isolation, visibility and invisibility, light and darkness, shining glory and

[27] Dietz (2000: 101).

[28] Ibid.

[29] Nancy Rosenblum characterizes liberal democracy according to this Shklarian orientation. Rosenblum (1998b: 48).

[30] Bernard Yack describes some of this confusion, especially as it relates to recent republican or civic humanist arguments whose authors look to Arendt for support. Yack (1993: 9–14).

[31] As George Kateb rightly notes, "we can learn from Arendt without endorsing every segment of her theory." Kateb (2000: 144).

shadowy pariahdom, immortality and oblivion.[32] The first half of each pair consistently shares the positive and praiseworthy connotations of the public, the political, public happiness, and freedom. Just as consistently, the second half shares the negative connotations of the private, the social, mass loneliness, and the abnegation of freedom (in the form of necessity or enslavement). This dichotomous pattern, systematically invoked, illuminates an additional, overarching dichotomy that pervades Arendt's work.[33] One can distinguish between a positive or visionary political theory representing political ideals to be pursued or preserved, and a negative or cautionary political theory describing those twentieth-century horrors whose reappearance must be prevented.[34]

Margaret Canovan contributes two ideas essential to my interpretation. First, she draws attention to the concept of "plurality" in Arendt's political theory;[35] second, she argues for a "contextual" reading of Arendt's work that views her political theory (at least in part) as having emerged in reaction to totalitarianism's horrors.[36] However, Canovan does not expand on the vital connection between these two points: Arendt's focus on plurality is itself a response to totalitarian and pretotalitarian conditions. Arendt champions plurality as a contrast to what she portrays as its harmful opposite, widespread isolation. A clear pattern emerges when one examines the broad sweep of Arendt's writings, from *The Origins of Totalitarianism* through *The Life of the Mind*. The unfavorable imagery that Arendt uses to characterize bourgeois individu-

---

[32] While *monism* might be a more literal antonym of *plurality*, Arendt repeatedly uses *isolation* and I follow her intentions.

[33] "Arendt's approach was, in her own terms, 'systematic' . . . one can discover order without insisting that that there is a final, total order into which all statements or trains of thought fit, leaving no loose ends." Young-Bruehl (1982: 74; see also 473).

[34] In this vein, James Miller distinguishes between constructive and nonconstructive strands of Arendt's political theory. Miller (1979: 202). Young-Bruehl distinguishes between Arendt's "negative reactions" and the "positive outcome of her impressions" in a situation regarding Arendt's reaction to nonpolitical intellectuals before the war. Young-Bruehl (1982: 109). I must stress that visionary and cautionary are thematic distinctions. Some of Arendt's books, such as *The Origins of Totalitariansim* (hereafter *OT*), are mostly cautionary in orientation but contain elements that resonate with her visionary ideals. Others, such as *The Human Condition*, are mostly visionary in orientation but still contain cautionary elements. *On Revolution* contains a mixture of cautionary and visionary orientations, the former in evidence when Arendt describes the French Revolution and the latter when she describes the American Revolution. Finally, some writings are only peripherally related to either cautionary or visionary orientations. *Eichmann in Jerusalem* (hereafter *EJ*) fits into this category although it does contain passages that relate to each type of theory.

[35] Canovan (1992: 281). See also Villa (1996).

[36] Canovan (1992: 7). See also Benhabib (1994) and Dietz (2000) for endorsements of such a contextual reading.

alism, imperialism, and totalitarianism finds an almost perfect mirror image in the positive imagery she uses to characterize political participation and the free political realm. Arendt probably employs this dichotomous structure to make a series of subtle points rather than a simplistic reversal of the earlier harms, but while the results are often illuminating her method harbors flaws that prove fatal to her intrinsic defense of political engagement.

This chapter proceeds in three discrete stages, each of which addresses several related issues. The first section outlines Arendt's visionary project: her ideals of a free political realm, the politically engaged life, and the associated rewards of public freedom, public happiness, earthly immortality, and glory. It covers familiar territory but also advances the original claim that Arendt associates politics, action, and freedom with the concepts and metaphors of plurality, light, visibility, political virtues, shining glory, and immortality. The second section outlines Arendt's cautionary project, her warnings against the rampant materialism and deadly totalitarianism that threaten her ideals. It also describes her association of the social, marginalization, enslavement, and totalitarian domination with the concepts and metaphors of isolation, darkness, invisibility, bodily needs, and the eternal nothingness of oblivion. The third section analyzes these dichotomous patterns, interprets Arendt's intentions, and evaluates her execution. Neither a completely literal nor completely figurative reading of Arendt's work can account for the logical inconsistencies in her arguments as well as the linguistic consistencies that connect her visionary and cautionary theories. I propose a combination of the two that acknowledges the difficulties with Arendt's intrinsic defense of political engagement while acknowledging her many other insights into politics.

Arendt's Visionary Political Theory

We should begin with plurality. In Arendt's account, plurality is "specifically the condition . . . of all political life," and political life is the locus of human freedom.[37] Each human being requires the presence of others in order to exercise the distinctively political capacities for speech and action. With these capacities, translated into word and deed, "we insert ourselves into the [plural] human world."[38] Such political activity, undertaken in the presence of others, is "not forced upon us by necessity, like

[37] HC: 7. Young-Bruehl writes that for Arendt, "the political realm, not the social, is the realm of heroism and freedom." Young-Bruehl (1982: 256).
[38] HC: 176.

labor, and it is not prompted by utility, like work."[39] In other words, for Arendt the political life is "good in itself."[40]

Human plurality plus human uniqueness equals human diversity, the wealth of distinct perspectives regarding a common world. Through their communications with one another diverse persons can generate a "common sense," the phenomenon by which we form and enunciate reliable perceptions of reality.[41] It is only because we can share our perceptions that "the other sense perceptions are known to disclose reality and are not merely felt as irritations of our nerves or resistance sensations of our bodies."[42] Even freedom is only experienced with certainty under conditions of plurality.[43] Thus the condition of plurality, in addition to separating people from the animal kingdom by facilitating speech and action, attaches people to worldly freedom through their own common sense and facilitates a fellowship that is good for its own sake. Plural participants in political life experience "the joy of inhabiting together with others a world whose reality is guaranteed for each by the presence of all."[44]

Politics generates political power, but (at least in her visionary political writings) Arendt employs a unique definition. Rather than the traditional association of power with coercion, Arendt's power excludes coercive force and appears only where people act together. Power "corresponds to the human ability not just to act but to act in concert . . . it belongs to a group and remains in existence only so long as the group keeps together."[45] Plurality is thus the precondition not only for political action and the creation of a public space but also for generation of the power that "keeps the public space in existence."[46]

Plurality is a necessary but not sufficient condition for political life. Throughout her works Arendt metaphorically associates politics and political freedom with visibility and light.[47] Plurality makes politics possible but visibility makes it good. Visibility means that people can see and be seen by their fellow citizens, appearing in word and deed and revealing aspects of their essential identities. Canovan writes that plurality satisfies

[39] HC: 177. Arendt adds that "liberation . . . from the necessities of life" is a necessary (but not sufficient) condition for the more complete freedom of political life. BPF: 148.

[40] Kateb (1983: 1).

[41] "The reality of the public realm relies on the simultaneous presence of innumerable perspectives and aspects in which the common world presents itself." Arendt, HC: 57.

[42] HC: 208–9. See also Arendt, OT: 476.

[43] "Whenever the man-made world does not become the scene for action and speech . . . freedom has no worldly reality. Freedom as a demonstrable fact and politics coincide and are related to one another like two sides of the same matter." BPF: 148–49.

[44] HC: 244.

[45] "On Violence," in Arendt, Crises of the Republic (1972: 143). Hereafter CR.

[46] OT: 200 and 244–45.

[47] For example, Arendt, OR: 253.

"the need for an audience to see and remember what is done."[48] That much is true, but the point must be extended. Without visibility and light, the actors and audience would sit blindly in the dark. Plurality without visibility could describe the "lonely crowd" of mass society.[49] People can live mutely and blindly alongside one another, unable to make the meaningful, public connections that sustain common sense and political stability. Just the same, visibility without plurality could describe panopticism, a single person's one-directional gaze over many.[50] Arendt's vision of a revitalized public space demands what we might call "visible plurality" in which "everything . . . can be seen and heard by everybody."[51]

With a stage, an audience, and conditions of visibility, people can engage in speech and action—humankind's distinctive, political capacities— to "show who they are, reveal actively their unique personal identities."[52] The political realm, then, is a "revelatory" arena, a "space of appearances"; only through political action with and before others can we disclose our *daimonia* (unique identities) to our fellows and thus ground ourselves "in the human world."[53] Lacking conditions of visible plurality, "the misery of the mortals" would indeed be "their blindness toward their own *daimon*."[54] And just as we require plurality to generate common sense, we can trust our own eyes only in the space of appearances: "to men the reality of the world is guaranteed by the presence of others, by its appearing to all."[55] Identities and relationships must be seen to be believed, with seeing understood as a cooperative activity.

Appearance relies upon a public realm and the public relies on "the world itself," that "interspace" between persons that, "like every in-between, relates and separates men at the same time."[56] Publicity requires a spatial proximity in the same sense that visibility requires perspective; the public realm "gathers us together and yet prevents our falling over each other." Figuratively as well as literally, people can only appear to one another if they are neither too close together nor too far apart to see

---

[48] Canovan (1992: 7). For a similar point, see Villa (1996: 84).

[49] Arendt cites David Riesman's *The Lonely Crowd* to illustrate "modern loneliness as a mass phenomenon." Arendt, *HC*: 59.

[50] For panopticism, see Foucault (1977).

[51] *HC*: 50. In her metaphorical emphasis Arendt departs from Heidegger, who claims that philosophy relies too much on *seeing* metaphors and proposes that we turn more exclusively to *hearing*.

[52] *HC*: 179. For politics as a stage for appearance, see Arendt *BPF*: 154.

[53] *HC*: 193. Arendt devotes two sections of *The Human Condition* (28 and 29) to the "space of appearance," linking appearance to plurality, speech, action, cooperative power, and politics. *HC*: 199–212.

[54] Ibid., 193.

[55] Ibid., 199.

[56] Ibid., 52.

and be seen clearly. But with the proper conditions, free political activity can generate a "flaming light" that, while ephemeral, is "the only authentic light we have," illuminating "men acting in freedom and fighting for it."[57]

Visible plurality provides the conditions or arena in which politics might thrive. But politics involves a vital human element as well: innate capacities that, under conditions of visible plurality, can generate political action and deeds worth remembering.[58] Arendt associates the political virtues of *courage, competitiveness, pride,* and *natality*[59] with the concepts of plurality, visibility, light, appearance, and political freedom. Under conditions of visible plurality, political virtues facilitate and inspire political action and excellence.

Arendt calls *courage* "the political virtue *par excellence.*"[60] Courage fortifies human beings for the first, frightening step of political life: leaving the sometimes-comforting darkness of privacy for the glaring light of the public realm.[61] It toughens them for the competitive, agonal atmosphere of performative politics (and the potential onset of stage fright). Only courage enables actors to face the future unflinchingly despite the irremediably unpredictable nature of action.

Competitiveness (or *love of distinction*) ensures that political actors want to achieve great deeds and be seen in the process. Arendt's performative politics are famously agonistic, with participants competing for the public eye, for self-revelatory opportunities, and for the "shining brightness" of glory (visibility's most enduring manifestation). In *The Human Condition* Arendt mentions the Greeks' "passionate drive to show one's self in measuring up against others,"[62] and in *On Revolution* she endorses it. She agrees with John Adams that "'the passion for distinction' . . . [is] 'more essential and remarkable' than any other human faculty." The drive has both a "virtue" and a "vice," the former being "the 'desire to excel another'" and the latter "aim[ing] at power as a means of distinction." Arendt adds that "psychologically speaking, these are in fact the chief virtues and vices of political man."[63]

---

[57] *OT*: 502; see also 482.

[58] Canovan (1992: 102) writes that *The Human Condition* is about "fundamental human activities that bear upon politics." It is also, however, about fundamental human capacities that bear upon political activities.

[59] Natality is synonymous with the power to create and to begin anew.

[60] *HC*: 36. Also *BPF*: 156.

[61] *HC*: 186. Arendt also associates courage with leaving the private realm in *BPF*: 156.

[62] *HC*: 194. Given the context Arendt presumably means "agonistic" rather than the words she uses, "agonal," which actually means "associated with agony."

[63] *OR*: 119.

Pride is Arendt's third political virtue; the quest for excellence and "its subsequent pride" are indispensably public and political.[64] The achievement of excellence begets pride, given a public audience before whom one can shine. Pride, in turn, fuels further aspirations of high achievement, "mak[ing] possible . . . the erection of the human artifice."[65]

Arendt refers to *natality* and initiative as the capacities of inserting oneself into the world and making new beginnings. Initiative is bound up with speech, action, and appearance before others.[66] Natality, the capacity to begin, is "the supreme capacity of man" and the essence of political freedom.[67] Without natality human beings would lack the creative energy to actualize great plans. Perhaps the paradigmatic "new beginning" is the activity of "founding," the establishment of a polis through whose life the founders can achieve lasting glory.

Judgment, while not simply a political capacity, is "the most political of man's mental abilities" and hence an honorary member of this list.[68] In the absence of judgment—in the presence of thoughtlessness—people can condone or perform egregious actions (with Adolf Eichmann representing the thoughtless individual par excellence).[69] Thoughtless individuals still have cognition, which Arendt describes as mere "instrumental reason" divorced from courage, conviction, or moral sense.[70] She implies that in an era of scientific breakthroughs and nuclear capabilities, unless we muster the moral resolution to "think what we are doing" we may end the world with a bang, not a whimper.[71]

Together, these political capacities and virtues form the core and raison d'être of political action. Courage bolsters action in its incipient stages. Competitive love of distinction provides action with a goal. Pride sets

[64] "No activity can become excellent [without] . . . the constituent elements of the public realm." *HC*: 49.

[65] *OT*: 458.

[66] "Speech and action . . . are the modes in which human beings appear to each other . . . *qua* men. This appearance, as distinguished from mere bodily existence, rests on initiative." *HC*: 177. See also *OT*: 455.

[67] "What Is Freedom?" in *BPF*: 148–49. Freedom as an inner capacity is the capacity to begin; but beginning is also "politically . . . identical with man's freedom."

[68] "Thinking and Moral Considerations": 446, cited in Canovan (1992: 269).

[69] Of Eichmann Arendt writes: "There was no sign in him of firm ideological convictions or of specific evil motives . . . it was not stupidity but *thoughtlessness*." Arendt, *Life of the Mind* (1978: 4). Hereafter *LM*. Later in the essay Arendt writes that "wickedness may be caused by absence of thought." *LM*: 13.

[70] Michael Gottsegen notes that Arendt regards "these forms of instrumental and practical rationality as antithetical to the manifestation of plurality." Gottsegen (1994: 221–22).

[71] *HC*: 5 and 262. Hanna Pitkin points out that Arendt presents bureaucracy as, "'the most social [and hence apolitical] form of government,' as "an abdication of human initiative and judgment." Pitkin (1998: 79).

high standards for the goal: excellence rather than mediocrity. Natality and initiative provide the energy for actualization. Finally, judgment prompts political actors to resist moral disengagement and thus to defend the public realm against threats to its integrity.

While Arendt associates all of her political ideals with light and visibility, the more praiseworthy the goal the more intense the metaphor. Politics takes place in the light of the public; revolutionary action can generate a "flaming light" of freedom; hard-won fame carries its own "radiant power." Most instances of public light—even most achievements of political fame—are sporadic or fleeting.[72] But true excellence can "make shine through the centuries whatever men may want to save from the natural ruin of time."[73] The practices of storytelling and historiography enshrine great words and deeds in accessible, durable indices of greatness, the "full light of recorded history."[74] Thus truly excellent action in "its full appearance" can achieve lasting visibility in the "earthly immortality" and "shining brightness we once called glory, which is possible only in the public realm."[75] While obviously not a promise of eternal life, Arendt's immortality is a paean to the specifically political capacities, a reminder of our potential for excellence, and a plea for noble actions in world of otherwise "inherent futility."[76]

Arendt's Cautionary Political Theory

As many frustrated readers have noted, what I call Arendt's "visionary" political theory is full of unsupported assertions and begs more questions than it answers. Why should freedom depend upon politics or plurality? Why should a reliable reality depend upon the presence of many? Why should power be producible only by people acting in concert? Why should courage, natality, and pride be so essential for politi-

[72]This helps to explain why Arendt was uneasy about fame and hostile toward "the European 'society of celebrities' which had existed between the wars." The celebrities "whose distance from the nonfamous multitudes brought them blindness and sometimes susceptibility to collaboration with oppressors" had not earned their fame through feats of true greatness. Their repute was thus likely to be "transient" and unstable, as opposed to the enduring fame of great deeds such as political foundings. Young-Bruehl (1982: 461).

[73]OT: 120 and HC: 55. Further, action "creates the conditions for remembrance, that is, for history." HC: 8–9.

[74]HC: 173–74; also "The Crisis in Culture," in BPF.

[75]HC: 180. Kateb acknowledges that glory does not always motivate those engaging in authentic politics (as in the case of the Hungarian revolutionaries). Kateb (2000: 139). But those revolutionaries can still achieve glory if their story is preserved in human memory, and that glory will constitute part of their greatness.

[76]OR: 220.

cal freedom? Why should the "shining brightness" of glory and earthly immortality be relevant political goals or ideals? A partial answer lies in what I call Arendt's "cautionary" theory and the dichotomous pattern of concepts and metaphors she employs throughout both sets of writing. By scrutinizing her cautionary alongside her visionary writings we can illuminate, in the latter, the "presence of the absence": the implicit, pervasive admonition "or else."[77] Arendt's "plurality" is ever shadowed by its inverse, isolation, an unhealthy state that obtains in its absence. The same is true of visibility, light, political capacities and virtues, and the shining brightness of glory and immortality. Each forms half of a dichotomous pair, with the negative halves predominating throughout Arendt's cautionary theory. The cautionary writings describe conditions in which the visionary metaphors and concepts are endangered and then eradicated. This is not to claim that Arendt's cautionary writings dictate the content of her visionary theory; it is only to insist that the two are intimately connected.

Now begin with isolation. Plurality is so vital to Arendt that its negation, isolation, seems worse than physical death.[78] In fact, she indicts Adolf Eichmann not primarily for his role in systematic genocide but for his refusal to "share the earth" with others—his refusal to acknowledge the fundamental condition of plurality.[79] Isolation frustrates innate capacities essential for human dignity and flourishing. It obscures people's access to ethical sources, deforms their political orientations, and threatens a phenomenon of mass loneliness that can weaken political society to the point of destruction. Of course, isolation is not the only condition that negates plurality; absolute unity accomplishes the same end. Whether experienced as the "iron band" into which totalitarianism compresses its subjects[80] or the "collective nature of labor" that finds all participants "labor[ing] together as if they were one individual," nonplurality or monism—the "unitedness of many into one"—is "basically antipolitical" and hence the realm of nonfreedom.[81] However, Arendt invokes the specter of severe isolation much more frequently than absolute unity, and I follow her emphasis.

[77] The phrase is from Jacques Derrida's work on intertextuality; see Derrida (1983). Mary Dietz uses a similar metaphor to write about the consistent presence of the Holocaust in Arendt's writings, drawing on Harry Berger's insight into the "felt absence" of themes that are "conspicuously exclu[ded]" from great works. Our uses of these felicitous concepts developed separately.

[78] Arendt uses "isolation" and "atomization" almost interchangeably but uses the former term far more frequently.

[79] EJ: 279.

[80] "Total domination . . . strives to organize the infinite plurality and differentiation of human beings as if all of humanity were just one individual." OT: 438.

[81] HC: 212–14; OR: 94; OT: 501 (Epilogue).

Totalitarianism isolates subjects from one another, from the outside world, and from any connection to a reliable moral code.[82] But totalitarianism only radicalizes unhealthy processes that developed less offensively. Isolation can be imposed on a populace but voluntarily incurred as well, embraced by citizens more interested in commercial or familial pursuits than political engagement. Arendt's concern about the "flight . . . from the world into the self,"[83] the illusory attractiveness of "escape from the frailty of human affairs into the solidity of quiet and order," recalls Alexis de Tocqueville's description of democratic individualism.[84] Arendt worries that such self-isolation, while freely chosen at first, may eventually become the mass phenomenon of loneliness.[85]

Arendt traces this mass phenomenon to the growth of bourgeois individualism as justified by Thomas Hobbes. She casts Hobbes not only as the philosopher of the bourgeoisie but also as a prophet of the atomizing forces that culminated in totalitarianism.[86] Rather than blame Hobbes for the ensuing disasters she means to draw out the practical implications of his political philosophy if taken to logical extremes. In Arendt's view, Hobbes wrongly assumes that "the individual will consider his advantage in complete isolation" and thus "will realize that he can pursue and achieve his interest only with the help of some kind of majority" (which can help him to obtain power). For Hobbes's isolated individual, "desire for power must be the fundamental passion."[87]

> Excluded [by a centralized authority] from participation in the management of public affairs that involve all citizens . . . [he] loses his rightful place in society and his natural connection with his fellow-men. He can now judge his individual private life only by comparing it with that of others, and his relations with his fellow-men inside society take the form of competition.[88]

Isolated from a common world and a common set of concerns, the bourgeois individual turns inward and undergoes a moral deformation.[89]

[82] The only truly reliable moral code is "based entirely on the presence of others." *HC*: 238. Nazi totalitarianism, conversely, isolated victims and executioners alike; even Nazi storm troopers were kept in "total separation from normality," so that "they could not possibly get used to and take root in any other part of the ordinary world." *OT*: 372.

[83] *HC*: 6.

[84] *HC*: 222. See also Tocqueville, *DA*, vol. II.

[85] *OT*: 474–79.

[86] *OT*: 143 and 157. In the analysis that follows I only explain Arendt's interpretation of Hobbes rather than endorse or judge it.

[87] *OT*: 139.

[88] Ibid., 141.

[89] My term *moral deformation* implies the corruption of some preexisting standard. In the previously cited passage. *OT*: 141. Arendt implies that all people have a "rightful place" in society and public affairs, a right that derives at least partly from the "natural connection" among "fellow-men." That connection is deformed in Hobbes's isolated individual.

Arendt accepts Hobbes's diagnosis; she agrees that if individuals consider their advantage in complete isolation they will recur to competitive acquisition and power politics. In her account of African history, Boer settlers lived "in complete isolation" and consequently "lost . . . their civilized feeling for human fellowship," ruling over the natives "in absolute lawlessness, unchecked by 'kind neighbors.'"[90] Under conditions of isolation those who have lost a grasp on "common sense" are "indeed no more than animals who are able to reason, 'to reckon with consequences.'"[91]

But those observations, to Arendt, weigh against isolation and in favor of visible plurality. She accuses Hobbes of endorsing an isolated, politically disengaged populace for the sake of stability. To Arendt, "political concepts are based on plurality, diversity, and mutual limitations" lest the public realm become a Hobbesian state of nature or an arena of domination.[92] Without the mutual limitations that accompany conditions of plurality and diversity, power becomes conceptualized as coercive force, acquisition of power becomes an end in itself, and the ensuing attitudes spell doom for the public realm: "not the beginning of humanity but its end."[93]

While the conditions of bourgeois society may isolate the citizenry, its effects are incidentally incurred and gradually experienced. But for the totalitarian leader, isolation is a program and a tool, deliberately pursued and violently imposed. With force and precision enhanced by technology the leader isolates subjects and government functionaries alike.[94] By eradicating plurality the totalitarian leader eliminates the realm of political action ("to be isolated is to be deprived of the capacity to act") and, by extension, the people's capacity to generate cooperative power.[95]

No isolation can compare with the concentration camp's complete and consummate seclusion, which embodies the ideals of totalitarian organization:

> Just as the stability of the totalitarian regime depends on the isolation of the
> fictitious world of the movement from the outside world, so the experiment of

[90] *OT*: 193. In characterizing the Boer's moral isolation, Arendt abstracts away from the fact that many of them lived with their families.

[91] *HC*: 284. See also *OT*: 342.

[92] Arendt (1993), *Men in Dark Times*: 81. Hereafter *MDT*.

[93] *OT*: 157. Most of *OT* dwells on coercive as opposed to cooperative power, and coercive power—which Arendt's visionary theory seeks to delegitimize—is associated with invisibility rather than visible plurality. "The only rule of which everybody in a totalitarian state may be sure is that the more visible government agencies are, the less power they carry." *OT*: 403.

[94] "Isolation of atomized individuals provides not only the mass basis for totalitarian rule, but is carried through to the very top of the whole structure." *OT*: 407.

[95] *HC*: 188.

total domination in the concentration camps depends on sealing off the latter against the world of all others, the world of the living in general.[96]

Inmates disappear from the outside world as if they had never existed. The absolute absence of plurality ensures a sterile and virtually inhuman environment. Gone are action, freedom, spontaneity, and natality; in their stead are victims reduced to wholly predictable "bundles of reactions."[97]

All types of isolation, ranging from the utter seclusion of the concentration camp to the relatively mild self-involvement of bourgeois individualism, confound human perception with an atmosphere of unreality. Arendt's comment on the human heart applies to her perception of all isolated spaces: "whatever goes on in its obscurity can hardly be called a demonstrable fact."[98] While isolated individuals can perceive sense data, they lack the means of holding on to their perceptions:

> The impact of factual reality, like all other human experiences, needs speech if it is to survive the moment of experience, needs talk and communication with others to remain sure of itself. Total domination succeeds to the extent that it succeeds in interrupting all channels of communications.[99]

People deprived of the public world are "deprived of reality"; for them the world "comes and passes away like a dream."[100] Dreamlike haziness encompasses the Boer imperialists isolated on the "dark continent," the atomized masses in pretotalitarian eras, the terrorized individuals under totalitarian domination, and the dehumanized concentration camp inmates. The former two groups, lacking a moral perspective grounded in the *sensus communis*, grasp at ideological fictions to give their lives meaning. The latter two groups, torn from the world and shrouded in darkness, lack the certainty even to confirm their own suffering.[101]

Earlier I questioned why, in Arendt's visionary theory, freedom relies upon political activity and conditions of plurality. Her cautionary writings indicate that freedom perishes when those conditions are absent. Isolated bourgeois individuals are enslaved by an endless cycle of production and consumption; atomized masses wander in obscurity, lacking proof of their freedom or a forum in which to exercise it; totalitarian-

[96] *OT*: 438.
[97] Ibid.
[98] *BPF*: 149.
[99] *OT*: 495.

[100] *HC*: 199n29. Arendt agrees with Heraclitus that "the world is one and common to those who are awake, but everybody who is asleep turns away to his own."

[101] A concentration camp survivor "is often assailed by doubts with regard to his own truthfulness, as though he had mistaken a nightmare for reality." *OT*: 439.

ism's isolated subjects encounter the ultimate realm of nonfreedom. I questioned why power is producible only through cooperative plurality. Arendt's cautionary writings indicate that isolation encourages the competitive pursuit of coercive force masquerading as power. Lacking any truly political applications, this pseudo-power destroys the realm of politics altogether. I questioned why a reliable morality and even a reliable reality must depend upon communication between associated individuals. In Arendt's negative account we see isolated individuals losing touch with the ethical sources and *sensus communis* that sustain human association and flourishing. In Arendt's visionary theory common sense anchors people to a "moral code" that is "based entirely on the presence of others."[102] In each of these cases the conditions that characterize Arendt's visionary and idealistic political theory are defined in opposition to their negations. This oppositional pattern extends to the complementary dichotomy of visibility and invisibility. Visibility and invisibility help Arendt to clarify the damage done by isolation and the remedy that plurality must effect.

Arendt consistently uses images of darkness or invisibility to characterize isolation's negative effects. Invisibility variously describes the agonizing atomization of marginalized individuals and disaffected masses in modern societies, the isolation of victims in totalitarian regimes, the dangerous unaccountability of totalitarian governments, and the utter darkness to which totalitarianism consigns individual victims and entire populations. In some instances this metaphorical pattern simply reinforces the force of isolation's ill effects.[103] However, just as Arendt's light metaphors allude to certain benefits of politics that plurality by itself cannot connote (benefits bestowed, for example, by the light of history, the radiance of fame, or the shining brightness of glory), darkness and invisibility evoke a new type of injury.

Some kinds of invisibility can be tolerable for a while; when the public realm has lost its luster the darkness of self-seclusion can seem a welcoming refuge. The condition of "pariah peoples"—whose lives are "an obscurity in which a man who is himself hidden need no longer see the visible world either"—exactly opposes the condition of publicity in which political participants see and are seen.[104] Whereas political actors

---

[102] *HC*: 238.

[103] For example, to enter the public realm is to appear to one's fellows, to "see and be seen" in the public light. Conversely, to be private is to be invisible, "that is . . . deprived of seeing and hearing others, of being seen and being heard by them." *HC*: 58. Whereas plurality and politics involve a public appearance that confirms participants' unique identities, private isolation represents disappearance: "as far as [others] are concerned, private man does not appear, and therefore it is as though he did not exist." Ibid.

[104] *MDT*: 16.

are situated with proper space between them and hence the perspective for mutual visibility, pariah types exist among "closely-packed human beings" for whom "the interspace we have called world . . . has simply disappeared."[105] But the pariahs' experience is not always wretched, as the juxtaposition with the public realm might lead one to expect. At least in the short run such privacy can deliver a wealth of warmth and familial closeness.

In the long term, however, grim danger looms. Withdrawal may be most attractive when the political realm seems inhospitable or inaccessible, but those are precisely the times when participation is most important. Those who abdicate their place in the plural world lose the ability to improve their condition or prevent its deterioration, since "power only arises where people act together."[106] But Arendt appeals not only to pariahs' long-term self-interest; she invokes an obligation to appear in the political realm.[107] There are occasions when withdrawal into darkness "need not harm an individual," but it always injures the world; "with each such retreat an almost demonstrable loss to the world takes place."[108] One who ignores his or her obligation to the world ignores the human condition of plurality.

The absence of spatial proximity and visual perspective entails further negative consequences. Scientists view the earth from an Archimedean point—from a vantage outside the earth—and they do so against humanity rather than for it. When the earth is viewed from such a great distance (as if from a satellite or as a molecule under a microscope) individuality blurs into a mass; people's lives and actions "appear not as activities of any kind but as processes."[109] Social science has been similarly guilty, prompting us to "look and live in this society as though we were as far removed from our own human existence as we are from the infinitely small and the immensely large."[110] Public appearance must have appropriate visual perspective, neither too great a distance between people nor too little. The same applies to modern science, a discipline of surprisingly great "political significance" and action, lest it dehumanize humanity or unleash unearthly forces on the world.[111]

---

[105] *MDT*: 16 and 13.

[106] *MDT*: 22.

[107] Arendt describes a "natural connection" among "fellow-men" that could form the foundation of such an obligation. *OT*: 141.

[108] *MDT*: 4.

[109] *HC*: 322. In Arendt's works processes are connected with laboring and biological necessity as opposed to acting and political freedom.

[110] *HC*: 323.

[111] For scientists' political significance, see *HC*: 322. For her fear of nuclear annihilation see *EJ*: 273.

While voluntary withdrawal threatens long-term dangers, forced marginalization entails a much graver harm: repression of the essential human capacity for visibility. Slaves, paupers, and ghetto dwellers suffer a "shadowy existence" that brings a pain unrelated to physical deprivation. To some this condition may be "bearable," but even then it cannot match the reality or fullness of a life lived in public.[112] No longer able to see the world or be seen by it, the marginalized individuals undergo "a fearful . . . atrophy of all the organs with which we respond to [the world]")— in other words, the specifically political organs.[113] Not only invisible but politically blind they fall short of full humanness, trapped in a "worldlessness" that is "always a form of barbarism."[114]

Those for whom the experience is not bearable undergo a more grievous injury. Invisibility to the world painfully insults their dignity or pride because, in John Adams's characterization, "to be wholly overlooked, and to know it, are intolerable." Arendt strongly agrees, suggesting that "darkness rather than want is the curse of poverty."[115] Upon reflection we recognize this apolitical darkness as the very opposite of glory's shining brightness, and the injured capacities of dignity and pride as the very forces that impel public actors to political success.

As if those "curses" of "darkness" were not enough, the utter blackness of concentration camp existence (in which people "disappear" without a trace "under cover of the night")[116] annihilates the political capacities that Arendt's visionary theory celebrates. Even when concentration camps do not kill the physical human being they murder human dignity, courage, pride, spontaneity, and initiative. In an extreme mutation of bourgeois privacy (in which "private man does not appear, and therefore . . . whatever he does remains without significance and consequence to others"[117]) concentration camps seal off human masses from the eyes of the world, "as if what happened to them were no longer of any interest to anybody."[118] Through a total deprivation of human attention the camps

---

[112] HC: 50.

[113] MDT: 13.

[114] Ibid. George Kateb aptly challenges Arendt's insistence that all "world-alienation" is bought at great cost. See Kateb (1983: 148–83). I agree with Kateb's point but am only concerned here with presenting Arendt's argument.

[115] OR: 69. Arendt adds that "the predicament of the poor after their self-preservation has been assured is that their lives are without consequence, and that they remain excluded from the light of the public realm where excellence can shine; they stand in darkness wherever they go." Adams's Discourses on Davila, from which Arendt frequently quotes, seems strongly to influence her choice of metaphors.

[116] OT: 434–35, 442.

[117] HC: 58.

[118] OT: 445.

destroy their victims' identities. Minds and bodies may be left intact but not the vital, political capacities that make them distinctly human.

Against the political virtue of courage, totalitarianism's main principle is pervasive, dominating terror. Victims and executioners alike are stripped of the ability or inclination to resist, protest, or even commit suicide.[119] Against competitiveness or love of distinction, which demands visible plurality for fulfillment, totalitarianism isolates victims in "holes of oblivion" that no light can penetrate or escape. It reduces them to completely interchangeable "bundles of reactions" among which no distinction is possible, and it attempts to obliterate their identities from all human memory.

Against the political capacity of pride, totalitarianism reduces people to "something that even animals are not"; its ideological "supersense" "destroyed the element of pride."[120] Against natality, totalitarianism compels each individual to "surrender his inner freedom," his "capacity to begin."[121] Against judgment, totalitarianism "eliminates responsibility" among its executioners and inculcates an instrumental reason that approaches pure thoughtlessness (as embodied in Eichmann), which neither questions nor judges the leader's orders.[122]

While totalitarianism thus negates the political capacities that Arendt associates with light, visibility, appearance, and freedom, her cautionary theory describes a further negation: the unhealthy proliferation of bodily functions, needs, and emotions that she associates with darkness, invisibility, and necessity, the antipolitical realm of the social. Indeed, to Arendt bodily functions and desires are inherently apolitical and hence the opposite of our political capacities. While speech and action characterize politics and freedom, "pleasure and pain, like everything instinctual, tend to muteness."[123] While visibility and light incorporate the political realm, Arendt locates "passions and the emotions" in "the human heart,"[124] but elsewhere asserts that "the human heart, as we all know, is a very dark place, and what goes on in its obscurity can hardly be called a demonstrable fact."[125] While courage and the spirited "desire to excel another" are political virtues, bodily needs and desires destroy political freedom. The French Revolution failed largely because of its "misplaced emphasis on the heart as a source of political virtue."[126]

---

[119] *OT*: 455.
[120] *OT*: 458.
[121] *OT*: 473. See also *OT*: 455.
[122] *OT*: 437.
[123] See *MDT*: 15–16; also *HC*: 119.
[124] *OR*: 95–96.
[125] *BPF*: 149.
[126] *OR*: 96.

Perhaps for these reasons, Arendt's visionary theory not only celebrates the political capacities and virtues but also excludes everything related to the body, necessity, and the social.[127] Prohibited from politics and the public realm are bodily desires and biological functions,[128] love,[129] pity,[130] compassion, and "givenness," meaning all of those innate physical and mental characteristics "which usually can become articulate only in the sphere of private life."[131]

Enslavement, whether to biological necessity or totalitarian terror, is a grievous injury but not the worst condition imaginable. Violent death is grave, as well, but, as Arendt insists against Herman Broch in *Men in Dark Times*, "we know today that killing is far from the worst that man can inflict on man . . . and unfortunately there can be far harsher punishments than the death penalty."[132] Even worse than the darkness of poverty or the isolation that makes one "literally dead to the world," the eternal nothingness of "oblivion" is a perfect contrast to Arendt's ultimate political goal of brilliant glory and "earthly immortality."[133]

Individuals lost in the biological life process, whether as part of a "primitive" culture or the sweeping process of bourgeois materialism, suffer the ultimate indignity of uncommemorated death. They are born and die alone, as transitory cells in an organism that neither distinguishes between its constituents nor remembers the dead. "The tragedy of savage tribes," according to Arendt, is "that they live and die without leaving

[127] To Arendt, bodily functions not only represent necessity—the opposite of freedom—but also are antiplural in nature. As biologically needy beings all humans are the same and can be grouped as a single organism. *HC*: 213. The masses who stormed into broad view during the French Revolution were unitary and apolitical because "the cry for bread will always be uttered with one voice. *OR*: 94. Further, "while it is true that freedom can only come to those whose needs have been fulfilled, it is equally true that it will escape those who are bent upon living for their desires," as Arendt claims of the poor. *OR*: 139.

[128] Aristotle's political "good life" "was 'good' to the extent that by having mastered the necessities of sheer life . . . and by overcoming the innate urge of all living creatures for their own survival, it was no longer bound to the biological life process." *HC*: 37.

[129] "Love . . . is killed, or rather extinguished, the moment it is displayed in public." *HC*: 51. Further, the heart deals with "problems of darkness" but "it has no solution for them, since a solution demands light, and it is precisely the light of the world that distorts the life of the heart." *OR*: 96–97.

[130] Pity can become an "all-devouring passion" whose "very boundlessness . . . seems to kill human dignity." *OT*: 329.

[131] Nazi propaganda appealed to the equality of all Germans based on "nature, and their absolute difference from all other people." Conversely, Arendt insists upon excluding "givenness" from political consideration, which denotes "all that is given in us by birth and which includes the shape of our bodies and the talents of our minds . . . those qualities which usually can become articulate only in the sphere of private life." *OT*: 296.

[132] *MDT*: 127.

[133] *HC*: 176.

any trace."[134] Individuals victimized by totalitarian domination endure a similar tragedy, which is perhaps more awful for being violently imposed: total nothingness, the erasure of the individual from sight and memory. Concentration camps are "veritable holes of oblivion into which people stumble by accident" and leave no "ordinary traces of former existence." While the free political realm is a space of *appearance* in which human beings can reveal their unique identities, the totalitarian regime effects a "complete *disappearance* of its victims;" through its secret police it tries "to erase the identity of [the] victim from the memory of the surviving world."[135] Free human beings might aspire to greatness recorded "in the full light of recorded history." But concentration camp victims, "expelled from humanity" and even "from human history," are doomed to eternal darkness and a "hellish" fate worse than death.[136]

Interpretation

Thus far I have shown that the metaphors and concepts of Arendt's cautionary political theory perfectly oppose the metaphors and concepts of her visionary political theory. In her cautionary theory, "the social" and totalitarian oppression (which she portrays as a malignant version of the social run amok)—along with instrumental calculations and predictable behavior (conditioned by materialistic desires or totalitarian terror)—impose necessity and enslavement along with the ultimate afflictions of uncommemorated death and oblivion. Arendt systematically associates all of the preceding with the conditions of isolation, the capacity for biological needs and private emotions, and the metaphors of darkness, disappearance, and invisibility.

In Arendt's visionary theory, the political and its creative, spontaneous, noninstrumental action make possible human freedom, public happiness, and the ultimate rewards of shining glory and immortality. Arendt systematically associates all of the preceding with the conditions of plurality, the capacity for political virtues and public excellence, and the metaphors of light, appearance, and visibility.

The parallels are too close to be ignored. Arendt's visionary political theory almost certainly represents some kind of reaction to its earlier, cautionary inversion. The question remains, what kind of reaction? Literal readings of Arendt's political ideals are not well equipped to grapple with these questions; they have difficulty making sense of Arendt's inti-

---

[134] *OT*: 296.
[135] *OT*: 434–35; stress added.
[136] *OT*: 439 and 445.

mately connected cautionary and visionary theories. But while figurative readings fare better they are not without perils, and their shortcomings shed additional light on Arendt's limitations.

As I noted earlier, one type of literal interpretation reads Arendt's visionary political theory in the service of civic republican goals, endorsing political engagement as the road to human flourishing. But that reading, situated in the broader context of Arendt's cautionary writings, encounters a number of discomforting dilemmas. To take Arendt literally regarding the singular joy and freedom of public life is to expose her to the charge of hypocrisy.[137] Arendt eschewed "the pursuit of public happiness" and lacked "the taste of public freedom" that she praised as requisite political virtues.[138] She preferred the private kinship of like-minded friends and colleagues, as did many of those whom she most deeply admired.[139] Of course, failure to live by one's espoused values does not necessarily invalidate one's teachings.[140] While we can still learn from those values we should strengthen our resolve not to impose them on others.

More significantly, reading Arendt literally as a civic republican theorist leaves her defenseless against the charges of political elitism and economic conservatism pressed by her more critical literal readers.[141] If Arendt intended her visionary theory as a prescription for remaking modern politics she would be advocating an environment hostile to the uncompetitive or those with an undeveloped facility for "great words and deeds." When read literally, Arendt seems to endorse such exclusions; for example, while praising Thomas Jefferson's participatory ideals she acknowledges that only the few "politically best" will participate in public happiness.[142] In a similar vein, if Arendt favored expelling economic considerations from the free, public realm she would be promoting a system that conserves the status quo. When the needy cannot advocate politically for their interests then politics loses its potential for promoting distributive justice.[143] Further, excluding economics would mean foreclosing politics to those whose initial impetus to leave the private realm involves

[137] The references are to HC: 244 and OR: 434–35.

[138] OR: 275. Arendt calls these capacities the required "political passions," by which term "she also means virtues, in this context." Kateb (2000: 136).

[139] Cf. Young-Bruehl (1982: 461–63).

[140] One of the best examples is Rousseau's admission that he is naturally good but without political virtue, and that he could not have been a citizen in the Social Contract's strictly regimented republic. Rousseau (1992: 77 and 83).

[141] Cf. Wolin (1983); Pitkin (1998); Benhabib (1994).

[142] OR: 254; see also 275–80, where Arendt accepts the idea of participation by an elite as long as that elite is self-selected, based on political passions and virtues. Reinhart (1997) also notes Arendt's apparent comfort with noninclusive politics.

[143] Pitkin (1981) criticizes Arendt on these grounds.

a desire to pursue material interests. Public engagement can expand one's horizons and enlarge one's viewpoint, so that initially self-involved concerns need not remain narrowly self-interested.[144] While the exclusive priority of political virtues would ensure widespread inability to participate in Arendtian politics, the exclusion of bodily needs and economic interests would ensure widespread inattention or apathy.[145]

To validate those criticisms would be to acknowledge internal contradictions that threaten Arendt's intellectual credibility. Time and again she warned against the privations of darkness and marginalization; "it is precisely the human person in all his subjectivity who needs to appear in public in order to achieve full reality."[146] If Arendt's political ideals were designed as the domain of the political elite (or if they effectively kept economically motivated people from joining the debate) she would be consigning the apolitical masses to the very darkness to which she had alerted us. Thus the civic republican reading holds an untenable position. Without taking Arendt's ideals at face value one can hardly draw support for the special excellence of political action. But in taking Arendt's ideals literally one cannot avoid exclusionary and elitist implications.

One can avoid those implications by refusing to read Arendt's political ideals literally in the first place. Indeed, the highly critical literal readings of Arendt falter primarily because they go too far.[147] For Arendt simply to have ignored the inconsistencies that literal critics allege, she would have manifested a blindness inconsistent with her demonstrated acuity. She would have manifested a split personality as well. Over the course of many decades Arendt keenly observed rough-and-tumble politics—politics often concerned with claims of economics and necessity—and wrote hardheaded political analysis in *Crises of the Republic*. To comment approvingly on instrumentally oriented politics while formulating a theory

[144] As Alexis de Tocqueville suggests, while "at first it is of necessity that men attend to the public interest," in time their involvement may be "by choice." Eventually, the initially self-concerned individual may "find his self-interest in forgetting about himself." Tocqueville, *DA*: 510–12.

[145] While Arendt approvingly cited David Reisman's *Lonely Crowd*, Nathan Glazer recounts that Riesman rejected Arendt's disdain for "the social": "Riesman saw not only that [the social] existed . . . but that it too had its virtues." Glazer also implies that Riesman rejected Arendt's cultural elitism, or what Glazer calls her "disdain for the 'bourgeoisie.'" Glazer (2000: 27–33).

[146] *MDT*: 72.

[147] Roy Tsao's persuasive, literal reading of Arendt's *Human Condition* chastises other literal interpreters for not reading Arendt closely enough. According to Tsao, Arendt must not be interpreted as an unqualified enthusiast for the Greek conception of politics, a view that has prompted many literal readers to portray her as a nostalgic elitist. Tsao argues that a careful scrutiny of Arendt's words reveals a hostility toward the Greek "ambition to attain 'everlasting remembrance' without a Homer, to make deeds imperishable entirely on their own." Tsao (2002: 111). Nonetheless, Tsao's interpretation does not show Arendt to have rejected the Greek *aspiration* to permanence or glory (with which I align her) but only to have disdained their foolish means of achieving it (i.e., without dependence on storytellers).

that rejected that paradigm entirely would have bordered on the bizarre, the left hand unaware of what the right hand was doing.

I can envision only one other literal-minded explanation for the shape of Arendt's political ideals that could avoid accusing her of an unlikely blindness. Perhaps the relationship between Arendt's visionary and cautionary theories is one of severe overreaction. Perhaps she was so overwhelmed by the twentieth century's depredations—by the darkness, isolation, and loss of creativity and spontaneity incurred by bourgeois materialism and the radicalization of those harms under totalitarian oppression—that she enshrined as ideals whatever those evils had tried to eradicate. That interpretation could explain why Arendt opposes isolation with plurality, darkness with light, invisibility with visibility, and oblivion with immortality. It could explain why she lionizes exactly those political capacities that totalitarianism threatened with extinction, and why her idealized political realm omits everything associated with the ever encroaching "social."

But diagnosing Arendt as a knee-jerk reactionary introduces another potentially devastating, but implausible, internal contradiction. Arendt repeatedly inveighs against "automatic reactions," because reactions represent necessity and not freedom. Through the political capacity of forgiveness we achieve "freedom from vengeance," freedom from "the natural, automatic reaction to transgression," and freedom from a "relentless automatism."[148] In other words, freedom means not falling into reactionary traps. Arendt's visionary theory surely represents some kind of response to her cautionary writings, but an automatic, necessitous reaction would be completely incompatible with her entire project.

For these reasons I find strictly literal interpretations unpersuasive. Figurative readings are better able to account for Arendt's visionary political theory and its relationship to her cautionary writings without exposing her to charges of hypocrisy, blindness, or severe inconsistency. Nonetheless, they harbor difficulties of their own.

Earlier I reviewed two types of figurative interpretations, each of which reads Arendt's stylized political ideals as a response to undesirable forces or trends. As an example of the first type, James Miller suggests that Arendt's idealized political characterizations might be seen as stylized rhetoric aimed at "restoring a sense of balance" to an era dominated by instrumental reasoning and materialistic values.[149] As an example of the second type, Mary Dietz envisions Arendt's idealized rhetoric as part of a larger response to her cautionary *summum malum*—as "a profound response to the trauma inflicted upon humanity by the Nazi regime."[150]

[148] *HC*: 240–41.
[149] Miller (1979).
[150] Dietz (2000: 90).

Miller's suggestion of rhetorical balancing can account for some of the apparent discrepancies in Arendt's cautionary and visionary theories—discrepancies that the literal readings could not forgive. For example, Arendt's oddly inconsistent use of the word "power" appears on closer analysis to be just the kind of "balancing act" that Miller has in mind. Throughout most of the *Origins of Totalitarianism* Arendt uses "power" in a fairly traditional manner, meaning states' legitimate monopoly of coercive force.[151] But she reaches a turning point midway through volume II, concluding that conditions of isolation produce an "endless process of power accumulation" that erodes the public space of appearances, undermines "all natural connections with . . . fellow men," and leads inexorably to competitive destruction.[152]

As if to circumvent the entire operation—as if by denying its legitimacy she might eliminate destructive, competitive acquisition from human consideration—Arendt revokes the name "power" from the practice of power politics.[153] Throughout the rest of the *Origins* (and throughout her later visionary writings) Arendt insists that true power results only from the concerted action of equals, and that what had sometimes been called "power politics" is merely brute strength or coercion.[154]

Arendt's essay "On Violence" contrasts cooperative power with violence or force and supports the supposition that her earlier rhetorical reversal was a calculated maneuver. She regrets that almost all of the era's political theorists "equate political power with 'the organization of violence,'" and against them she insists that "it is only after one ceases to reduce public affairs to the business of dominion that the original data in the realm of human affairs will appear, or, rather, reappear, in their authentic diversity."[155] Consistent with Miller's figurative reading, in this

---

[151] For example, "violence has always been the *ultima ratio* in political action and power has always been the visible expression of rule and government." (*OT*: 137; also 5, 15, 23, 51, to cite only a few instances).

[152] *OT*: 157. Cecil Rhodes personified the inexorable progress: "[no] matter what individual qualities or defects a man may have, once he has entered the maelstrom of an unending process of expansion, he will, as it were, cease to be what he was and obey the laws of the process, identify himself with anonymous forces that he is supposed to serve in order to keep the whole process in motion." *OT*: 215. These words anticipate Arendt's description of totalitarianism's ideological devotees.

[153] Arendt's approach here recalls the Hebrew aphorism "asu s'yag la'Torah," translated as "make a fence around the law"—found in Tractate Avot of the *Mishnah*. The aphorism directs religious Jews to forego activities that are not forbidden by Jewish law, but whose consequences might inadvertently lead to unwanted violations. Eliminating the middle activity breaks the chain of potential harm. *Mishnayot* 4 (1963).

[154] In "On Violence" Arendt deplores the "traditional concept of power," which holds that "power is expansionist by nature." She implies that changing the terms of the theoretical debate may decrease the likelihood of "violence [being] justified on the ground of creativity." *CR*: 171–72.

[155] *CR*: 134 and 143.

instance Arendt seems to have changed her terminology to counteract (or protest) the prevailing, pernicious conflation of power with violence.[156]

But the interpretation of "rhetorical overstatement" cannot fully explain the relationship between Arendt's cautionary and visionary theories. Surely some of Arendt's idealized political characterizations aim at countering the reach of economic and sociological reasoning. By insisting upon the purity of politics Arendt might inoculate readers against the ever-creeping logic of "the social." But Arendt's cautionary writings encompass harms far more serious than instrumental reasoning's encroachments. The metaphors of darkness, invisibility, and oblivion characterize excessive privations and oppression—including totalitarian domination—that no amount of overstated rhetoric could counteract. So while the interpretation of "rhetorical balancing" explains a portion of Arendt's visionary and cautionary theories, her direst warnings (and their visionary opposites) fall beyond its explanatory scope.

Only Dietz's type of figurative reading can account for Arendt's visionary and cautionary political theories and explain their mutual relationship. Dietz depicts Arendt's political ideals of action, glory, and the free public realm as figurative attempts "to confront and counter . . . the existential unreality of 'death-yet-not-death, life-yet-not-life': the living death/deathly life that was the horrific specter of the Holocaust."[157] Arendtian action could be "a powerful and compelling rebuke" to totalitarianism's depredations, "a 'recreative escape,' a chance to give one's self over to the radiance of the represented world."[158]

Because Arendt's visionary theory does not address politics and political engagement as we normally conceive them, literal interpreters might not think it "adequate to the task of capturing what politics requires or entails." Dietz anticipates that critique but still rejects the literal reading for "a better way to make sense" of Arendt's political ideals: a figurative interpretation that views Arendt's stylized politics as an "attempt to conjure a magnificent transfiguring illusion" with the power to restore faith and hope in human capacities.[159]

In spite of its many virtues, Dietz's figurative reading has difficulty affirming Arendt's practical value to contemporary readers. Faith and hope may be forces for good; an "optimistic illusion" is often preferable to a pessimistic one (although it is not always preferable to realism). But Arendt's cautionary writings go beyond merely describing past horrors whose memory must be overcome. They also warn of immediate, dire

---

[156] For these reasons I agree with Jeffrey Isaac's claim that in reading Arendt, "a purist understanding of power would be misleading." Isaac (1992: 135).

[157] Dietz (2000: 99).

[158] Ibid., 102.

[159] Ibid.

threats to our collective future. At the end of the *Origins* Arendt warns of potentially disastrous consequences for marginalized people "if we continue to think of our world in utilitarian terms."[160] In *Eichmann in Jerusalem* she warns of "the possibility of a repetition of the crimes committed by the Nazis," made all the more chilling by the means of modern automation and nuclear weapons "beside which Hitler's gassing installations look like an evil child's fumbling toys."[161] And in her epilogue to the *Origins* Arendt warns against "the worst": Soviet leaders' refusal to grasp the facts of mutual assured destruction, unmitigated by a "*sensus communis* that might penetrate their ideological haze. Arendt gloomily reflects that "freedom as well as survival may well depend upon our success or failure to persuade the other part of the world to recognize facts as they are and to come to terms with the factuality of the world as it is."[162]

If we conceptualize Arendt's visionary political theory as a response or reaction to her cautionary writings, as Dietz proposes, and if Arendt's visionary political theory is primarily a poetic, figurative rebuke to assaults on human creativity and dignity, then while Arendt's ideals might inspire hope and faith they remain powerless to address or prevent her own depiction of "the worst." Warning readers of literal, apocalyptic peril and then responding with a "grand, optimistic illusion" offers cold comfort at best.

This failure points to a problem not with Arendt's figurative interpreters but with her own political writing. We cannot read her cautionary theory in a strictly figurative manner, because many of her warnings are in fact deadly serious. But neither can we read her visionary theory literally without labeling Arendt elitist, exclusionary, or blind to her own contradictions (labels that I find extremely implausible). By vividly depicting dangers whose resolution she ignores, Arendt forces sympathetic interpreters between a rock and a hard place. Figurative interpreters must confront the possibility that regardless of Arendt's intended meaning, her poetic rhetoric obscures it to most of us.[163] Whatever other praise or blame she receives, Arendt should be held accountable simply for failing to write clearly what she meant. If she intended to rebut the era's "subtle sociology" and "finely tuned economics," and to expose excessive

---

[160] At greater length: "today, with populations and homelessness everywhere on the increase, masses of people are continuously rendered superfluous if we continue to think of our world in utilitarian terms," and "totalitarian solutions may well survive the fall of totalitarian regime." *OT*: 459.

[161] *EJ*: 273.

[162] *OT*: 492.

[163] Tsao's literal reading also acknowledges that much of the confusion around Arendt stems from her own oblique argumentative structure, which "obscures the critical thrust" of her core insights. Tsao (2002: 99).

materialism's dehumanizing effects, she could have done so quite plainly without tying her critique to a dubious, visionary theory or making numerous political claims that she probably did not intend literally. Arendt famously endorsed the critical method of "pearl diving," mining texts for ideas that assume fresh meaning when removed from their original context.[164] But Arendt practices pearl *hiding* as well, sinking her own insights "full fathoms five" where they frequently elude even sympathetic interpreters.[165]

Holding Arendt accountable for her opaque formulations and misleading political ideals does not undermine her contributions to political theory. Ironically, however, while Arendt addresses her visionary writings to the concerns of modern democracies, her cautionary writings may prove more germane to those very concerns. Arendt's visionary theory cannot demonstrate that political engagement constitutes human flourishing, but her cautionary theory helps us to understand what destroys it. She cannot establish cooperative political engagement as the path to true freedom, but she does argue persuasively that conditions of extreme atomization jeopardize meaningful freedom. She cannot prove the connection between visible plurality and a morally responsible "common sense," but she sensibly warns that extreme isolation and atomization can lead to potentially disastrous moral disengagement or thoughtlessness. Thus for students of pragmatic politics Arendt has less to teach about the ends we should pursue than about the social and political outcomes we should avoid.

For students of all kinds of politics Arendt continues to inspire and instruct, as great political theorists generally do. My concern has been to temper our inspirations by examining the implications of various interpretive approaches. To do that is to recognize that her intrinsic defense of political engagement falls flat. Of course, Arendt does not make the mistake of valuing politics only intrinsically; her cautionary writings illustrate political engagement instrumental value as well. But her intrinsic defense of politics and visionary theory have gained far more purchase among contemporary theorists than her instrumental defense and cautionary theory, even though the former aspects of her writing hold up least well to close scrutiny. Political engagement's intrinsic defenders invoke Arendt's writings frequently, as if her authority could legitimize their claims. It cannot. Arendt probably does not intend her claims about politics' shining excellence literally, and she certainly does not continuously recommend political engagement to all or even most

---

[164] Arendt attributed this method to Walter Benjamin but is widely regarded as having embraced it herself. Hannah Arendt, "Walter Benjamin," in *MDT*: 205–6. See also Young-Bruehl (1982: 95).

[165] The excerpts are from Shakespeare's *The Tempest*, the lines that Arendt famously quotes in her exposition of pearl diving. "Walter Benjamin," in *MDT*: 193.

people. Just because Arendt cannot provide participatory democrats with a foundational argument for political engagement's intrinsic worth does not in itself close the book on the intrinsic defense. Chapter 5 will consider several other versions of that defense. For now, however, I turn to Alexis de Tocqueville and a different orientation toward political engagement and disengagement. Tocqueville, like Arendt, fears widespread withdrawal from public life but defends political engagement in less lofty, and more strategic, terms than Arendt. He understands the appeal of self-centered pursuits, the need for collective action, and the acceptability of collective action motivated by relatively self-centered or at least instrumental concerns. Tocqueville's versions of social and political engagement might not promise self-revelation or eternal, worldly glory, but they show how ordinary citizens can satisfy their own reasonable desires in the long run.

Chapter 4

POLITICAL ENGAGEMENT AS INSTRUMENTAL GOOD

TOCQUEVILLE, ATTENTION DEFICIT, AND ENERGY

> That constantly renewed agitation introduced by democratic government into political life passes, then, into civil society. Perhaps taking everything into consideration, that is the greatest advantage of democratic government, and I praise it much more on account of what it causes to be done than for what it does.
> —Alexis de Tocqueville, *Democracy in America*

I N THE LAST CHAPTER I focused on Hannah Arendt, the most influential proponent of political engagement's intrinsic value, and found Arendt's argument inconsistent and unpersuasive. Now I turn to Alexis de Tocqueville as the most influential proponent of political engagement's instrumental value. Tocqueville's political works support my conception of political engagement as a combination of attention and activity, an investment of mental focus and physical energy that are closely related, instrumentally valuable resources for effective democratic governance. Tocqueville's insights into attention and energy and their importance for sustainable self-government comprise one of his more original, and overlooked, contributions to political theory.[1] Often misread as an unqualified enthusiast for so-called civic engagement in America, Tocqueville actually distinguishes between political and social engagement, explains why political attention and energy will probably flag in most liberal democracies, and suggests a number of avenues for resisting those tendencies.[2] Here I explore Tocqueville's analysis of political engagement and the obstacles it faces when citizens are free to invest their time and resources as they like.

---

[1] *Énergie* is the term Tocqueville uses throughout his works, meaning roughly the same in French as in English. "Attention" simply describes the concept of mental focus or regard that Tocqueville uses many different terms to denote, including the French nouns *attention* and *regard* and the verb *s'occuper*.

[2] Most notably in Bellah et al. (1985) and Putnam (2000).

Many readers regard Tocqueville's *Democracy in America* as a how-to manual for sustaining healthy democracies, frequently citing his enthusiastic accounts of the New England townships and their bustling community spirit and energy.[3] But Tocqueville also predicted voluntary isolation, political withdrawal, and governmental centralization. Having achieved the freedom to participate politically and administer common affairs, citizens can also choose the corollary freedom to abstain from political matters and focus on personal business. As their attention wanders and energy divests from the public realm, citizens' interests and freedom can suffer in the long term. Thus democracy's citizens need, but often lack, the proper perspective on their own long-term interests. Those with clear vision realize that long-term self-interest requires cooperative social engagement and participation in self-government. Not only does clear vision direct citizens to social and political engagement, but the experience of social and political engagement can also further clarify this "big picture" perspective.[4] They are mutually reinforcing—for some, at least. This is where Tocqueville and Arendt cross paths.

As I argue in chapter 3, Arendt portrays political engagement as an intrinsic good, but one that is only available to the few "politically best" individuals who muster the necessary energy and attention (and who cannot live without public freedom). Arendt has difficulty explaining why most people will never choose the political life and never experience the highest good. That makes her account less accessible and democratic than she might have intended. At the same time she intentionally neglects the instrumental benefits sometimes ascribed not only to political engagement but also to social engagement. Tocqueville's and Arendt's visions converge far more than they diverge, as I note in chapter 1, but with regard to engagement's practical value their subtle differences favor Tocqueville. Tocqueville, like Arendt, considers political engagement to be intrinsically choice worthy and good for some human beings, not all. However, he also catalogs a range of instrumental benefits that explain the importance of widespread political engagement and suggest the means of combating voluntary withdrawal. While Arendt bars economic and material concerns from the political realm, Tocqueville acknowledges their existence in everyday politics (while cautioning against excessive materialism) and hence has something to say about the engagement of ordinary

---

[3] Putnam (2000: 292) calls Tocqueville the "patron saint of social capitalists." See also Roark (2004).

[4] Tocqueville claims that if the Old Regime had not been so atomized, "the slightest contact with 'self-government' would have changed it profoundly and would quickly have transformed or destroyed it [and its inequality]." In the original French Tocqueville uses the English term "self-government," and he means the experience of administering common affairs in common. Tocqueville, *The Old Regime and the Revolution* (1998: 340), hereafter *ORR*.

citizens. Tocqueville thus explores the broad, middle ground that Arendt abandons, hoping to counter the human tendency of "choosing between two excesses."[5]

Tocqueville's repeated concern for balance and equanimity make him a theorist of moderation in the Aristotelian tradition.[6] On ten different occasions in *Democracy in America* he laments the human tendency to vacillate between extremes instead of cleaving to a reasonable mean. In observing the slippery slope of partial press censorship, he warns that soon "you have gone from extreme independence to extreme servitude without finding a single spot where it was possible to rest on that long journey."[7] Such vacillations "attest the inferiority of our nature, which, unable to hold firmly to what is true and just, is generally reduced to choosing between two excesses."[8] Equanimity is difficult because "the same energy which makes a man break through a common error almost always drives him on beyond what is reasonable."[9]

With regard to political engagement, democracy's citizens are ever torn between withdrawal into private life and excessive agitation in civil and political society, which Joshua Mitchell calls "inward" and "outward" directions.[10] At the individual level, Tocqueville's endorsement of the doctrine of "self-interest well understood" dictates a mean between inner-directed, enervated materialism and outer-directed, overenergetic ambition. At the collective level, associational life and political engagement constitute a mean between excessive self-absorption and unwanted public tumult. The goal is a middle ground between individualism and collectivism. But without a vibrant associational life (combining political and social engagement) as well as responsive political institutions that give citizens a sense of voice and efficacy, democracy tends toward extremes that none of its citizens need or want.[11] For Tocqueville, social and

---

[5] *DA*: 43.

[6] Aurelian Craiutu has persuasively emphasized Tocqueville's moderation as a vital feature of his work and his worldview. Craiutu (2005: 602).

[7] *DA*: 181.

[8] *DA*: 43. Aristotle, in the *Eudemian Ethics*, demonstrates that opposites often desire each other not because they truly wish to become their negation but because of a misinterpreted wish to attain a middle ground. For example, people suffering from extreme cold may move toward a fire, but not because they wish to suffer extreme heat. "If when people have got too cold they are subjected to heat, and when they have got too hot to cold, they reach a mean temperature, and similarly in other matters; but without such treatment they are always in a state of desire, because they are not at the middle points." (1935: 1239b20).

[9] *DA*: 597. The Mayer-Lawrence translation of *Democracy in America* (cited here) uses the term "energy" where "effort" would be a more suitable rendering.

[10] Mitchell (1995: 5).

[11] Mitchell phrases the problem thusly: "if the self is inclined either to fall quietly into itself—Tocqueville's term for this phenomenon is 'individualism'—or to be anxiously carried away, then the more moderate, intermediate disposition is not given in the nature of things

political engagement provide a path to the healthy middle, although he is more eager to avoid widespread social and political disengagement than to promote unlimited participation.

One might object that Tocqueville values political engagement not only for what it can prevent but also for what it embodies: intrinsically valuable freedom.[12] Indeed, Tocqueville does esteem freedom as the highest good, valuable for its own sake: "Whoever seeks for anything from freedom but itself is made for slavery."[13] In democratic nations freedom would not be possible without social and political engagement, but those engagements cannot truly be said to constitute freedom. (In a letter written around 1841 Tocqueville distinguishes between democratic politics and freedom, greatly preferring the latter: "I passionately love freedom, legality, the respect for rights but not democracy. This is the base of my soul."[14]) Tocqueville's freedom includes aspects of solitude and self-reliance: "being able to speak, act, and breathe without constraint, under the government of God and the laws alone."[15] Further, he often defines freedom negatively, as the absence of restraint or dependence on another, since "what peoples who are made for freedom hate, is the evil of subjection itself."[16] If one could remain self-reliant without formal politics, as Tocqueville envisioned some of the "quasi-aristocratic" Native Americans to have done—living in accord with their "indomitable love of freedom"—Tocqueville never indicates a principled objection.[17] But most people cannot remain their own masters without participating in a political community. We citizens must abandon at least a bit of our unlimited freedom by assuming an otherwise unwanted responsibility (unwanted by all but the noblest souls, that is) in order to secure any

---

but rather must be achieved over and over again" (1995: 5). Mitchell emphasizes religion's role in securing the intermediate disposition; the current project focuses on political and social engagement as well as political institutions.

[12] For those who appreciate it fully (and certainly for Tocqueville himself), freedom is "a good so precious, and so necessary, that no other could console [lovers of freedom] for its loss." *ORR*: 217.

[13] *ORR*: 217.

[14] Zunz and Kahan (2002: 219–20).

[15] *ORR*: 217.

[16] *ORR*: 216. By claiming that Tocqueville often defined political freedom or liberty negatively I do not mean to go as far as Edward Banfield, who unjustifiably claims that "what Tocqueville meant by liberty was no more than the absence of despotism." Banfield (1991: 244). Tocqueville associates love of liberty with some of the noblest human pursuits.

[17] *DA*: 29. One might reasonably respond that in the earlier passage from *The Old Regime and the Revolution*, Tocqueville writes that the "passion for political freedom . . . in all times, has made men do the greatest things that humanity has accomplished." *ORR*: 216. Thus Tocqueville seems to reserve his highest praise for freedom linked with politics, although not necessarily democratic politics. But that does not indicate that all admirable freedom must be constituted by political engagement.

meaningful freedom in the long run. This active defense is vital because for Tocqueville, as for Madison, "power is of an encroaching nature."[18] Those citizens who simply want to rest amid material well-being will eventually be governed by someone else.[19]

Unfortunately, most people naturally ask little more from freedom than to be to be left alone in their private, materialistic pursuits. The problem is not necessarily that most citizens eschew freedom but that they misconstrue and undervalue it. While "democratic peoples have a natural taste for liberty," they often value other goods more dearly: "their passion for equality is ardent, insatiable, eternal, and invincible."[20] Taste pales before passion, so the passion for equality perpetually threatens to overwhelm the taste for freedom—at least among the majority. But while Tocqueville looks down on those who seek only "ease, well-being, and often riches" from their freedom, he refuses to recommend forced political engagement or self-development. Political laziness is a shame, not a crime. It becomes a matter of wider concern, and a subject for Tocqueville's "new political science," if many individuals turn inward, because that endangers the entire community's freedom: "Men who prize only these kinds of goods have never enjoyed freedom for long."[21] Widespread political disengagement elicits centralized administration, which infringes on everyone's independence, and it renders the myopic individualists less fit for self-government should they decide to participate.[22] And should an officious, centralized administration and individualistic public mores become predominant forces, the environment might stifle self-development among the few who incline toward meaningful individuality. The ultimate risk is either harsh or soft despotism. Harsh despotism means cruel rule by a tyrant, the abnegation of freedom—which makes it Tocqueville's *summum malum* and greatest fear.[23] Soft despotism, more likely in the modern era, means the gradual assumption of all meaningful decisions by

---

[18] Hamilton, Madison, and Jay (1999: 332, Paper 48). Tocqueville's insistence that withdrawal invites encroachment evokes G. K. Chesterton's criticism of conservatism, perhaps more accurately classed as a criticism of disengagement: "All conservatism is based upon the idea that if you leave things alone you leave them as they are. But you do not. If you leave a thing alone you leave it to a torrent of change." Chesterton (1909: 212).

[19] "As those who work are unwilling to attend to public affairs . . . the role of government is left unfilled. . . . When the great mass of citizens does not want to bother about anything but private business, even the smallest party need not give up hope of becoming master of public affairs." *DA*: 540–41. See Walzer: "There is no escape from power and coercion, no possibility of choosing, like the old anarchists, civil society alone" (1992: 102).

[20] *DA*: 506.

[21] *ORR*: 216–17.

[22] Consider the disengaged French citizens who had no "daily involve[ment] in regional administration" during the late eighteenth century and became easy dupes for bad advice and irresponsible mobilization during the revolution. *ORR*, book 3, chap. 1.

[23] "Those words ['despotism' and 'blessing'] can never join together in my thoughts." *DA*: 226.

a "schoolmaster government" seeking to keep citizens in a perpetual infancy.[24] Tocqueville also implies that soft despotism, once in place, could turn harsh with little resistance.

How can democracy sustain meaningful freedom through widespread social and political engagement if most citizens lack a natural love of liberty or an innate drive toward politics?[25] The answer lies in what Pierre Menant calls Tocqueville's "democratic art,"[26] the art of enticing citizens to experience associational life, self-government, and democratic freedom, if not by appealing to their love then to their tastes, and if not to their tastes then to their passions (including their hatred of being despotically ruled).[27] From the experience of self-government a newly strengthened taste or even love for freedom may emerge, a process not so much art as alchemy.[28]

Tocqueville's unique combination of political theory and a social scientific approach—Jon Elster calls Tocqueville the first social scientist—qualifies him especially well for my purposes.[29] Tocqueville approaches democracy as something of an engineer: looking at American democracy he seeks to understand what works, with the ultimate goal of securing reasonable democracy in America and elsewhere. Although at times he expresses his own preferences or biases (as when he laments the passing of aristocratic virtues), Tocqueville maintains a focus on identifying practical solutions, sometimes locating alternative means of supplying public goods or social functions that were once supplied by a now-outmoded source. The materials with which he works include citizens' collective perspective, energy, and attention. The rest of this chapter addresses those materials, Americans' means of sustaining them, and Tocqueville's fears for the future of citizens' political attention and energy. Although Tocqueville eventually grew disillusioned with American democracy, I close with several Tocquevillean reasons for hope and several remedies inspired by his insights (although I only develop those remedies in chapter 6).[30]

---

[24] DA: 690.

[25] The desire to be free only "enters of itself into the great hearts that God has prepared to receive it," so "one must give up on making this comprehensible to the mediocre souls who have never felt it." ORR: 217.

[26] Manent (1998: 79–84).

[27] Tocqueville's point recalls Aristotle's observation in *The Politics*: "the many do not chafe as much at being kept away from ruling—they are even glad if someone leaves them the leisure for their private affairs—as they do when they suppose that their rulers are stealing common [funds]" (1984: 1308b35).

[28] Although taste for freedom is innate, the experience of self-government increases and empowers it. Involvement with communal institutions gives the people "both a taste for freedom and the skill to be free." DA: 287.

[29] See Elster (2009). However, Elster contends that Tocqueville was not a political theorist, a position from which I demur.

[30] For Tocqueville's increasing disillusionment after 1840 see Craiutu and Jennings (2004).

Sustaining Freedom by Pooling Citizens' Energies

Citizens' energies, for Tocqueville, comprise one of democracy's most vital resources. Energetic democracies might not always succeed, but enervated democracies—the citizenry completely dependent upon its government and "fear[ing] it will die if it makes an effort"—are sure to end badly.[31] In stressing that point Tocqueville articulates a concern of long standing in the political theory tradition. Philosophers from Plato to William James have regretted democracy's potential to go soft, to sacrifice martial discipline and toughness for fur coats and the fatted calf. The worry is that rigor, discipline, and energy may bring about commercial success that undermines those very traits and virtues. Warriors become merchants become sybarites, eventually falling prey to any disciplined, energetic enemies who raise their fists. Free regimes, in which citizens can enjoy the fruits of their energies, require active measures (and a new political science) to prevent their energies' dissipation while tempering their excesses.

Public affairs will never attract citizens' energies enduringly if they do not first attract and hold citizens' attention, so Tocqueville focuses on both of those resources: energy and attention. A third resource fills out the Tocquevillean triumvirate: long-term perspective, or what the first President Bush once dismissed as "the vision thing." Citizens need, but often lack, clear perspective on their own long-term interests, which include a sustained investment of attention and energy in the occasionally unappealing business of self-government. Perspective, attention, and energy occupy a far greater portion of Tocqueville's new political science than most readers have supposed. Tocqueville's new political *engineering* might be an equally appropriate description, because he aims to pool, channel, and limit citizens' energies through the use of various tools: institutional design, political education, moral suasion, and other appeals to citizens' attention.

At the very outset of *Democracy in America* Tocqueville sets the tone for his project by worrying about French democracy's warped political perspective, inadequate political attention, and insufficient political energy. Each citizen "loses sight of the very aim he was pursuing," people "give the least attention" to understanding democracy's needs, and they lack "the courage and energy" to preserve democratic freedom.[32] In the rest of his magisterial work Tocqueville elaborates on the connections among perspective, attention, energy, and sustainable freedom. When

[31] *DA*: 16.
[32] *DA*: 16.

political attention disperses, when political energy wanes, and when political perspective gives way to shortsighted individualism, meaningful self-government faces an uncertain future.

Tocqueville identifies both the innate impulses and the environmental factors that impel people toward self-enclosure and the voluntary removal of their energies from collective projects, focusing on four primary factors: equality, materialism, individualism, and isolation.[33] The latter two are intimately related and when taken together resemble what we now call political disengagement. Equality and materialism can promote that disengagement, so they join individualism and isolation in threatening to undermine political perspective, disperse political attention, and absorb political energy in private pursuits. As political engagement declines—as citizens withdraw their attention and energy from self-government in order to focus on materialistic projects—they may appoint a third party to oversee their common affairs. The results are governmental and administrative centralization that may undermine democratic liberty. Hence, Tocqueville's "principal goal in writing this book has been to combat" the forces impelling democracy toward the related perils of societal atomization and administrative centralization.[34] To be clear, these perils do not stem from abusive government, predatory big business, or foreign adversaries; they arise from within the citizen body. Citizens' own judgments and actions are largely to blame, because their perspective, attention, and energy are limited. Nonetheless, combating disengagement is not a matter of the government compelling citizens to participate in public life. Attention and energy cannot be coerced or they lose their spontaneity and power. Democratic government must try to elicit political energy and attention with a soft touch, through persuasion, education, and inducement, and then channel and limit those resources responsibly rather than attempt the kind of self-defeating coercion that "unconsciously drives away the very thing it wants."[35]

[33] As one example of voluntary disengagement: Democratic citizens' "habits and their feelings predispose them to accept" and even to welcome concentration of political power. "Not only are [democratic citizens] by nature lacking in any taste for public business, but they also often lack the time for it. In times of democracy private life is so active and agitated, so full of desire and labor, that each individual has scarcely any leisure or energy left for political life." *DA*: 671.

[34] Ibid. Tocqueville's analyses of citizen disengagement and its causes are far too complex for simple encapsulation. I aim only to draw out those elements of Tocqueville's analysis that connect citizen disengagement and atomization to difficulties with civic attention, energy, and perspective. The limitations of those human capacities can explain sufficiently, albeit not exhaustively, why citizens might voluntarily disengage from politics and self-government at the risk of their long-term interests.

[35] *DA*: 539. The context of this quote comes from Tocqueville's admonition against excessive greed that undermines the very objects of its affection.

What Is Energy?

Throughout *Democracy in America* Tocqueville refers to energy (*énergie*) fifty times, giving astonishing prominence to a term more commonly found in physics texts than in political philosophy.[36] Tocqueville's energy describes the motive force behind action, the fuel for achievement of any human ends. Energy undergirds individual and collective action, part psychological and part physiological. Thus energy encompasses Aristotle's distinctions among *dunamis*, *kinesis*, and *energeia*—human potential, activity, and actualization—which are rooted in the human psyche as well as the biological world.[37] Energy signifies much more than mere desire, which, lacking motive force behind it, cannot accomplish anything of value. Consider Tocqueville's complaint about his homeland:

> Each man [in France] feels what is wrong, but none has the courage or energy needed to seek something better; men have desires, regrets, sorrows, and joys which produce no visible or durable result, like old men's passions ending in impotence.[38]

Tocqueville repeatedly claims that desire alone, without the courage, energy, or power for actualization, leaves one's goals unfulfilled. When commenting on the scarcity of great learning in democracies, Tocqueville observes that "both the will and the power to engage in such work are lacking."[39] Effective work requires not only the will to choose an object but also the energy or power to get the job done.

Energy exists to be actualized, and energetic characters hate illegitimate constraint or arbitrary rule. Thus Tocqueville often places energy alongside *thymos's* corollaries, courage and love of freedom.[40] Tocqueville criticizes French aristocrats for their debauched cruelty but praises their energy, their "pride of heart," and the "manly mores" that make them "the most resistant part of the social body."[41] Similarly, Tocqueville honors the early Native Americans as a quasi-aristocratic race possessing

---

[36] Here I refer to the original French and include various forms of *énergie*, including *énergique* (energetic) and *énergiquement* (energetically or vigorously).

[37] Aristotle, *De Anima* (1988: 412a22-8); *Nicomachean Ethics* (1985: 1153a10).

[38] *DA*: 16.

[39] *DA*: 56.

[40] See Aristotle, *The Politics*, on the relationship of *thymos* (or spiritedness) to politics and also freedom: "Both the element of ruling and the element of freedom stem from this capacity [*thymos*] for everyone: spiritedness is a thing expert at ruling and indomitable." (1985: 1328a5).

[41] *ORR*: 173.

"the energy of barbarians," a "proud spirit," "courage," and an "indomitable love of freedom."[42] Indeed, energy without courage often falters, as Tocqueville observed of his European contemporaries. In France "society is tranquil . . . it fears it will die if it makes an effort."[43] And in Germany, Tocqueville regrets the disappearance of "the activity, the energy, the communal patriotism, the fertile and manly virtues" that had once been inspired by municipal institutions.[44]

Governments as well as individuals require energy to act swiftly and effectively, to execute their goals and defend their independence. As the people are democracy's ruling element, the institutions of government are essentially tools or mechanisms for achieving the people's collective ends and the public good. Like all mechanisms they require inputs of energy in order to function. Throughout his political works Tocqueville draws upon mechanistic metaphors to hammer home the importance of institutions fueled by citizens' collective energy. In New England townships "everything is in motion around you, but the motive force is nowhere apparent. The hand directing the social machine constantly slips from notice."[45] In *The Old Regime*, Tocqueville insists that the "greatness and power of a people" cannot be adduced to "the mechanism of its laws alone; for, in this matter, it is less the perfection of the instrument than the strength of the motors that determines the result."[46] Collective energy is the fuel that facilitates society's activity, supplies the "motive force," and tends the "strength of [its] motors."[47]

Motive force and activity, in turn, are closely associated with freedom itself. Consider the well-known passage in which Tocqueville inveighs against administrative centralization.

> What does it matter to me . . . that there should be an authority always on its feet, keeping watch that my pleasures are tranquil . . . if this authority, at the same time that it removes the least thorns on my path, is absolute master of my freedom and my life, if it monopolizes movement and existence to such a point that everything around it must languish when it languishes, that everything must sleep when its sleeps, that everything must perish if it dies?[48]

[42] "No famed republic of antiquity could record firmer courage, prouder spirit, or more obstinate love of freedom than lies concealed in the forests of the New World." *DA*: 29.

[43] *DA*: 16.

[44] *ORR*: 104. In French: "mais l'activité, l'énergie, le patriotisme communal, les vertus mâles et fécondes qu'elles ont inspirées ont disparu."

[45] *DA*: 72.

[46] *ORR*: 221.

[47] Joshua Mitchell also emphasizes the importance of motion in Tocqueville's thought, although for wholly different reasons relating to the psychological effects of boundaries and restraints on people's motion. Mitchell (1995: 29–33).

[48] *DA*: 88.

Freedom and *life* should be read as a pair, alongside *movement* and *existence*. When government is the master of the first pair, it monopolizes the second. Thus life parallels existence—a rather obvious equation—but also, more provocatively, freedom parallels movement.

In his chapter on the ubiquity of energetic activity throughout the United States Tocqueville contrasts free and nonfree countries in terms of their activity. In free countries "all is activity and movement; here [in France], all seems calm and immobile."[49] In his eyes "the greatest advantage of democratic government" may be the "agitation, constantly reborn," introduced by democratic government and carried into civil society.[50] Because energy and activity are the engines of self-government's independence, political science—"that great science of government"—must teach "how to understand the general movement of society."[51]

Individual and Collective Energy

While energy is a capacity residing in every individual, it functions best when utilized collectively. Energetic individuals face overwhelming odds when they act by themselves, as shown by the case of the failed reformer: "He exhausts himself trying to animate this indifferent and preoccupied crowd and finds at last that he is reduced to impotence, not because he is conquered but because he is alone."[52] To be enduringly successful, collective energy must be voluntary as well: "One will never encounter ... genuine power among men except in the free concurrence of their wills."[53] Tocqueville often contrasts the efficacy of freely combined energies with the futility of coercion. When a centralized, despotic government forces people to work toward imposed goals it courts disaster, because "it is not on such terms that one wins the concurrence of human wills" necessary to produce "genuine power." Slavery, the ultimate coercion of energy and effort, is not only unjust but also inefficient: "the masters make the slaves work without any obligation to pay them, but they get little return from their work, whereas money paid to free workers comes back with interest from the sale of what they produce."[54] Thus, while isolated or coerced

[49] *DA*: 231.
[50] *DA*: 233.
[51] *ORR*: 198.
[52] *DA*: 638.
[53] *DA*: 89.
[54] *DA*: 346. While energy, movement, and freedom are intimately connected, the same holds true for the obverse combination (enervation, immobility, and the absence of freedom): "humanity is so constituted that it prefers to stay still rather than march forward without independence toward an unknown goal." *DA*: 92.

individuals are immobile and ineffective, a society of energetic individuals working in overlapping projects generates an important store of power (even if it falls short of aristocratic greatness). That power makes possible impressive, collective efforts as well as a viable, common defense against the encroaching power of domestic governments and foreign threats.

Tocqueville's emphasis on collective energy prefigures Arendt's insistence on the cooperative nature of power.[55] For both Tocqueville and Arendt, energy and power must be used or risk atrophy. Should democratic citizens abandon their collective, energetic pursuits, they abandon their primary resource for resisting despotism's sway. While the relentless activity produced by widespread liberty may seem frightening or exhausting, citizens should not yield to the temptation to withdraw from public life: "I know that in our day there are many honest people . . . who, fatigued by freedom, would like to rest at last far from its storms. But they know very poorly the port toward which they direct themselves."[56]

The Democratization of Energy

Energy must reside in any regime's ruling element: healthy aristocracies must have an energetic nobility; healthy democracies need an energetic citizenry. The nobility's tastes, loves, and habits decide the goals toward which aristocracies direct their collective energies; in democracies, popular tastes (and social conditions) dictate the same. Aristocracies, moved by what Tocqueville considers to be "great" loves, can "act strongly on all [other nations] . . . attempt great undertakings and . . . great actions."[57] The resulting rewards, however, are distributed inequitably; aristocratic laws "tend to monopolize power and wealth in the hands of a few, because in the nature of things an aristocracy is a minority."[58] Conversely, one of the "true advantages" of democracy is that "it spreads throughout the body social a restless activity, superabundant force, and energy never found elsewhere, which . . . can do wonders."[59] The democratization of energy results in greater overall prosperity but also lower goals, because of democracy's prosaic tastes. Nonetheless, while democracy's goals and achievements may not be as impressive, Tocqueville praises democracy less for its outcomes than for its processes—the continual motion evoked

[55] For Arendt, true power (as opposed to brute force) "corresponds to the human ability not just to act but to act in concert . . . it belongs to a group and remains in existence only so long as the group keeps together." Arendt, "On Violence" in CR: 143.

[56] DA: 298–99.

[57] DA: 234–35.

[58] DA: 232.

[59] DA: 244.

by democratic institutions and continued throughout civil society—that he believes essential to sustaining widespread freedom.

While the people are democracy's ruling element, Tocqueville realizes that in modern democracies citizens must delegate a share of their power to a centralized government.[60] To govern justly and well, central government requires energy and firmness. As Madison writes in *Federalist 37*, "Energy in government is essential to that security against external and internal danger, and to that prompt and salutary execution of the laws which enter into the very definition of good government."[61] Tocqueville cites the *Federalist* approvingly, never disagreeing on the importance of governmental energy, but he emphasizes a complementary point. Madison, writing during a period of unstable, ineffective government, tries to ensure sufficient energy for the Union. Tocqueville, with fifty years' hindsight, insists that energetic government must be balanced by equal energy in the citizenry. Thus while all of the *Federalist*'s (thirty-one) references to political energy concern the energy of government, all but one of *Democracy in America*'s references to political energy concern the energy of the people.[62]

Too often, political science scholarship focuses on policy proposals and government initiatives as if government itself were the regime's ruling element. Tocqueville's insights are a reminder that democracy's ruling element must always be the people, and if their energy departs, so does democracy. Even though he lacks the twentieth-century term *bureaucracy*, Tocqueville recognizes that concept as the logical and regrettable outcome should centralized administration ever monopolize political energy. Tocqueville associates bureaucratic monopoly with the end of meaningful democracy and a likely step toward harsh or soft despotism.[63]

Tocqueville frequently uses the metaphors of water and molecules to enhance his descriptions of human relations.[64] When molecules are too

[60] "I cannot conceive that a nation can live, much less prosper, without a high degree of centralization of government." Note that centralized government is not the same as centralized administration. The former consists of concentrating "certain interests . . . common to all parts of the nation . . . in the same place or under the same directing power." The latter consists of concentrating "other interests of special concern to certain parts of the nation, such, for instance as local enterprises." Administrative centralization—remote, bureaucratic oversight of local interests and affairs—saps local energy, limits the experience of self-government, and dulls the taste for the experience of freedom. DA: 87–89.

[61] Hamilton, Madison, and Jay (1999: 226, Paper 37).

[62] Tocqueville's one exception appears in volume II, book 4: "One should never expect a liberal, energetic, and wise government to originate in the votes of a people of servants." DA: 694.

[63] Tocqueville's writings on soft and harsh despotism strongly influenced Hannah Arendt, who writes that "the rule by nobody is not necessarily no-rule; it may indeed, under certain circumstances, even turn out to be one of its cruelest and most tyrannical versions." HC: 40.

[64] "It seems as if the French people were like those supposedly elementary particles inside which, the more closely it looks, modern physics keeps finding new particles." ORR: 161.

far apart, their energy can dissipate or evaporate; when they are too close together, they are frozen and immobile. In Tocqueville's words, "despotism . . . walls [citizens] up inside their private lives. They already tend to keep themselves apart from one another: despotism isolates them; it chills their relations; it freezes them."[65] Individuals and their political energy require proper proximity to one another—neither the "iron bands" of despotism nor the atomization of mass society.[66] Even with the proper distance between its sources, energy must also be channeled effectively. Otherwise, collected energy could flow in many directions and thus deplete its potential, or could flood all at once and cause great damage. Consider Tocqueville's choice of metaphors: "municipal bodies and the administrations of counties therefore form so many hidden shoals that delay or divide the flood of the popular will," and political associations are a "dike to hold back tyranny" of the majority or of an oppressive faction.[67] The same metaphor holds regarding governmental energy: in France, an inefficient system of public employment "was like an irregular and badly constructed dike which divided the central power's strength and dissipated its shock."[68] If the collective energies are limited and channeled toward representative institutions that allow them expression, they can be harnessed toward useful projects and sometimes even great ones.

If energy is such a vital component of political and economic success, the idea of limiting it might seem puzzling. But just as freedom must be limited to be enjoyed in the long term—if all people do exactly as they like, anarchy looms on the horizon—the people's collective energy must be limited, circumscribed, and directed. Otherwise, collected energy tends toward entropy. Energy that is not pooled and directed can stagnate or wither, just as energy that is pooled but not limited can rage out of control and end in anarchy. Tocqueville observes both of these conditions in France before the revolution:

> The progress of government often slowed and sometimes stopped: public life was as suspended. At other times, it was by excess of activity and self-confidence that the new governments sinned . . . wanting to make everything better, they ended up confusing everything.[69]

Thus collective energy must not only be channeled toward useful projects but also kept within appropriate limits. The most important of

[65] ORR: 87.
[66] "Iron band" is Arendt's term for the over-close compression that totalitarianism enforces; "mass society" is her term for atomized individuals. Both apply well to the social and political extremes that Tocqueville fears.
[67] DA: 250, 192.
[68] ORR: 172.
[69] ORR: 237.

these limiting influences include laws and political institutions, "habits of the heart" (customs and mores), and one of the most important influences, organized religion.[70] Religion can restrain people's actions within a bounded moral universe and, perhaps more importantly, "impose a salutary control on the intellect." Absolute freedom to invest energy and attention can be worrisome or even maddening. In both religion and politics, "men are soon frightened by the limitless independence with which they are faced." In Tocqueville's view (to which Durkheim would later assent), freely accepted limitations on thought and action make meaningful freedom a possibility in the first place.[71] Faced with an endless riot of possibilities, energy would soon dissipate: "Such a state inevitably enervates the soul, and relaxing the springs of the will, prepares a people for bondage."[72]

America's moral and political landscapes are marked by restless and productive energies as well as salutary limitations and order.

> Everything in the moral field is certain and fixed, although the world of politics seems given over to argument and experiment. So the human spirit never sees an unlimited field before itself; however bold it is, from time to time it feels that it must halt before insurmountable barriers. Before innovating, it is forced to accept certain primary assumptions and to submit its boldest conceptions to certain formalities which retard and check it.[73]

Tocqueville would have it no other way; if a democracy were not both energetic and limited in the American manner, its leaders would have to find other ways of making it so. Later in volume two Tocqueville reiterates, "The task should be to put, in advance, limits beyond which [ambition] would not be allowed to break. But we should be very careful not to hamper its free energy within the permitted limits."[74] Tempering energy and ambition with judgment requires not only respect for moral standards but also a long-term perspective on the individual's and community's well-being.

---

[70] Joshua Mitchell expertly analyzes Tocqueville's reliance upon religion to restrain democratic energy while maintaining democratic freedom. See Mitchell (1995), especially chapter 4, "Christianity and Democracy."

[71] See Durkheim, *Suicide*: "It is not true, then, that human activity can be released from all restraint. Nothing in the world can enjoy such a privilege. . . . Man's characteristic privilege is that the bond he accepts is not physical but moral." (1951: 252). Also see Schwartz (2004). Note that Tocqueville does not endorse state censorship of thought and expression, and he protests against the "tyranny of the majority" over the same. Apparently he considers religious strictures to be "salutary" because individuals can more easily defy or leave a religion than they can defy or leave their state or society.

[72] *DA*: 444.

[73] *DA*: 292.

[74] *DA*: 632.

Perspective: Self-Interest Well Understood

Among its several roles, *Democracy in America* is a meditation on vision. Throughout this work (and also in *The Old Regime*) Tocqueville draws on metaphors of clear and far-reaching vision and contrasting imagery of blindness and obfuscation.[75] In *Democracy in America* he proposes "to see not differently but further," and in *The Old Regime* he desires "to see into the heart of the old regime, so close to us in years, but hidden from us by the Revolution."[76] Further, on more than a dozen occasions in *Democracy in America* Tocqueville distinguishes what is apparent "at first glance" (*au premier coup d'ôeil*) and what turns out to be true when one examines the facts more attentively (*un examen plus attentif l'explique*).[77] Those choices underscore Tocqueville's deep concern with democracy's long-term perspective and the factors that habitually cloud its sight.

Every legitimate regime requires a long-term perspective on the goals it can sustain and the means necessary to achieve them. Aristocracy, in spite of its many shortcomings, is well equipped for clear vision. At its best, aristocracy can set glorious, far-reaching goals, form the sound judgment necessary to pursue them, and achieve fruition by overcoming short-term desires. Government by nobility, "being master of itself . . . is not subject to transitory impulses; it has far-sighted plans and knows how to let them mature until the favorable opportunity offers."[78] For all of democracy's advantages over aristocracy—most notably, its greater justice—long-term perspective frequently eludes its grasp. Tocqueville notes that "it is this clear perception of the future, based on judgment and experience, which must

---

[75] Tocqueville's stated purpose in *Democracy in America* is "to see not differently but further." *DA*: 20. In *The Old Regime* he desires "to see into the heart of the old regime, so close to us in years, but hidden from us by the Revolution." *ORR*: 84.

[76] *ORR*: 84.

[77] *DA*: 640.

[78] *DA*: 232. Note that France and the other European aristocracies that Tocqueville takes as his historical subjects—being based on inherited wealth and privilege rather than virtue or wisdom—surely do not represent aristocracy at its best (and leave us to wonder whether a "best" aristocracy is purely hypothetical). Tocqueville observes considerable corruption and pettiness in those societies, and with regard to the coming revolution the French aristocrats suffered from a "strange blindness" because "their minds had frozen in their ancestors' point of view." *ORR*: 198.

I do not claim, or care to verify, that aristocratic perspective was ever as clear and far-reaching as Tocqueville occasionally suggests. I claim only the following: Tocqueville's account of clear perspective enduringly describes the foresight and judgment that democracy needs but struggles to attain.

often be lacking in a democracy."[79] Why should this be the case? Citizens have a difficult time judging appropriate long-term goals for their society because their materialistic desires direct them toward present satisfactions, and because the immediacy of those desires undermines the deep reflection required of good judgment. As Tocqueville laments: "In democratic centuries when almost everyone is engaged in active life, the darting speed of a quick, superficial mind is at a premium, while slow, deep thought is excessively undervalued."[80] Further, most people "see less clearly than the upper classes what can be hoped or feared for the future," in part because democracies lack a class of life-long statesmen, imbued with a respect for past and future generations.[81] Thus most citizens lack the aristocratic elites' experience with public affairs. Not only that, but democracy's "natural instincts"—its love of equality and mistrust of superiority—"lead the people to keep men of distinction from power."[82] For their part these distinguished figures often shun public office, either to avoid its frequent tawdriness or to pursue greater fortunes in private life.

Despite these obstacles, democracy must develop and sustain some kind of clear perspective on its long-term interests, its achievable desires, and the appropriate relationship of citizens to one another.[83] Tocqueville calls this the "doctrine of self-interest well understood." Note: well understood, not best understood. Less rigorous than Aristotle's virtue of practical wisdom (*phronēsis*), which evaluates virtuous ends and the means to achieve them, self-interest well understood—which I identify with democratic "perspective"—takes the people's ends as given and evaluates the means to achieve them imperfectly but enduringly. Self-interest well understood is "the general theory which helps [Americans] to combine their own advantage with that of their fellow citizens."[84] It dictates that individuals pay attention to and act in accordance with those norms "appropriate to the times," which include toleration, reciprocity, cooperation, and interpersonal trust. It tells citizens that they must help one another in order to accomplish their own ends, even if they find cooperation temporarily unpleasant.

[79] *DA*: 223. Tocqueville's insights echo Hamilton's: "the people always intend the public good, but they often mistake the means," Hamilton, Madison, and Jay (1999: 432, Paper 71). Tocqueville quotes this very passage at length. *DA*: 152–53n.

[80] *DA*: 461.

[81] *DA*: 223.

[82] *DA*: 198–99.

[83] Providing such perspective is one function of the "new political science" that "is needed for a world itself quite new." *DA*: 12. Tocqueville can look upon America with fresh eyes, unlike some of the chauvinistic Americans whose perspective is warped by their patriotic attachment.

[84] *DA*: 525.

As Tocqueville describes it, "enlightened self-love continually leads them to help one another and disposes them freely to give part of their time and wealth for the good of the state." Tocqueville endorses self-interest well understood as a flawed but undeniably useful asset that is the best moral doctrine available to most people.[85] The doctrine of self-interest well understood and its corollary norms are democratic virtues because, while they do not dictate phenomenal sacrifices or individual excellence, they are accessible and appealing to all. In their absence— should citizens no longer be touched or moved by "those great and powerful public emotions" that can motivate communal undertakings or the mingling of self-interest with the commonweal—then self-government and democratic freedom would be jeopardized.[86]

Tocqueville claims that among Americans the doctrine of self-interest well understood had "come to be universally accepted," but acceptance does not equal active emulation; it may mean that people pay attention to social and moral norms without an energetic follow-through.[87] Tocqueville's observations imply that a citizenry steered by self-interest well understood is more of an ideal than an empirical observation.[88] In practice, long-term vision often falters:

> It is no use telling [the people] that by this blind surrender to an exclusive passion [for equality] they are compromising their dearest interests; they are deaf. It is no use pointing out that freedom is slipping from their grasp while they look the other way; they are blind, or rather they can see but one thing to covet in the whole world.[89]

In other words, it must be hoped but cannot be guaranteed that the people will have a taste for what they truly need. We might hope that reason or calculation will inform or shape desire, but we cannot always depend on it.[90] (The Constitution represents one institution by which the people decide, in advance, what they are not allowed to desire.) For all of his attention to the doctrine of self-interest rightly understood, and his insistence that people must be educated to its tenets, Tocqueville does

[85] "The doctrine of self-interest well understood seems to me of all philosophic theories the most appropriate to the needs of men in our times. . . . Even should [modern moralists] judge it imperfect, they would still have to adopt it as necessary." *DA*: 527.

[86] *DA*: 645.

[87] *DA*: 526.

[88] *DA*: 302. For Tocqueville's observations regarding the difference between New England and the American West, see *DA*: 55. For the South, see *DA*: 345–48.

[89] *DA*: 505. Against the people's habitual blindness, or at least myopia, Tocqueville plays the role of King Lear's loyal Kent: "See better, Lear, and let me still remain / the true blank of thine eye." Shakespeare (1970: 1.1).

[90] To recall Hamilton's phrase, such an occurrence is "more ardently to be wished than seriously to be expected." Hamilton, Madison, and Jay (1999: 33, Paper 1).

not expect reason alone to clarify democracy's vision and forge its morals. Reason requires the additional influence of moderate habituation and the restraint provided by organized religion that can temper people's desires and help to enlarge their perspectives.[91] Together with these supporting influences, self-interest well understood may not put reason in the seat of power but may make passions and interests more reasonable.[92]

Moderation and restraint are seldom aligned with nobility and greatness, as Tocqueville occasionally laments. Nonetheless, democracy's special excellence resides in its potential for facilitating widespread freedom—the freedom to invest time, energy, and attention as individuals see fit. But to fulfill that potential, citizens must invest attention and energy not only freely but also wisely, with an eye toward sustainability and long-term consequences. Otherwise, conditions of maximal freedom can produce conditions in which that freedom disappears: "by demanding too much freedom one gets too much slavery."[93]

Attention

Every regime's ruling element must attend to political affairs. Without political attention, collective problems and public interests would go without redress. Encroachments against liberty would proceed unchecked. And yet in modern times representative democracy has become virtually synonymous with delegated political attention. Citizens elect representatives to look after political affairs and turn their own attention to other pursuits. Tocqueville fears that energy will accompany attention in the headlong flight from political affairs and self-government. In his understanding—and this is *extremely* important if we are to grasp Tocqueville's "new political science"—energy generally follows attention. If a subject does not hold people's attention it will not enduringly attract their energy and activity. If the people's attention, and hence energy and activity, leave the political realm altogether, they are left with a government that "monopolizes movement and existence to such a point that everything around it must languish when it languishes."[94]

---

[91] The limited scope of this project prevents a proper exposition of religion's role in Tocqueville's analysis. That job has been ably undertaken by many scholars, including Mitchell (1995) and Kessler (1994).

[92] In other words, while "One must . . . expect that private interest will more than ever become the chief if not the only driving force behind all behavior," still "we have yet to see how each man will interpret his private interest." *DA:* 527.

[93] Tocqueville cites this French maxim in *ORR:* 199. Its message closely echoes Socrates' observation of democratic excesses in the *Republic*: "too much freedom seems to change into nothing but too much slavery, both for private man and city." Plato, *Republic* (1991: 564a).

[94] *DA:* 88.

Tocqueville considers whether attention might follow reason or rational self-interest, in other words, whether people tend to pay attention to issues and activities that affect their long-term interests as well as short-term desires. Unfortunately for democracy and political engagement, attention is largely a function of tastes—and while tastes can be educated by reason and shaped by moral values, those educative influences have their limits.[95] In most instances attention follows tastes, and energy follows attention.[96] A taste for freedom might direct attention and energy to self-government, but a passion for material well-being, leisure, or for being left alone may divert democracy's resources (and influence its political health) in a different direction altogether.[97] Tocqueville implies that people can only be engaged with—that is, active in and attentive to—a limited number of issues or concerns. He finds Americans to be completely consumed by their activities: "[Americans] are not only busy, but passionately interested in their business. They are always in action, and each action absorbs all their faculties. The fire they put into their work prevents their being fired by ideas."[98] Because of their many distractions they do not even pay much heed to respected leaders and officials; "even when one has won the confidence of a democratic nation, it is a hard matter to attract its attention [*d'obtenir son attention*]."[99] Political affairs must compete with commerce, entertainment, and the pleasures of private life for the scarce resources of attention and energy. To attract attention and energy they must appeal to people's tastes. As early as 1832, then, Tocqueville warns that we should not be surprised to see politics as spectacle:

[95] In this regard Tocqueville follows Aristotle, whose *Rhetoric* addresses the nature and manipulability of attention. Aristotle writes that "all men are accustomed to devote their attention to what they like and admire," and that, with regard to aural attention, "hearers pay most attention to things that are important, that concern their own interests, that are astonishing, that are agreeable." Aristotle (1926: 1415b).

[96] William James's psychological theories also strongly support Tocqueville's contentions: "No matter how scatterbrained the type of a man's successive fields of consciousness may be, if he really care for a subject, he will return to it incessantly from his incessant wanderings, and first and last do more with it, and get more results from it, than another person whose attention may be more continuous during a given interval, but whose passion for the subject is of a more languid and less permanent sort." James (1899).

[97] Consider Tocqueville's comparison of Ohio and Kentucky, the former a free state and the latter a slave state where the ideal of labor has been devalued. Whereas Tocqueville finds Ohioans to be industrious and thrifty, the average Kentucky citizen "has the *tastes* of idle men; money has lost some of its value in his eyes; *he is less interested in wealth than in excitement and pleasure and expends in that direction the energy which his neighbor puts to other use.*" *DA*: 347; stress added. The French for the italicized portion reads, "il poursuit moins la fortune que l'agitation et le plaisir, et il porte de ce côte l'énergie que son voisin déploie ailleurs."

[98] *DA*: 642.

[99] Ibid.

When he is drawn out of himself, he always expects to have some prodigious subject put before him, and that is the only consideration which would induce him for one moment to tear himself away from the complicated little cares that are the excitement and joy of his life.[100]

Commerce gives politics stiff competition for citizens' limited attention and energy. Commerce appeals not only to Americans' taste for material goods but also for the impassioned activity that is sometimes associated with politics: "In democracies nothing has brighter luster than commerce; it attracts the attention of the public and fills the imagination of the crowd; all passionate energies are directed that way."[101] The danger is apparent: commerce or other brilliant involvements may charm popular attention and energy from involvement with self-government, even though the latter channels, pools, and mingles people's energies, upholds democratic freedom, and hence enables pursuit of commerce in the first place.

In special instances politics may outpace its competitors. Political crisis, for instance, can focus citizens' attention on political affairs.[102] But as soon as the trouble has passed, attention and energy wander after tastes once again. Further, the focusing effect of crisis is not only impermanent but also indeterminate. Crisis can focus attention and energy on self-government and the common defense, but can just as easily disperse them. Tocqueville writes of the American Revolution and aftermath.

The consequent prosperity itself made men forget the cause that had produced it, and with the danger passed, the Americans could no longer summon the energy or the patriotism which had enabled them to get rid of it. Their anxious preoccupations gone, they readily returned to their normal everyday habits, letting their usual inclinations have their head.[103]

For all of these reasons Tocqueville fears that democratic citizens will always struggle to focus their attention on political affairs, and hence will always be at risk of a political energy crisis.

When citizens withdraw their attention and energy from public and collective affairs they court a condition that Tocqueville calls isolation, and that condition can encourage the warped perspective of individualism (and ultimately egoism). And in spite of his current fame as a civil society enthusiast, Tocqueville is much more concerned with avoiding

---

[100] DA: 488.

[101] DA: 553. In *The Old Regime* Tocqueville depicts the French royal court's public appeal in the same manner, as a "brilliant" force attracting public regard: "they were, in short, that which most struck contemporaries' eyes and too often monopolizes posterity's attention." ORR: 121.

[102] Research in cognitive and political psychology supports this commonsense point. See, for example, Marcus and MacKuen (1993).

[103] DA: 386.

undue isolation and individualism than with promoting unlimited associationism and community. Political associations and social togetherness have their downsides, the former potentially undermining political order and the latter potentially quashing free thought and expression. Political engagement is not guaranteed to teach the art of ruling well; township government is inefficient and messy, and in pre-revolutionary France associations contributed to a thoroughly uncivic culture. But while political engagement brings uncertain rewards, widespread political disengagement almost certainly undermines political capacities and self-government. We need look no further than the eighteenth-century French intellectuals who lacked any exposure to active engagement, and who viewed politics from "an almost infinite distance from practice."[104] Their fellow citizens had no "daily involve[ment] in regional administration," and hence were susceptible to the extraordinarily bad political advice, the "contempt for existing facts," that French intellectuals offered them.[105] Tocqueville suggests that the French Revolution's excesses were due in no small measure to the debilitated political perspective resulting from widespread political disengagement.

Political energy suffers as well as political and moral perspective. By definition, isolated citizens withdraw their energy and attention from public affairs. Tocqueville worries that isolated energies may not only stagnate but also diminish. As we saw earlier, Tocqueville suggests that in the absence of continual agitation and progress, energy tends toward disuse and atrophy. Energy responds with special ardor to circumstances that allow for personal distinction, but isolated individuals are out of the game. Energy unused becomes energy squandered, both at the individual and collective level.

> If the citizens continue to shut themselves up more and more narrowly in the little circle of petty domestic interests and keep themselves constantly busy therein, there is a danger that they may in the end become practically out of reach of those great and powerful public emotions which do indeed perturb peoples but which also make them grow and refresh them.[106]

Tocqueville worries not simply that people will fail to exercise the "great and powerful public emotions" that stir them, but that, through this inactivity, the rousing force may become "practically out of reach" even if the people want or need them. "Ambition may lose both its spark and its greatness," base materialism may "loosen the springs of action," and an

---

[104] ORR: 197.
[105] ORR: 195–202.
[106] DA: 645.

enervated people may lose the ability even to maintain its independence, let alone accomplish anything of lasting importance.[107]

The conditions of social equality promote political disengagement in the form of individualism and isolation; equality "tends to isolate men from each other so that each thinks only of himself."[108] But equality also "lays the soul open to an inordinate love of material pleasure," and materialism is Tocqueville's fourth great concern for sustainable self-government.[109] Under conditions of social equality most individuals could never hope to achieve fame or political power. But wealth and material pleasures are available to many, and thus conditions of social equality encourage pursuit of worldly goods: "the same causes which make the citizens independent of each other daily prompt new and restless longings and constantly goad them on."[110]

Materialism, in turn, can increase citizens' isolation. We seek privacy in which to enjoy the fruits of our labor, and the experience of private enjoyment sharpens our desires: "the soul cleaves to [these petty aims]; it dwells on them every day and in great detail; in the end they shut out the rest of the world and sometimes come between the soul and God."[111] In American and also French democracy Tocqueville laments the increasing "desire to enrich oneself at any price, the preference for business, the love of profit, the search for material pleasure and comfort." These "most widespread desires" often "occupy men's minds and turn them away from public affairs."[112]

Materialism damages all three qualities that Tocqueville's new political science seeks to promote: perspective, energy, and attention. The blind passion for wealth perverts political perspective and self-interest well understood:

[107] "What frightens me most is the danger that, amid all the constant trivial preoccupations of private life, ambition may lose both its force and its greatness, that human passions may grow gentler and at the same time baser, with the result that the progress of the body social may become daily quieter and less aspiring." *DA*: 632.

[108] *DA*: 444. The French is "elle tend à les isoler les uns des autres, pour porter chacun d'eux à ne s'occuper que de lui seul." Tocqueville generally uses the verb *s'occuper* in the sense of occupying one's own attention, so another way of rendering this passage is that equality brings each citizen "to focus his attention on himself" (as the Reeves translation of *Democracy in America* has it).

[109] Ibid.

[110] *DA*: 635. Elsewhere, analyzing the democratic danger of military coups, Tocqueville blames "the love of material enjoyments and taste for well-being that equality naturally suggests to men," which is naturally opposed to energy, to "virile mores," and is "antipathetic to the military spirit." Were the nation to become thus softened, "the army would take up its arms without ardor and would use them without energy." *DA*: 702, note XXIII.

[111] *DA*: 533.

[112] *ORR*: 87.

> Intent only on getting rich, [citizens] do not notice the close connection be-
> tween private fortunes and general prosperity. . . . They find it a tiresome in-
> convenience to exercise political rights which distract them from industry. . . .
> Such folk think they are following the doctrine of self-interest, but they have a
> very crude idea thereof, and the better to guard their interests, they neglect the
> chief of them, that is, to remain their own masters.[113]

Material desires focus on immediate or imminent satisfactions while
democratic freedom requires long-term perspective on citizens' interests.
Immediate satisfactions are also easy pickings and, because they do not
require well-invested energy, a life of short-term gratification lets energy
stagnate. Early in *Democracy in America*, in an apparently unimportant
account of South Sea Islands, Tocqueville foreshadows his concern with
democracy's enervating materialism. In the tropical "enchanted islands,"
where everything "seems devised to meet man's needs or serve his pleasures," Tocqueville identifies "some enervating influence which made men
think only of the present, careless of the future."[114] He reiterates similar
worries throughout the following political analyses. Individuals absorbed
with material pleasures are "more prone to become enervated than debauched," and at the collective level a kind of "decent materialism" can
"loosen the springs of [societal] action."[115]

For the time being, Tocqueville's Americans maintain their springs'
tautness by investing their energies in cooperative projects and thus looking after their own affairs (as far as possible). Tocqueville addresses three
different kinds of participation that modern scholarship often includes
under the catchall rubric of "civic engagement": township administration, political associations, and civil associations. In Tocqueville's eyes
they are particularly desirable because they all attract and embody citizens' collective political attention and energy. That differentiates them
from activities such as voting, which some political scientists regard as
the quintessential measure of political participation. For Tocqueville,
political engagement is good insofar as it means that citizens' attention
and energy are focused on their common affairs and the business of self-
government. Were political engagement to consist primarily in periodic
voting—even if most citizens voted—Tocqueville would lament the declining habits and spirits of independence: "citizens quit their state of
dependence just long enough to choose their masters and then fall back
into it."[116] Tocqueville's preference for political engagement that directly
involves citizens' energies in cooperative activities and self-government

---

[113] *DA*: 540.
[114] *DA*: 26.
[115] *DA*: 533.
[116] *DA*: 693.

speaks to recent political science literature that highlights so-called voter ignorance. That literature questions whether citizens know enough about complex national politics to do more good than harm.[117] Tocqueville himself observes a kindred nineteenth-century phenomenon:

> here is one sort of ignorance which results from extreme publicity. Under despotisms men do not know how to act because they are told nothing; in democratic nations they often act at random because there has been an attempt to tell them everything. The former do not know; the latter forget. The main features of each picture become lost in a mass of detail.[118]

But Tocqueville does not lose hope in democracy, and even if today's citizens exhibit the lack of knowledge regarding politicians, policies, and platforms that scholars ascribe to them—which seems difficult to dispute—it would not make Tocqueville's vision of democracy less feasible. Citizens participating directly in self-government and local administration do not exhibit the kinds of ignorance that some political scientists fear, because they are not being asked for blanket opinions on vast, complex, national and global issues. Not only does direct participation in local affairs involve citizens' attention and energies in self-government to a far greater extent than periodic voting—they are closer to the issues and can see the results in action—but it also puts those energies to a more efficacious use.

Township Administration

Tocqueville's chapter on American townships is probably the most commonly consulted section of his most commonly consulted book. Nonetheless, scholars seldom cite more than a line or two from that chapter, and even less commonly do they situate it within the context of Tocqueville's larger project (which must also include *The Old Regime*). It deserves a closer look. Tocqueville lauds the township system because it provides incentives for self-serving individuals to become public-serving citizens. Indeed, the political engagement of township administration does not begin as public-spiritedness or virtue. Rather, Tocqueville describes nineteenth-century Americans as what rational choice theorists might call "utility-maximizing" individuals who turn their attention and energy to cooperative ventures when the individual benefits are obvious and the costs of participating are low.[119] Desire and taste are the initial lures: "desire

[117] See Caplan (2007); Somin (1998).

[118] *DA*: 610–11.

[119] Rational choice theory specifies that "in acting rationally, an actor is engaging in some kind of optimization," which may be construed as "maximizing utility." Coleman and Fararo (1992: xi).

for esteem, the pursuit of substantial interest, and the taste for power and self-advertisement" "excite men's interest" to the township's ample resources.[120] The township is "the mainspring of public administration" because it is "the center of men's interests and their affections."[121] While Tocqueville observes that township government "is to [citizens'] taste as well as of their choice," in truth it is "of their choice" because it is suited to their taste.[122]

But even prodigious rewards, if inaccessible, rarely excite people's attention or energy; for example, "only a few can exercise influence" in federal offices, so "no ambitious man would make them the fixed aim of his endeavors."[123] The township's resources in Tocqueville's America, however, are not only ample but also readily available. Citizens see the township as "a free, strong corporation . . . which is worth the trouble of trying to direct," and so "a vast number of people are interested in administration for selfish reasons."[124] They perceive their own potential efficacy, and that perception may further shape their tastes toward local political engagement.[125] Tocqueville's Americans, who possess a "taste for power and attention," develop a taste for local political engagement as well because that is the venue in which they feel most efficacious.[126]

Once the township's "advantages" have "excited men's interest" and "attracted the hot hearts of ambitious men," the average citizen "invests his ambition and his future" in township administration—invests his energy and activity—sharing there in decision and office.[127] Earlier I noted Tocqueville's insistence that individual energies must be pooled, limited, and channeled toward useful ends. The township serves those purposes admirably. By appealing to the tastes and hence attracting the attention and energy of self-interested individuals, it embodies "a natural vitality"

[120] DA: 69. When Tocqueville writes that "the New England township combines two advantages [independence and power] which, wherever they are found, keenly excite men's interest," he uses the term "interest" (*l'intérêt*) in the sense of "attention" or "regard." The township's advantages appeal to people's desires and hence excite their attention. Interest construed as "self-interest" would make no sense in this context.

[121] DA: 81.

[122] DA: 70.

[123] DA: 69.

[124] DA: 69.

[125] Almond and Verba's classic study of citizen engagement employs the term "subjective competence" to describe citizens' self-confidence and perceptions of political efficacy: "a subjectively competent citizen . . . is more likely to be an active citizen." Almond and Verba (1963: 182). See also Verba, Schlozman, and Brady (1995: 346–47).

[126] Jon Elster calls the adaptation of tastes to match perceived efficacy "adaptive preference formation." Elster (1983: 110).

[127] DA: 68–69.

and engenders "a continual gentle political activity that keeps society on the move without turmoil."[128]

The initially selfish engagement holds transformative potential, because tastes can be shaped and perspective can be educated.[129] The experience of cooperative engagement enlarges citizens' political perspective by drawing them outside of themselves and their narrow concerns. Those pursuing short-term resources come to realize that their long-term self-interest requires continued political engagement: this is self-interest well understood. Even when people manage public affairs "very badly"— which is often the case, in Tocqueville's view—"their concern therewith is bound to extend their mental horizon and shake them out of the rut of ordinary routine."[130] The citizen engaged with local government "in the end accumulates clear, practical ideas about the nature of his duties and the extent of his rights."[131]

The political engagement of township administration can set in motion a beneficial, self-reinforcing cycle (or "virtuous circle"). As citizens experience self-government and the pleasures of local freedom they develop a stronger taste for the same and grow better equipped to identify encroachments by hostile powers.[132] And as citizens treat common problems in common, their initially self-involved perspectives often widen to include notions of duty and reciprocal responsibility. The experience of self-government enlarges political competence as well as political perspective. Just as juries are schools for citizenship, "the institutions of a township are to freedom what primary schools are to science; they put it within reach of the people" because they "make them taste [freedom's] peaceful employ and habituate them to making use of it."[133] For Tocqueville, hands-on experience can teach political responsibility and the necessity of self-government in a uniquely powerful way, and townships

---

[128] DA: 71 and 69.

[129] "At first it is of necessity that men attend to the public interest, afterward by choice. What had been calculation becomes instinct. By dint of working for the good of his fellow citizens, he in the end acquires a habit and taste for serving them." DA: 512–13. Note that "of necessity" does not mean "by coercion"; citizens serve the public interest because they need one another. They perceive the necessity as a natural occurrence, or at least one not imposed by another's will. In Tocqueville's analysis, people do not adapt so willingly to compulsory participation.

[130] DA: 243.

[131] DA: 70.

[132] "In democracies the people, constantly occupied as they are with affairs and jealous of their rights, prevent their representatives from deviating from a general line indicated by their interests." DA: 233. The experience of political engagement not only keeps citizens' attention alerted to possible encroachments; additionally, the occasional disorders of public life, "the little shocks that freedom continually gives the most secure societies," and "keep[s] awake public prudence" against long-term threats to self-government. ORR: 199.

[133] DA: 57.

provide a much more accessible venue than state or national governments. Thus "in this restricted sphere that is within his reach," the locally engaged citizen "tries to govern society."[134]

Nonetheless, local self-government is frequently inefficient and messy, although in Tocqueville's view its benefits more than outweigh the costs. He compares efficient, centralized administration in France to American townships "whose budgets are not drawn up on methodical and above all uniform plans," and sides strongly with the American.

> I see most of those French communes, whose accounting system is so excellent, plunged in profound ignorance of their true interests and overtaken by such invincible apathy that society there seems to vegetate rather than live; on the other hand, I see in those American townships, with their untidy budgets lacking all uniformity, an enlightened, active and enterprising population . . . a society always at work.[135]

France's centralized efficiency, which monopolizes administration, lacks each of the essential political goods that I associate with political engagement: political perspective ("ignorance of . . . true interests"), political attention ("invincible apathy"), and political energy or motion ("vegetate rather than live"). America's messy townships, in which average citizens administer common affairs, produce the opposite results—despite their inefficiencies.

But as Tocqueville realizes, inefficient engagement is a hard sell with commercially oriented citizens, even if it promotes long-term self-interest. Much more likely is a rapid loss of patience with local governments' untidiness and inefficiency; citizens may "find it a tiresome inconvenience to exercise political rights which distract them from industry."[136] Impatience may lead citizens to delegate administration to an efficient, centralized power. And it precedes the slow slip into soft despotism.

Political Associations

Tocqueville extends his analysis of associations beyond the "municipal freedoms" of township administration to include the attentive activity of political associations.[137] While township administration constitutes formal government—an institution of the state—political associations are of private origin, established "solely due to the initiatives of individu-

[134] DA: 65.
[135] DA: 92–93, footnote 51.
[136] DA: 540.
[137] DA: 192.

als."[138] Tocqueville's political associations are thoroughly instrumental: "An association simply consists in the public and formal support of specific doctrines by a certain number of individuals who have undertaken to cooperate in a stated way in order to make these doctrines prevail."[139] The motivation to associate need not represent the expression of an intrinsically political human nature or the fulfillment of humankind's highest capacities, as civic republican theorists sometimes portray it. Rather, stated in flatly mechanistic terms, "an association unites the energies of divergent minds and vigorously directs them toward a clearly indicated goal."[140] Of course, political associations could embody a rich public freedom and an intrinsically good exercise for certain individuals at certain times. But those are not the grounds on which Tocqueville recommends political associations. They do not play that intrinsically fulfilling role for all (or even most) people at all times, whereas they reliably evince instrumental benefits. Political associations protect citizens' freedom without actually constituting it. Tocqueville acknowledges that democratic citizens could do without political associationism for significant periods, and while "their independence would run great risk . . . they could keep both their wealth and their knowledge for a long time."[141] How could an important but periodically dispensable activity constitute the freedom of people who remain free during its temporary absence? But even if not constitutive of freedom for all, political associations vitally facilitate freedom's protection.

Individually, political associations have any number of ends; categorically, they serve one overarching purpose. Political associations are sites of resistance, those institutions "by which men seek to defend themselves against the despotic action of the majority or the encroachments of . . . power." While a citizen might join any particular political association to support a "specific doctrine," he or she learns there "to combine with his fellows to preserve his freedom at a time when he individually is becoming weaker and so less able in isolation to defend it."[142] Political associations form a "dike to hold back tyranny" of centralized government or an oppressive, democratic majority.[143] They act as powerful individuals in aristocratic nations: "An association, be it political, industrial, commercial, or even literary or scientific, is an educated and powerful body of citizens which cannot be twisted to any man's will or quietly trodden

[138] DA: 189.
[139] DA: 190.
[140] Ibid.
[141] DA: 514.
[142] DA: 513.
[143] DA: 192.

down, and by defending its private interests against encroachments of power, it saves the common liberties."[144] Tocqueville differentiates between those political associations with a social element and those whose bond is "purely intellectual," the latter apparently resembling what present-day scholars call "mailing list associations."[145] Only in those political associations where members meet personally can ideas and opinions be "expressed with that strength and warmth which the written word can never attain."[146]

bonding

Tocqueville also implies that many political associations, being fundamentally insular and partisan, do not promote moral virtues such as generalized tolerance and mutual respect. Political associations can actually encourage moral disengagement because, as in France, "by the single act of uniting" citizens can make "a complete sacrifice of their judgment and free will," which "greatly diminishes their moral strength."[147] This is not to say that political associations are immoral or amoral, or that political associations cannot involve moral engagement. But in general they do not enlarge the heart in the manner of nonpolitical, and often nonpartisan, civil associations.

While Tocqueville offers high praise for political associations at their best, he maintains grave reservations about their prospect for causing harm. Precisely because they are energetic and partisan sites of resistance, a bulwark against tyranny of the majority, political associations can also threaten stability and order. The degree of their utility depends on the larger societal context. They are necessary and good in nineteenth-century America, because Americans enjoy long-standing traditions of nonviolent association and deliberation. Further, in America "difference[s] of view are only matters of nuance," so violent struggles are (in general) uncommon.[148] Tocqueville's France, conversely, lacks America's stable mores and traditions; there, political associations are viewed as catalysts to action and often violence, real threats to the political order. In other words, taking a step back from America, the political engagement of political associations may or may not support healthy democracy depending on a nation's prior resources and traditions. That admission need not mute our enthusiasm for political associations in the contemporary United States or developed, liberal democracies. If nothing else, Tocqueville's observations should chasten any contemporary political scientists

---

[144] *DA*: 697. We should note that Tocqueville here groups together political and civil associations and lists a political purpose that even civil associations can serve. But serving a political purpose does not make them political associations, as we will see in the following section.

[145] See Skocpol (1997b: 455–79).

[146] *DA*: 190.

[147] *DA*: 195.

[148] *DA*: 194.

who look to the American system as a model for developing democracies worldwide.[149]

Civil Associations

Tocqueville pointedly distinguishes between political and civil associations. The latter encompass "those associations in civil life which have no political object."[150] Many contemporary scholars insist that participation in nonpolitical organizations stimulates political involvement and interest.[151] But Tocqueville made that point first; he shows how civil associations can enlarge citizens' moral as well as political perspective by bringing people together, emphasizing their commonality, and demystifying their differences. Civil associations are essential because "feelings and ideas are renewed, the heart enlarged, and the understanding developed only by the reciprocal action of men one upon another."[152] Once citizens learn the art of associating they may put it to political uses; "civil associations pave the way for political ones."[153] However, that positive influence is not automatic; civil associations can just as easily divert people's attention and energy from political involvement.[154] At their best, civil associations can stabilize society by developing the art of association while balancing the agitation of political associations. At their worst, civil associations can wall people off in enclaves that neither interact with nor care about the larger public, a danger that looms should the state be unable or unwilling to provide members with needed benefits and demand a measure of respect in return.[155]

bridging

While participation in civil associations can promote political associationism, even more frequently the causal arrow points the other way: "One may think of political associations as great free schools to which all citizens come to be taught the general theory of association."[156] We cannot judge one type of associationism as superior in Tocqueville's eyes; regarding both civil and political associations he offers empirical and contextually specific claims rather than timeless verities. For example, Tocqueville observes that in Jacksonian America citizens may be more

[149] See Weaver, Rock, and Kusterer (1997).

[150] DA: 513. For a distinction between political and apolitical (but cooperative) engagements, see also Zukin et al. (2006).

[151] See Verba, Schlozman, and Brady (1995: 79).

[152] DA: 515.

[153] DA: 521.

[154] DA: 523. Civil associations, "far from directing public attention to public affairs, serve to turn men's minds away therefrom."

[155] ORR: 162–63.

[156] DA: 522.

inclined to join political than civil associations, not for reasons of intrinsic priority or deep-seated preferences but for reasons of simple risk-
aversion: "One cannot take part in most civil associations without risk-
ing some of one's property; this is the case with all manufacturing and
trading companies. Men who have as yet little skill in the technique of
association . . . have less hesitation in joining political associations, which
do not strike them as dangerous because they do not risk losing their
money."[157] Conditions have changed. Citizens no longer risk their property by joining civil associations, so Tocqueville's logic gives us no reason
to suppose that they will enduringly choose political before nonpolitical
associations. Thus I disagree in degree, rather than in kind, with scholars who read Tocqueville as definitely prioritizing the political—political
associations and engagement—over other kinds of associations and engagements, in all circumstances and contexts.[158]

This much is clear from Tocqueville's analysis: regardless of which precedes the other, both political and civil associations are vital for democracies' health. Political associations develop the art of self-governance, the
love of liberty, and the ability to resist encroachments against it. Civil associations further promote the art of associating even as they divert some
of society's copious energy away from immediate investment in politics,
thus "keep[ing] society on the move" without excessive political agitation
or instability. While Tocqueville finds full freedom of civil association
essential to all forms of democracy at all stages of their democratization, political associations are most valuable in democracies with long
traditions of stable, constitutional government and rule of law. In newly
democratizing countries political associations may undermine stability
and promote civil chaos. And both stable and developing democracies
might possibly survive the loss of their political associations for a while,
although not in the long run. But no democracy can endure the absence
of civil associations' transmission of cooperative norms and social connectedness. Tocqueville fears for "the morality and intelligence of a democratic people" if government were to crowd out private associations, but
not if political associations were imperiled.[159]

At any rate, in Tocqueville's United States both the political participation of township administration and political associations, and the social
engagement of civil associations (which reciprocally reinforces political
participation) keep citizens' attention and energy focused on self-government. The perspective of self-interest well understood steers people
toward that productive engagement and away from the corrosive individualism and isolation that can undermine democratic freedom. For these

---

[157] DA: 520.
[158] Villa (2008, chap. 4).
[159] DA: 514–15.

reasons American democracy resists, for the time being, the pernicious influences that Tocqueville glimpses more fully in his native France. Nonetheless, Tocqueville can only muster muted optimism about democracy in America, and even less than that about democracy in Europe. For all of its merits, American democracy seems to represent an unstable equilibrium that might easily be tilted toward excessive inattention, enervation, and disengagement.[160] Why?

First, the township system that earns Tocqueville's praises comprised only a fraction of American democracy. Tocqueville admits that "what I have just said about New England" regarding public education and civic perspective "should not be taken to apply to the whole of the rest of the Union indiscriminately."[161] In Southern slaveholding states and in the sparsely populated Western territories he finds little of New England's established civic habits and tastes, focused political attention, and usefully channeled energies. Indeed, in slaveholding Kentucky, the average citizen "has the *tastes* of idle men," and since attention and energy follow tastes "he pursues fortune less than agitation and pleasure, and he applies in this direction the energy that his neighbor [in free Ohio] deploys elsewhere."[162] And the American West represents "democracy in its most extreme form," with few social networks and no civic traditions—an inhabited territory "but not as yet a society."[163] Thus while many present-day political scientists quote only a few enthusiastic passages from *Democracy in America* praising Americans' public-spiritedness and political engagement, they do not capture the entire picture.

Second, even the socially and politically engaged regions such as New England are marked by intense dedication to commerce and material gain. Excessive love of those pursuits threatens to crowd out civic attention and absorb all available energy, regardless of the religious influences that can sometimes keep materialism in check. In spite of civic traditions and norms of cooperation, if people love their private pursuits sufficiently they always flirt with the temptation to delegate public business to a professional bureaucracy and withdraw into their individual worlds.

Finally, tastes change. Tocqueville's Americans exhibit a strong taste for public life and political engagement. They find it a pleasurable diversion:

> To take a hand in the government of society and to talk about it [the American's] most important business and, so to say, the only pleasure he knows . . . even the women often go to public meetings and forget household cares while

[160] Tocqueville himself hints at this wariness in volume II of *Democracy in America*, but he openly states his disillusionment in correspondence and other texts written after 1840. Cf. Craiutu and Jennings (2004).

[161] *DA*: 302.

[162] *DA*: 333.

[163] *DA*: 55.

they listen to political speeches. For them clubs to some extent take the place of theaters.[164]

Elsewhere, Tocqueville tells us that "as yet very few [Americans] go to the theater at all . . . the stage is not very popular in America."[165] We are left to wonder whether Americans' civic attention is likely to survive once theatergoing catches up with clubs and political assemblies in popular esteem and entertainment value.[166] Do popular tastes comprise a sufficient hook on which to hang one's hopes for enduring, widespread civic attention and ensuing civic activity? The answer is discouraging. In great detail Tocqueville chronicles the fickleness of popular tastes,[167] and we can surmise that while at the time of his writing Americans comprised a remarkably engaged citizenry—both active in and attentive to treating "common problems in common"—he does not expect their tastes, attention, and hence energies to seek out public affairs forever.

> Not only do they [democratic citizens] not naturally have the taste to occupy themselves with the public, but often they lack the time to do it. Private life is so active in democratic times, so agitated, so filled with desires and work, that hardly any energy or leisure remains to each man for political life.[168]

In American democracy Tocqueville observes a relentless activity encouraged by the relatively new, and sometimes overwhelming, impact of free choice and independence. Able to choose their occupations, business, and leisure pursuits Americans become jacks of many trades but masters of none.[169] While political power or lasting fame may be out of the question, myriad material goods are not; "therefore [the American] does everything in a hurry," and "he is more bent on knowing a lot quickly than on knowing anything well."

---

[164] DA: 243. Similarly, regarding American associational life around the turn of the twentieth century, Robert Putnam and Gerald Gamm speculate that small and medium-sized cities were the sites of many civic associations because they lacked other entertainment options. Gamm and Putnam (1999: 549).

[165] DA: 492–93.

[166] Benjamin Franklin, recounting the success of his early lending library, stresses the absence of competing attractions for the people's attention: "Reading became fashionable; and our people, *having no public amusements to divert their attention from study*, became better acquainted with books, and in a few years were observed by strangers to be better instructed and more intelligent than people of the same rank generally are in other countries." Franklin (1996: 61; stress added).

[167] For example: "The Anglo-Americans . . . admit that what seems good to them today can be replaced tomorrow by the better that is still hidden." DA: 359.

[168] DA: 642.

[169] "Unable to be an expert in all, a man easily becomes satisfied with half-baked notions." Ibid.

Of course, these limitations apply to politics as well as business and leisure pursuits. While Tocqueville famously praises Americans' political participation, few scholars acknowledge this biting accompaniment: "their actions are often ill-considered because they give but little time and attention to each matter." Because attention is limited but political information is vast, "the main features of each picture become lost in a mass of detail." Tocqueville depicts a manic pace and shallow depth of daily life that could just as easily apply to today's society, and he closes with this powerful but little-known pronouncement: "Habitual inattention must be reckoned the great vice of the democratic spirit."[170] Since Tocqueville strongly suggests that energy follows attention, political inattention threatens political lethargy.

Rather than viewing the United States as a model polity that will show the world how to avoid democracy's perils, Tocqueville sees an impressive but unstable balancing act. It stands in a tenuous equilibrium maintained (for the moment) by an interplay of culture, ideology, tastes, habits, and political institutions, all of which can change and hence upset the balance. Indeed, nine years after his initial visit to America Tocqueville ends volume two with the very same worries that had inaugurated volume one: lack of political attention, which he calls the "general apathy," and a generalized enervation that could lead future democracies into despotism or anarchy.

> Both [license or tyranny, anarchy or despotism] are equally to be feared, and both could spring from one and the same cause, that is, the general apathy, the fruit of individualism. . . . We should therefore direct our efforts, not against anarchy or despotism, but against the apathy which could engender one or the other almost indifferently.[171]

The soft despotism of a "schoolmaster" government "hinders, restrains, enervates, stifles, and stultifies" inattentive individualists. So in spite of American democracy's countervailing forces, the continual pull of individualism and isolation gives Tocqueville concern for its future prospects.[172]

---

[170] *DA*: 611. Tocqueville's critique recalls the 1787 essay, "Vices of the Political System," James Madison's extended complaint about the decline of Americans' civic virtue after the revolution and the return to the vices of private life. Madison, "Vices of the Political System" in Madison (1962).

[171] *DA*, Appendix I, note BB, pp. 735–36. When Tocqueville writes, in this footnote, of *l'apathie générale* he is referring to the condition of a people, "constantly circling around in pursuit of the petty and banal pleasures with which they glut their souls. Each one of them, withdrawn into himself, is almost unaware of the fate of the rest." *DA*: 692. Such a condition is exactly what I call a lack or absence of social and political attention and hence perspective.

[172] "I noticed during my stay in the United States that a democratic state of society similar to that found there could lay itself peculiarly open to the establishment of a despotism." *DA*: 690.

As I show in chapters 1 and 2, present-day political science scholarship finds these same worries about social and political disengagement hard at work, with the occasional implication that we were once better off. But Tocqueville helps us to understand that democracy has long struggled—and perhaps always will struggle—with the amount of attention and energy that citizens dedicate to self-government and cooperative endeavors. Tocqueville's concept of energy (and his concern about its supply) lays the ground for Putnam's writings on social capital. At the individual level, energy is the most important ingredient of what economists and sociologists call human capital.[173] Collective energy comprises a significant component of social capital, the interpersonal connections that facilitate collective action. For Tocqueville, individual and collective energy can serve civil functions but, when necessary, can be channeled into political institutions and the processes of self-government. But *energy* has an added advantage over *capital* for thinking about democracy's health: we can apply it to governments as well as to individuals and groups. Democracy requires an energetic citizenry but also an energetic government. Without the latter democracy would fall to internal crises or external enemies; without the former, citizens would be at their government's mercy. The same point is not so easily made with the *capital* metaphor.

Further, Tocqueville's work can provide many additions or revisions to the political science and political theory literature that cites him so frequently. As we have seen, a number of political theorists insist that political engagement, good in and of itself, must mute or chasten claims of self-interest, efficiency, and utility.[174] In Tocqueville's view, democratic politics must countenance those claims if only to engage initially self-interested citizens. At the same time, some scholars value social or political engagement (often lumped together under the civic engagement umbrella) precisely for their role in producing economic, political, and bureaucratic efficiency.[175] Tocqueville responds that efficiency should not always be democracy's goal—that political engagement can be messy and inefficient, but remains vital to democracy's long-term interests. Other scholars value economic associations and commercial enterprise as important sites of social and moral engagement, where social capital and bonds of generalized trust can develop. Tocqueville does not disagree but cautions that excessive materialism, born of commercial and industrial success, can undermine social and political engagement and even undermine materialistic goals in the long run. Still others promote social and political engagement for the sake of fostering widespread trust, which

---

[173] Coleman (1994).
[174] Cf. Arendt 1959 and 1963.
[175] See Fukuyama (1995); Putnam et al. (1993); Putnam (2000).

they regard as a vital democratic virtue.[176] Tocqueville cautions us that while interpersonal trust should be highly esteemed, citizens are well served by a healthy *mis*trust of government as long as they feel efficacious to counter threats to their independence. For that matter, Tocqueville stresses perceived efficacy much more heavily than most scholars realize. Long before the recent trend among social and political scientists to investigate the importance of perceived efficacy for political engagement and mobilization, Tocqueville used it to explain New Englanders' participation in township government.

Some scholars treat so-called civic engagement, meaning both political and social engagement, as the engine for "making democracy work."[177] Tocqueville distinguishes between political and social engagement and points out that not all political engagement is equal, that balkanized engagement is only a collective version of democratic individualism, and that to be useful in the long term citizens' energies must be mingled, channeled, and harnessed by appropriate institutions.[178] He stresses the importance of localized political engagement because citizens can gain a small measure of power, feel efficacious, and learn the skills of self-government. Present-day political scientists often pass over local political engagement because the real power resides at the state and national levels, but, as I will suggest in chapter 6, that might be a mistake.

Tocqueville's new political science further teaches that energy and attention must be encouraged, limited, and channeled toward various cooperative projects, and sometimes toward self-government, but that a soft touch may elicit better results than forceful coercion. In our current desperation to stem the tide of political apathy among the young, many middle schools and high schools are requiring so-called civic engagement, meaning compulsory voluntarism and community service outside the classroom.[179]

---

[176] Putnam (1995, 2000).

[177] Putnam et al. (1993).

[178] Theda Skocpol levels a version of this reproach against Putnam and like-minded social scientists. For her stress on the importance of federated linkages and of overcoming civic balkanization, Skocpol is truer to Tocqueville's principles than many contemporary political scientists. "How Americans Became Civic," in Skocpol and Fiorina (1999). In Putnam's defense, *Bowling Alone* does distinguish between "bonding" and "bridging" social capital, only the latter of which is allegedly associated with pluralism and generalized trust. The predominance of "bonding" social capital might look something like Tocqueville's "collective individualism."

[179] Note that I am not referring to "community-based learning" classes that may integrate volunteer work into curricular contexts, but rather compulsory, extracurricular volunteer work undertaken simply as a graduation requirement. Echoing Williams James's 1908 manifesto on national service, Senator Chris Dodd recently proposed that mandatory community service be instituted in high schools nationwide. Holly Ramer, "Dodd Urges Mandatory Community Service," http://abcnews.go.com/Politics/wireStory?id=3309445, July 2007.

Tocqueville supplies reasons to doubt their efficacy if not their sincerity, because they seek to attract energy and attention without "the concurrence of [students'] wills." Because "humanity is so constituted that it prefers to stay still rather than march forward without independence toward an unknown goal," such mandatory measures could, "unconsciously drive away the very thing it wants."[180] If we take Tocqueville seriously we must take citizens' tastes seriously as well, because quite often attention follows tastes (and energy follows attention). Rather than coercing attention and energy we can attempt to attract them to cooperative pursuits, including self-government, by appealing to people's tastes. The trick, of course, is to make politics appealing but not tawdry or shallow to the point of meaninglessness. We might also provide greater incentives for satisfying participation, delegating more power to localities, and hence helping local politics appeal to the "hot hearts of ambitious men" and women.[181] And aside from eliciting additional attention and energy to politics and self-government, we might revise our political institutions so that they utilize and channel existing political attention and energy more efficaciously. In chapter 6 I will consider several Tocquevillean possibilities—inspired but not authored by Tocqueville—for treating, if not curing, democracy's enduring attention deficit and energy crisis.

[180] DA: 92, 539.
[181] DA: 69.

Chapter 5

IS POLITICAL ENGAGEMENT BETTER THAN SEX?

> Therefore, for a democratic polity to exist it is necessary for a participatory society to exist, i.e. a society where all political systems have been democratized and socialization through participation take place in all areas . . . maximum input (participation) is required.
> —Carole Pateman, *Participation and Democratic Theory*

> The problem with socialism is that it takes up too many free evenings.
> —Oscar Wilde[1]

O NE OF MY PURPOSES has been to upset the commonplace practice of taking political engagement for granted, both its meaning and its value. We must specify clearly what political engagement means before we can decide whether it is inadequately supplied and, if so, why—and what, if anything, might be done to promote it. Toward that end, I argue in chapter 2 that we should understand political engagement as a combination of attention and activity: attention to, and activity in support of, political affairs, which can (but need not) be combined with social or moral engagement. In chapters 3 and 4 I favor Tocqueville's instrumental defense of political engagement over Arendt's intrinsic defense of its worth, although neither account satisfies completely. Assessing their relative merits comprises a necessary but insufficient step toward appraising political engagement's value. Here I review a broader range of arguments regarding the need for high and widespread political engagement, including Tocqueville's, and find none completely persuasive on its own. Each one represents piecemeal, circumstantial evidence of political engagement's importance. But the arguments also suggest a better approach for anyone wishing to advocate for increased political engagement, as I will do.

I begin with a foundational but often overlooked question: exactly which benefits does political engagement offer to individuals and com-

---

[1] The quote is widely attributed to Wilde but has not been found in his writings.

munities? My second step assesses the value of that value. How essential are political engagement's benefits to the health of liberal democracy, and how much is enough? Among the scholars who address the first step at all, most assume that if political engagement has some demonstrable worth, then (1) liberal democracies need as much political engagement as they can get, (2) democracies with more politically engaged citizenries are healthier than those with less, and (3) modest declines in political engagement give us cause for grave concern. Those assumptions do not hold.

To understand why, consider this tongue-in-cheek question: Is political engagement better than sex? On a literal level the answer will be a resounding *no* for all but the most dedicated participatory democrats. But on a figurative level political engagement may be analogous to sex—at least procreative sex, undertaken for the purpose of reproduction—in the way that individuals and communities assess its value. Any particular individual might esteem procreative sex or do without it entirely. Some might consider procreation and parenthood to be essential for a meaningful life; others prefer to live without the attendant responsibilities and burdens. But at least some individuals must reproduce if the community is to survive. Yet the community does not necessarily need as much procreation as it can get. Under some conditions (such as scarcity or overcrowding) too much procreation can lead to real harm.

Analogously, for some individuals political engagement may seem essential to a meaningful existence, while others eschew the attendant responsibilities and burdens, leading perfectly fulfilling lives without it. But democratic polities face woeful consequences if no (or very few) citizens invest attention and energy in political affairs and processes. Democracy would not be democracy, rule by the people, if most of the people had nothing to do with politics. It might be oligarchy or aristocracy or Arendt's version of bureaucracy—rule by no one—but it would not be democracy. And certain groups of citizens, those with few economic and educational resources, stand to fare especially poorly when they do not engage politically. But we cannot easily prove that democracies need ever more political engagement, or that governments may justifiably compel participation or dedicate scads of scarce resources to promoting it, short of an overwhelming public mandate. In fact, under some circumstances very high levels of political engagement can prove harmful.

That is the argument's short version. The longer version follows. I will consider some of the most influential claims regarding political engagement's worth and show that each one amounts to circumstantial evidence, incapable of establishing that high political engagement is essential for democratic polities. But when we assemble them as parts of a coherent narrative—an assembly project that no one has yet undertaken—these individually incomplete arguments suggest that political engagement is likely to bring at least some of a wide range of benefits to at least some of liberal democracy's citizens at least some of the time. Thus while we cannot regard political engagement as a solution to democracy's ills, as Pateman seems to do with her assertion that maximum participation in all spheres of society would promote self-development and eliminate many moral and political vices, neither can we be indifferent to political disengagement (as some theorists of elite democracy have been).[2] In the area of political engagement, liberal democracies' top priorities should be preventing radical disengagement, which threatens a variety of undesirable consequences, and promoting political engagement among those citizens whose disengagement most harms their own interests and the polity's ideals.[3]

Proponents of increased political engagement can rely on strategies such as political education, media campaigns, and material incentives to encourage voluntary, widespread political attention and activity. Alternately, they can use the power of law to require it. Both approaches aim to give citizens not only justifying but also motivating reasons to engage politically—not only normative reasons that explain why citizens ought to engage politically but also arguments that motivate them to do so. Justifying and motivating reasons may coincide but often do not. For example, an overwhelming majority of Americans accept the proposition that duty requires us to vote.[4] But a much lower percentage follows through at election time. Apparently, duty justifies better than it motivates political engagement in the form of voting.[5] As I will show in this chapter, many of the most influential and commonly cited arguments for political engagement's vital importance fail to justify or motivate high and widespread levels of engagement. Does the case for participatory democracy founder as a result, or can it be grounded more reliably?

Earlier I divided the defenses of political engagement into two distinct groups, those that stress its intrinsic worth and those that address its instrumental benefits. Intrinsic defenders value political engagement for its own sake, as a necessary component of human flourishing or the

[2] In this regard Pateman quotes G.D.H. Cole approvingly, affirming that in a "participatory society . . . the motive of 'greed and fear' would be replaced by the motive of free service." Pateman (1970: 40).

[3] In chapters 3 and 4 I describe some of the harms that can accompany severe political disengagement.

[4] In a July 2000 Pew Research Center poll, 89 percent of respondents agreed either "completely" or "mostly" with the proposition, "I feel it's my duty as a citizen to always vote."

[5] In the November 2000 general elections approximately 55 percent of the voting-age population actually voted. U.S. Census Bureau 2002 report, http://www.census.gov/prod/2002pubs/p20-542.pdf.

good life.[6] But intrinsic defenses cannot comfortably account for the overwhelming evidence of political ambivalence. If political engagement were intrinsic to human flourishing, why would so many people—now and throughout the ages—choose to do without it? Intrinsic defenders can respond, with Arendt and other canonical republican theorists, that most people are ill suited for authentic politics and that only a natural elite, who are "politically, the best," will choose the full rewards of public happiness.[7] Centuries before Arendt, Machiavelli affirmed a similar republican worldview. Machiavelli distinguishes the few, who possess "a great desire to dominate," from the masses who show "merely the desire not to be dominated."[8] Far from sympathizing with the power seekers, Machiavelli advises princes to take sides against them for the sake of enduring, republican freedom. But what does this republican freedom entail for most citizens? Not widespread, intensive political engagement but rather political stability and individual protection, a claim more reminiscent of Hobbes than of Aristotle: "the vast bulk of those who demand freedom, desire but to live in security."[9] And in Aristotle's view, political engagement comprises an exclusive good not simply because of the masses' insufficient political demand but also because of their insufficient ability. A small minority of humans can enjoy the freedom and leisure of Aristotle's political engagement, made possible through slave labor and the exploitation of women.[10] Thus an influential portion of canonical republican theorists regard political engagement as an elite good, desired, appreciated, or achievable only by a few. Contemporary advocates of political engagement's intrinsic worth frequently treat those canonical theorists as amici curiae, but with friends like them the intrinsic defense needs no enemies.[11]

---

[6] "Nationalists, by contrast [with liberals], are likely to attach intrinsic value to public life, and to adopt a republican view of citizenship, according to which the citizen should be actively engaged at some level in political debate and decision-making." Miller (1995: 194).

[7] As discussed in chapter 3, Arendt regards some citizens as "politically . . . the best" not because they possess greater abilities but greater drive and taste for politics; they cannot imagine life without the public happiness of politics.

[8] "If we ask what it is the nobility are after and what it is the common people are after, it will be seen that in the former there is a great desire to dominate and in the latter merely the desire not to be dominated." Machiavelli (1984: 116).

[9] Ibid., 155–56.

[10] Sandel, too, disavows these "exclusive" aspects of Aristotle's republicanism. "Aristotle . . . considered women, slaves, and resident aliens unworthy of citizenship because their nature or roles deprived them of the relevant excellences." Sandel (1996: 318).

[11] While Machiavelli is widely considered a republican fixture, most would not align him with an intrinsic defense of politics. But in establishing politics' intrinsic worth for the "politically best" Arendt cites Machiavelli's "poignant" description of Florentine patriots who defied the pope and thus "showed how much higher they placed their city than their souls." She continues: "The question, as Machiavelli saw it, was not whether one loved God

Most contemporary scholars would never overtly endorse such elitism, but few options remain for anyone wishing to promote political engagement's intrinsic value in spite of citizens' reluctance to embrace it. One could dodge the problem of low demand by specifying only a certain kind of political engagement as intrinsically valuable and necessary: the political engagement of small-scale, intensively participatory democracy among mutually respecting equals, which we might call pure political engagement.[12] According to this line of argument, only pure political engagement promotes self-development and the good life, and, while it has rarely been available, "if you build it they will come."[13] But the argument founders on multiple fronts. First, its specialized conception of politics combines political, social, and moral engagement, just as civic engagement often does in academic literature. Second, it commits the sin of spurious correlation, assuming that the political element of pure political engagement merits special praise while ignoring the possibility that the social and moral components might be responsible for any special benefits such as self-development and fulfillment. History and literature provide myriad examples of politically disengaged humans flourishing through the social and moral engagements of close friendships, religious communion, intellectual fellowship, and the like. Obversely, radical social disengagement correlates with a range of undesirable outcomes, and radical moral disengagement would characterize a sociopath, but for any individual selected at random the experience of voluntary political disengagement threatens no dire consequences.[14] Lauding political engagement while lumping it together with social and moral engagement ignores the significant distinctions between them and drapes political action in borrowed finery.

Some intrinsic defenders analogize citizenship with friendship to ennoble political engagement undeservedly, a confusion apparently stemming from misuse of Aristotle's "civic friendship."[15] The insinuation is

---

more than the world, but whether one was capable of loving the world more than one's self. And this decision indeed has always been the most crucial decision for all who devoted their lives to politics." Arendt (1963: 286). Michael Gottsegen supports Arendt's estimation of Machiavelli, claiming that citizens will love their cities more than their souls "where the right degree of identification with one's city has been attained." Gottsegen (1994: 262).

[12] Benjamin Barber employs similar reasoning when he distinguishes between democracy as ordinarily conceived and his ideal of "strong democracy." Barber (1984).

[13] Just as some defend communism against its twentieth-century failures by claiming that "real" communism has never been tried, this argument alleges that "real" politics and political engagement have never been tried and so cannot be judged a failure.

[14] For example, radical social disengagement correlates with physical, mental, and emotional health risks. Hortulanus, Machielse, Meeuwesen (2006); Hartog, Audy, and Cohen (1980); House, Landis, and Umberson (1988: 540–45).

[15] Bernard Yack cites Arendt and Benjamin Barber, who acknowledges Arendt's influence, among those misinterpreting Aristotle's writings on civic friendship. Yack (1993: 51–87).

that since Aristotle characterizes citizenship as friendship, and since many people value friendship as one of life's most important goods, then citizenship, too, might be constitutive of the good life. But Aristotle only describes the relationship between citizens as a certain kind of friendship, a relationship based on mutual utility as opposed to a deep, moral bond.[16] It scarcely resembles the intimate bond that many people might acknowledge as a component of human flourishing. To elide this distinction is to err in a way that Aristotle observes among his contemporaries, who "wish to have it both ways at once—they associate together for the sake of utility but make it out to be a moral friendship as between good men."[17] Further, Aristotle stipulates that even the utility-based bond of civic friendship could only be shared by a small number, far fewer than reside in the average American town, metropolis, or state.[18] Perhaps most importantly, when Aristotle praises political life in *The Politics* he refers to an activity unavailable to almost all modern citizens. Aristotle's political engagement relies, for its goodness, upon an intimate community of free, leisured men whose leisure relies, in turn, on slave labor. E. E. Schattschneider might have stated the point too severely, but his overall meaning still resonates: "what the Greek philosophers had to say about Athens, a city-state having a population of thirty thousand, three-fourths of whom were slaves, has very little to do with democracy in a nation of 180 million."[19] In sum, Aristotle's conception of civic friendship differs tremendously from the engagement of close friendship that many of us might cherish as a component of the good life, and at any rate his political milieu cannot and should not be reconstituted today.

Nor should Machiavelli's or Rousseau's. None of the canonical theorists commonly cited to bolster the intrinsic defense provides an at-

[16] Aristotle, *Eudemian Ethics* (1935: 1242a5). Aristotle lists two kinds of friendships based on utility, "the merely legal [*nomikai*] and the moral [*ethikai*]." Civic friendship falls under the former (legal) type; with regard to adjudication in disputes, "civic friendship, then, looks at the agreement and to the thing, but moral friendship at the intention; hence the latter is more just—it is friendly justice." Aristotle commends moral friendship for its intrinsic value and civic friendship for its instrumental value: "the moral friendship is nobler but friendship of utility more necessary" (1243a30).

[17] Aristotle (1935: 1243a30). Some scholars advocate political friendship while recognizing Aristotle's distinctions and realizing that contemporary political friendship could not possibly resemble the engagement of intimates. Cf. Allen (2004). But civility and a willingness to talk to strangers, the main attributes of Allen's political friendship, are so far below the standard that we usually associate with friendship that we might consider using a different word.

[18] D. Brendan Nagle estimates that "Aristotle's ideal state would have had a territory of about 60 km^2 with a population of 500 to 1000 households, that is, about 2% to 3% the size of Athens." Nagle (2006: 312).

[19] Schattschneider (1960: 142n2). Of course, we can doubt the relevance of the "good life" in ancient Athens without going as far as Schattschneider.

tractive or feasible model for contemporary politics. In Aristotle's view, citizens belong not to themselves but to the polis, which can mold and shape them according to its needs.[20] Machiavelli prescribes despotic rule and bloody purges to pave the way for republicanism in any cities that lack the requisite virtue (meaning most of them).[21] Rousseau defends egalitarian political engagement as an intrinsic good, coterminous with freedom and the opposite of modernity's corruption, self-delusion, and unhappiness. But only engagement in a very special kind of political community fits the bill: small, rural, homogeneous, economically egalitarian and uncomplicated, centrally planned, all citizens under the sway of a single culture protected by severe censorship, and all citizens subscribing to a single civic religion or facing threat of death.[22] In the end Rousseau raises doubts about his reforms' sincerity or practicality by proclaiming himself unfit for that politically engaged freedom.[23] Judith Shklar aptly warns against plans to foster intrinsic goods that the planners cannot endure; Rousseau's end-run from utopia well illustrates her meaning.[24]

Thus while contemporary advocates of political engagement's intrinsic value often ground their arguments by citing canonical theorists' authority, that ground proves unstable, riddled with elements of coercion or exclusion. Just as importantly the few canonical theorists who ascribe intrinsic value to political engagement generally establish their point by fiat rather than reasoned demonstration.[25] Carole Pateman stands out as one of the few participatory enthusiasts who reasonably attempt to use empirical evidence as a means of testing claims that we could and should make many areas of modern life tremendously more participatory. But the few experiments of workplace democracy that she considers provide

---

[20] Aristotle (1984: 1337a25).

[21] The coercive impulse endured among early American republicans as well. See, for example, Cotton Mather (1702): "But there is a civil, a moral, a federal *liberty*, which is the proper end and object of *authority*; it is a *liberty* for that only which is *just* and *good* . . . this *liberty* is maintained in a way of *subjection* to *authority*; and the authority set over you will in all administrations for your good be quietly submitted unto." Mather, *Magnalia Christi Americana* (1820 edition), quoted in Tocqueville (1969: 46).

[22] Rousseau (1968: book I, chap. vii), (1960: chap. xi). Rousseau is willing to permit freedom of religious conscience, but all must subscribe to a simple, civic religion; and "if any one, after publicly recognizing these dogmas, behaves as if he does not believe them, let him be punished by death" (1968: book VI, chap. xiii).

[23] "Virtue consists in overcoming [our inclinations] when duty commands, in order to do what duty prescribes, and that is what I have been less able to do than any man in the world." Rousseau (1992: 77).

[24] "The accusation of 'instrumentality' . . . amounts to a disdain for those who do not want to pay the price of utopian ventures, least of all those invented by other people." Shklar and Hoffmann (1998: 15).

[25] I note Aristotle's assertion of humankind's political nature in chapter 3.

scant support for the former claim and none at all for the latter.[26] She finds little empirical evidence that many workers experience increased participation as an intrinsically valuable activity, that it contributes to their meaningful self-development, or that it constitutes the good life for many of them.[27]

Nonetheless, she insists that a participatory society would be "self-sustaining through the educative impact of the participatory process. Participation develops and fosters the very qualities necessary for it; the more individuals participate the better able they become to do so," and the more they desire it.[28] If we set the participatory society in motion its repeated, positive feedback loop generates a virtuous circle. But empirical evidence does not bear her out. Workers sometimes choose less participation rather than more because "they fear that if and when they participate, their own behavior will be controlled by their coparticipants."[29] And as William Schonfield observes, were Pateman correct about participation breeding a capacity and desire for ever more participation, then states with mandatory voting requirements—upon rescinding the requirement—should continue to increase or at least maintain their high voting rates. The opposite has occurred.[30]

In spite of workers' and citizens' apparent distaste for greatly increased levels of participation (in the workplace or the formal political process), Pateman still seems ready to sanction an intensively participatory democratic society, although its achievement would require widespread coercion and ongoing governmental intervention.[31] She dismisses the workers' apparent lack of demand for participation, because "the atmosphere of

[26] Toward the end of *Participation and Democratic Theory*, Pateman claims only to have shown that we cannot completely dismiss the possibility of workplace democracy. Pateman (1970: 102). That retreat makes it all the more difficult to understand why she would earlier insist that society be democratized at all levels, including intimate areas such as family life. Ibid., 43.

[27] Pateman does argue that for many workers "even the mere feeling that participation is possible, even situations of pseudo-participation [in which workers' opinions are solicited but have no real effect on the firm's ultimate choices], have beneficial effects on confidence, job satisfaction, etc. It would be reasonable to suppose that actual participation would be more effective." But that last logical leap does not hold. Pateman's evidence suggests only that many workers feel better if allowed to exert minor influence over their environment.

[28] Pateman (1970: 25). Pateman attributes these claims to Rousseau but also endorses them in her aggregate "theory of participatory democracy."

[29] Michael Crozier, *The Bureaucratic Phenomenon* (1964: 204), cited in Schonfeld (1975: 152–53).

[30] Schonfeld (1975: 152n52).

[31] Philippe Schmitter classifies Pateman as a "preliberal" democratic theorist whose ideals do not match contemporary conditions. "Most important, preliberalism makes demands of individual citizens—especially upon their time and attention—that are unrealistic given the pace of contemporary life and the availability of so many more appealing ways of spending one's (always scarce) leisure." Schmitter (1995: 19).

hierarchical systems in general" allows workers only a "limited perspective."[32] Thus Pateman comes perilously close to claiming "false consciousness": most citizens cannot discern their own good, but under the right circumstances they will flourish, which justifies highly coercive political and economic upheaval.

Some contemporary participatory democrats disavow such coercive or exclusionary arguments in favor of a more pluralistic, broadly welcoming, and instrumentally oriented republicanism. Michael Sandel extols Tocqueville as the exemplar of reasonable republicanism—"unlike Rousseau's unitary vision, the republican politics Tocqueville describes is more clamorous than consensual"[33]—which accords with my reading, although Tocqueville is at least as much a liberal as a republican, and recommends political engagement primarily for its instrumental rather than intrinsic value.[34] Tocqueville also values individual autonomy, dreads excessive governmental involvement in citizens' lives, and, while he stresses the close relationship between individual and communal self-interest, stops far short of advocating a forced reconciliation or even forced public deliberation.[35] Thus a republicanism rooted in Tocqueville would not defend political engagement intrinsically and would resemble liberalism in most respects. To be sure, Tocqueville might join contemporary republicans in decrying atomistic or excessively individualistic strains of liberalism. But public-spirited liberals (including myself) can praise and support voluntary social and political engagement, and support governmental policies that facilitate political engagement, while leaving the ultimate choice up to citizens. In fact, choice—the opportunity to participate politically—may be more important for citizens' happiness and satisfaction than the act of participation.[36] On the flip side, a recent, cross-national study of political participation in Latin American countries finds a "robust negative relationship between enforced compulsory voting and average national life satisfaction."[37]

It was never my purpose to refute the intrinsic defense of political engagement completely, as if any subjective claim could be authoritatively proved or disproved. Political engagement could still have intrinsic worth for some, as might philosophy or artistic expression. But that acknowledgment may speak more about the value of engagement than of politics.

[32] Pateman (1970: 85; see also 106–7).

[33] Sandel (1996: 347).

[34] As I note in chapter 4, Tocqueville himself seems to value political engagement intrinsically but recognizes that most people will not, and he grounds his advocacy in instrumental reasons.

[35] On Tocqueville as the best hope for modern republicans, see Sandel (1996: 301–36). On Tocqueville's peculiar brand of liberalism, see Kahan (1992); Ossewaarde (2004).

[36] Frey and Stutzer (2000 and 2005) make this argument based on empirical studies of Swiss citizens.

[37] Weitz-Shapiro and Winters (2008: 16).

Virtually every philosophical, literary, and religious account of human flourishing, or the good life, has prioritized intensive engagement of some sort, whether intellectual, moral, social, religious, or aesthetic. Martha Nussbaum, examining a range of those accounts, finds the social-moral engagement of friendship—but not political engagement—so commonly esteemed by different traditions and cultures as to merit inclusion in a "thick, vague theory of the good."[38] Empirical psychological research agrees: people achieve meaning and fulfillment in a range of different ways, but engagement—"the merging of action and awareness"—unites their experiences across geographical and cultural boundaries.[39] Survey respondents claim to have experienced a wide range of engagements as "autotelic" or "intrinsically rewarding," although not because of any political component.[40]

In sum, the intrinsic defense of political engagement's value relies upon assertion rather than demonstration, and because it does not comport with most people's lived experience, cannot firmly establish political engagement as intrinsic to human flourishing. To persist in advocating compulsory political engagement because of its intrinsic worth would be undemocratic and illiberal: undemocratic, because it would disregard people's considered convictions in favor of an unproven assertion; illiberal, because it would grant government jurisdiction over individuals' personal fulfillment. Liberals ranging from Kant, Tocqueville, and Mill to Rawls, Shklar, and Nussbaum make the good life a matter of personal choice because reflection and the historical record cast doubt on any particular good's universality, and also because forced engagement undermines self-development and flourishing before they begin.[41] But the liberal objection is not to coercion per se; liberals countenance legal coercion when the public interest demands it, as in the case of potentially destructive collective action problems (such as the need to limit pollution). If voluntary political disengagement could be shown to harm the public interest severely, then liberals might join some republicans or participatory democrats in advocating compulsory political engagement.

[38] Nussbaum's "thick, vague theory of the good" attempts to catalog a range of human capacities and needs, recognized in many cultures and traditions as vital for a good life. Her core list includes "being able to live for and with others, to recognize and show concern for other human beings, to engage in various forms of familial and social interaction." Nussbaum (1992: 222).

[39] Csikszentmihalyi (1991: 53). Csikszentmihalyi's empirical research into the "good life" focuses on "optimal experience," a combination of energy and focused consciousness or "the merging of action and awareness," and while respondents from different cultures report different kinds of activities as particularly meaningful, the ways in which they undertake them—with focused attention and intense energy—"seem to be the same the world over." Ibid., 3, 48–49.

[40] Ibid., 67.

[41] Kant, *Theory and Practice*, in Kant (1991); Mill (1978); Shklar, "The Liberalism of Fear" in Shklar and Hoffmann (1998); Nussbaum (1992); Rawls (1971).

(Or they might not; Tocqueville's sympathizers will recall his concern that coerced attention and energy are rarely efficacious in the long run.) But once we frame the question thusly the promotion of political engagement depends upon instrumental considerations and lets us close the door on the intrinsic defense.

Scholars who promote political engagement for its instrumental value generally take one of two approaches, arguing that democracies must pursue very high levels of political engagement or that they must avoid very low levels. I will call these the visionary and the cautionary defenses of political engagement's instrumental worth, consistent with my categorization of Hannah Arendt's political theories. In scholarly literature the visionary instrumental defense appears more frequently. Many scholars associate high political engagement with a range of desirable results: rapid economic growth and bureaucratic efficiency,[42] high political legitimacy,[43] strongly performing schools, and psychological and physiological well-being,[44] for example. But as Putnam acknowledges, the relationship is one of correlation rather than causation.[45] Political engagement is certainly not *un*desirable per se, but its value depends upon the larger social, political, and institutional context. In certain circumstances very high levels of political engagement, understood as attention to and activity in political affairs and processes, can accompany economic stagnation, questionable legitimacy, and widespread malaise.[46] Unfortunately, many scholars do not understand political engagement so plainly but rather lump it into the umbrella category of civic engagement—as I have demonstrated—that commonly encompasses not only political but also social and moral engagement. Just as intrinsic defenders often do, many scholars lauding civic engagement on instrumental grounds throw laurels to political attention and activity that belong on different shoulders.

In other words, when Putnam and other scholars associate high civic engagement with a range of desirable outcomes—often implying that the former somehow promotes the latter—they run the risk of giving the same credit to political attention and activity as to social and moral engagement.[47] Virtually all of the available research suggests a close connection between social capital—which encompasses what I call social and also moral engagement—and economic and governmental efficiency,

[42] Putnam, Leonardi, and Nanetti (1993: 152–62, 176).

[43] Verba, Schlozman, and Brady (1995); Leighninger (2002).

[44] Przeworski et al. (2000).

[45] Putnam (1995).

[46] Kohli (1990).

[47] As noted earlier, Putnam does not construct the category of civic engagement unthinkingly or at random; he selects those indicators, some social and some political, that correlate with the performance of public institutions. Cf. Putnam (2000). But the breadth of his terminology unintentionally facilitated conceptual stretching that left scholars talking past one another.

high-performing schools, life satisfaction, and even life expectancy.[48] But political engagement as I define it—attention to and activity in political processes and affairs—bears no necessary connection to any of those phenomena. Italy, Indonesia, and South Africa all evince much higher levels of political interest and higher voting rates than the United States, but much lower levels of social capital and social engagement, and they rank lower in measures of economic and governmental efficiency, life satisfaction, public health, and other features allegedly correlated with so-called civic engagement.[49] Political attention and activity are often correlated with social capital, but when they diverge—when societies feature either high social capital or high levels of political attention and activity, but not both—those democracies with high levels of social engagement and bridging social capital almost always fare better in the relevant measures of efficiency, satisfaction, public health, and perceived legitimacy. Indeed, high levels of political engagement may impair economic efficiency when the politically engaged populace foments for greater economic equality through redistributive or protectionist policies.[50] That trade-off may be normatively justified, but it is a trade-off nonetheless and it contradicts some scholars' expectations of political engagement's uniformly positive impact on economic measures. Tocqueville reminds us that very high levels of political engagement can cause governmental inefficiencies as well, inefficiencies that centralized administrations might bypass. For similar reasons Madison expects "the confusion and intemperance of a multitude" should too many hands try to shape legislation.[51] Of course, Tocqueville prefers "the political advantages derived by the [inefficient] Americans" over the greater security and efficiency that might result "if the administration of the whole country were concentrated in one pair of hands."[52] But because governmental efficiency need not result from in-

---

[48] In Italy "norms and networks of civic engagement have fostered economic growth" and are "powerfully associated with effective public institutions." With regard to life satisfaction, "happiness is living in a civic community." Putnam, Leonardi, and Nanetti (1993: 173, 113). Putnam's Web site for the "Saguaro Seminar" at Harvard University, subtitled "Civic Engagement in America," links civic engagement with various "quality of life" benefits, including longer life spans. See http://www.ksg.harvard.edu/saguaro.

[49] International Institute for Democracy and Electoral Assistance, http://www.idea.int/vt/survey/voter_turnout_pop2.cfm. Also Norris (2005).

[50] Dennis C. Mueller and Thomas Stratmann, "The Economic Effects of Democratic Participation," January 2002. CESifo Working Paper Series No. 656. Available at SSRN, http://ssrn.com/abstract=301260.

[51] Hamilton, Madison, and Jay (1999: 342, Paper 55). To be fair, Madison is considering representatives' participation at the congressional level, and Tocqueville is considering citizens' participation at the township level, so Madison rejects and Tocqueville countenances the expected inefficiency. But both anticipate political disturbance and untidiness when participants proliferate.

[52] Tocqueville, *DA*: 93. Of course, Tocqueville prefers "the political advantages derived by the Americans" over the greater security and efficiency that might result "if the administration of

creased political engagement, the promise of the former cannot establish the latter's value.

Political engagement, no matter how widespread or earnest, can do little without responsive institutions that channel, process, and respond to it. Quite the contrary: without responsive institutions that can accommodate citizens' opinions, values, and demands, high political engagement and mobilization may promote destabilizing violence (as witnessed in the cases of post-Weimar Germany, Chile and Brazil in the 1970s, and the contemporary Palestinian Authority).[53] Alternately, without responsive institutions elites may be able to capture government and twist legislative agendas to favor their own narrow interests in spite of the politically engaged majority's expressed preferences.[54] Tocqueville in the nineteenth century, Arendt and Kornhauser in the mid-twentieth century, and contemporary scholars such as Samuel Huntington, Sheri Berman, Simone Chambers, and Jeffrey Kopstein all appreciate the need to ground discussions of political engagement against a backdrop of responsive political institutions.[55]

The visionary arguments I have canvassed thus far, favoring political engagement because of its alleged effects on citizens' material well-being, mental and physical health, or economic efficiency and growth, are primarily instrumental and only incidentally normative. But two of the oldest and most familiar visionary arguments for high political engagement focus on normative concerns. According to the first normative argument, higher levels of political engagement indicate greater democratic legitimacy, which itself is portrayed as an unlimited good; more is always preferable to less.[56] According to the second argument, attentive activity in one's political community comprises a fundamental citizen duty, regardless of whether one supports or protests against prevailing policies, representatives, and institutions. Criteria such as democratic legitimacy and citizen duty find supporters all along the political spectrum, unlike criteria such as economic efficiency or equality that are more commonly favored

---

the whole country were concentrated in one pair of hands." My point is only that increased governmental efficiency is not a reliable standard by which to gauge political engagement's value.

[53] Huntington (1981); Bermeo (2003).

[54] Li, Squire, and Zou (1998).

[55] Tocqueville, *DA*; Huntington (1981); Berman (1997); Chambers and Kopstein (2001). To reprise my argument from chapter 3: Berman agrees with Arendt that ineffectual institutions led to Germans' widespread political disengagement after Weimar, although Berman points out that while German citizens were disengaged politically they were highly engaged socially. Berman argues that the presence of widespread social engagement and social capital, combined with political frustration due to ineffectual political institutions, became a political powder keg that the Nazi Party exploited.

[56] Marshall Ganz goes so far as to claim that "any less than full and equal electoral participation puts democracy at risk." Ganz (1994: 100).

by those on the political left. Unfortunately, the available empirical evidence is decidedly mixed.[57] Very high political engagement can indicate high legitimacy but also the opposite—widespread dissatisfaction and perceived illegitimacy—as in the case of 1970s Chile and Brazil. In such cases citizens may be so dissatisfied with the existing state that they take up arms in public demonstration.[58] Conversely, low political engagement may sometimes indicate satisfaction with the status quo, the kind of political quiescence that many Americans now claim to desire and that seems to have characterized the prosperous Roaring Twenties.[59] One study of the European Union agrees that because types of, and motivations for, political engagement vary so widely, "it is not the case that more democracy would necessarily lead to more legitimacy; neither is it the case that more participation would necessarily mean more legitimacy."[60]

Perhaps more importantly, governments that promote increased political engagement for the sake of increasing political legitimacy put the cart before the horse. Increased political engagement hardly demonstrates legitimacy when achieved through coercion (as with the Athenian soldiers' red ropes) or bribery (as with Athenian citizens' paid political attendance), nor in the modern examples of compulsory deliberative juries, compulsory voting, or paid participation in a nationwide Deliberation Day.[61] Increased political engagement demonstrates legitimacy when it represents citizens' free expression of satisfaction, recognition, and efficacy. Yet if citizens feel satisfied, recognized, and efficacious then their government can probably claim high legitimacy even if the satisfied citizens choose not to engage politically. Where political legitimacy is concerned high political engagement matters only if freely chosen, and even

---

[57] Finkel (1985) links U.S. voting and campaign participation with heightened commitment to the elected representatives; Finkel (1987) links German citizens' voting between 1974 and 1976 with increased regime legitimacy. However, he also finds that other forms of political engagement—peaceful protest and aggressive protest, in particular—either have no effects or negative effects on regime support. Such studies encounter methodological problems such as selection bias—the voters, volunteers and activists may have been predisposed to trust or mistrust the candidates or the regime—and they are also few and far between.

[58] Bermeo (2003).

[59] Hibbing and Theiss-Morse (2002); Schudson (1998).

[60] Blondel, Sinnott, and Svensson (1998: 238).

[61] Bruce Ackerman and James Fishkin (2004: 146) take enhanced legitimacy so seriously that they propose a new, two-day holiday (Deliberation Day, replacing President's Day) during which millions of citizens might deliberate about political issues, policies, and candidate platforms. Acknowledging low citizen demand, they propose $150 daily stipends for each participating citizen. Should Americans still reject the deliberative political engagement, Ackerman and Fishkin foresee a grim future: Americans would be abandoning "their democratic faith," in which case "much more than Deliberation Day is at stake." Leaving aside the merits of their proposal, their dire premonition lacks empirical grounding. Citizens rejecting intensive political engagement, even for pay, need not spell the end of democracy.

then political engagement may matter less than citizens' feelings of satisfaction, efficacy, and inclusion.

Again, none of these points makes high political engagement undesirable; they simply show that its value depends upon the larger social, political, and economic context. If many democratic citizens suffer oppression, exclusion, or deprivation and do not engage politically, a state's political legitimacy might be called into question. But under those same conditions of inequality, even greatly increased political engagement will not always bring increased legitimacy unless political institutions are sufficiently responsive and effectual to give citizens hope of achieving desired change.

According to the second normative argument, political engagement comprises a duty of citizenship, the necessary counterpart to citizens' rights and a constitutive element of the community's moral fiber. This argument holds widespread influence, although primarily as a justifying rather than a motivating reason for political engagement. As discussed earlier, far more people acknowledge citizen duty as an abstract principle than act on its dictates.[62] A further problem also looms. In many liberal democracies poor, less well educated, and marginalized citizens are the ones most likely to be politically disengaged.[63] Inveighing with those less fortunate citizens to stop shirking their citizen duty would be something akin to blaming the victims. And were we to give this normative argument teeth and make voting (or other forms of political engagement) compulsory, with the threat of punishment for noncompliance, then poor and marginalized citizens would be the ones most likely to suffer.[64] Adding the injury of political punishment to the insult of poverty and invisibility would seem a harsh and unfeeling means of promoting citizen virtue.

Thus two of the most plausible normative arguments for very high political engagement—that it promotes democratic legitimacy and is required by citizens' duty—place a disproportionate onus on poor and marginalized citizens to change their behavior and priorities. But the arguments fail to show why those populations should be motivated by claims of legitimacy or duty in the first place, especially since those citizens' own shabby status might call both claims into question. And they fail to show that very high political engagement always equates with political legitimacy, especially if the engagement is forced. So none of these arguments by themselves can easily justify the use of scarce resources or legal coercion to promote high and widespread political engagement.

---

[62] See footnotes 3 and 4 in this chapter.
[63] Putnam (2000); Verba, Schlozman, and Brady (1995).
[64] Lijphart (1997).

Cautionary defenses of widespread political engagement avoid some of the problems that most visionary arguments encounter. Rather than aiming to achieve the desirable outcomes allegedly associated with high levels of political engagement, cautionary defenses aim to avoid the undesirable outcomes allegedly associated with very low levels. Very low political engagement allegedly threatens democracy with a variety of undesirable outcomes ranging from the apocalyptic (despotism or totalitarianism) to the simply bad (economic and bureaucratic inefficiency, pervasive discontent, or questionable legitimacy, for example). The cautionary defense's apocalyptic versions hold that without widespread, intensive political engagement "the potential for demagoguery and totalitarianism becomes that much greater."[65] Benjamin Barber advocates "strong democracy" and widespread political engagement only after connecting political disengagement with a range of public ills culminating in a "totalitarian temptation."[66] But Barber and other apocalyptic theorists improperly connect two unrelated assertions: first, that radical political disengagement threatens democracy with despotism or totalitarianism; second, that widespread political engagement is the necessary tonic.[67]

The first assertion boasts a respectable pedigree. Plato's Socrates warns that democratic citizens turning their attention to private pleasures may fall prey to crafty demagogues who then change into tyrants.[68] Tocqueville echoes that concern, worrying that disengaged citizens court disaster if they delegate all power to a central administration that could become incompetent or malicious. And in the twentieth century, Arendt links citizens' disengagement and political atomization with the rise of Nazism and the extinction of freedom. The only problem with the philosophers' stories is that they have never actually played out in the real world.[69] Political disengagement did not undo Plato's Athens or Arendt's Germany—just the opposite, in the latter case.[70] That observation does not invalidate the theorists' essential point if, as I suspect, they intend

---

[65] Curtis Gans, of the Committee for the Study of the American Electorate, quoted in Cooper (2000: 833). See also Callan (1997), which begins with a thought experiment linking widespread citizen disengagement with pretotalitarian conditions.

[66] Barber (1984: 109–11) warns against "liberalism and the totalitarian temptation," as if contemporary liberal culture and values always court the radical individualism and mean-spirited commercialism that could result in the rise of an ideological dictator. Daniel A. Bell (1993: 174) has such arguments in mind when characterizing communitarians (and others concerned with political disengagement) as fearing "the atomized mass society of mutually antagonistic individuals, easy prey to despotism."

[67] See Meyers (2008).

[68] Plato (1991: 562b–566d).

[69] At the very least, empirical evidence is extremely hard to come by.

[70] Historians have effectively destroyed Arendt's depiction of 1930s Germany as a radically disengaged, atomized, apolitical wilderness. Berman (1997).

their dire scenarios as stylized portraits of the perfectly disengaged polity. Plato and Arendt may be inviting us to measure actual states' political health against their ideal types, with the expectation that any state approaching the stylized extreme runs a grave risk of despotism. But since no contemporary liberal democracy comes anywhere near that stylized state, the warning is instructive but largely academic. Further, we cannot infer (as Barber and others seem to do) that if radical political disengagement threatens grave harm, very high political engagement prevents or reverses it. In the twentieth century, Germany, Brazil, and Chile—which lacked strong and responsive political institutions—succumbed to despotic overthrow in spite of high and widespread political engagement.[71] And while some scholars invoke the totalitarian specter in the context of Americans' declining political engagement, the United States—which features relatively strong and responsive institutions—is much more stable politically than many of its more politically engaged democratic brethren.[72] Yet the United States has never experienced the kind of radically low political engagement that Arendt depicts in Weimar Germany (and for that matter, neither has Germany).

Arendt provides an additional, valuable distinction between voluntary and involuntary political disengagement. Although Arendt praises the political life she well understands the temptations to flee publicity into the warmth of the private realm, and she recognizes the human goods that can flourish there.[73] But, as I discuss in chapter 3, forced disengagement imposes invisibility upon the marginalized, a painful condition of seeing the world around them while remaining unseen by it. Arendt agrees with John Adams's assessment that "to be wholly overlooked, and to know it, are intolerable," and goes further by claiming that that "darkness rather than want is the curse of poverty."[74] While it is difficult to establish political engagement's intrinsic goodness, Arendt more persuasively depicts forced disengagement—whether social or political—as intrinsically bad.

[71] In the years preceding Pinochet's dictatorial coup, Chilean political mobilization and civic associationism increased dramatically, and the size of the electorate expanded greatly. Bermeo (2003: 138–76). Cf. Berman (1997). And in Italy between 1919 and 1921, "fascism's greatest support came from Italy's most civic regions: the most densely organized, politically engaged and politicized." Wellhofer (2005: 37).

[72] Although voting is only one among many measures of civic engagement, comparative voting rates provide at least some illumination. Italy, Cambodia, Indonesia, Uzbekistan, and Iran are just a few of the states with much higher voting rates than the United States (since 1945); 113 states rank higher overall. Yet because of the United States' institutional and constitutional structure, its political culture, and perhaps its relatively high level of social engagement, the United States seems much less susceptible to despotic overthrow than most of the more electorally engaged countries.

[73] Arendt, MDT: 13.

[74] Arendt, OR: 69. For a contemporary reflection on "unjust and systemic exclusion," see Dovi (2002: 732).

One would be hard-pressed to find any persuasive grounds on which to defend forced political or social disengagement.

Thus in summary, high political engagement does not necessarily preclude overthrow by a despot, especially in the absence of strong and responsive political institutions; moderately low political engagement does not necessarily invite despotic overthrow; and, while radically low political engagement could plausibly allow a destructive faction to seize power, we cannot know for certain if that would happen because we have no relevant examples from which to judge. As a result, the cautionary defense's apocalyptic version can muster only two bits of circumstantial evidence for political engagement's value: the plausible (but inconclusive) claim that radically low political engagement should be avoided at all costs because it might give rise to despotism, and the more compelling claim that we should go to great lengths to ensure that no citizens are forcibly disengaged, whether through legal discrimination or more insidious forms of marginalization.[75]

The cautionary defense's nonapocalyptic version begins by observing that political disengagement threatens democracies with undesirable consequences less serious than despotism—economic and bureaucratic inefficiency, moral disengagement,[76] diminished political legitimacy,[77] and pervasive discontent,[78] for example. These claims fare well at first glance; as Putnam illustrates, a range of democracies marked by declining or very low political engagement have struggled with such ills.[79] But from their experiences we can only conclude that low political engagement correlates with the problems rather than causing them. The causal arrow could even point in the other direction; problems such as bureaucratic inefficiency or perceived illegitimacy might prompt disgusted citizens to disengage from politics. Alternately, entirely different phenomena might cause

[75] See Manza and Uggen (2004 and 2006) for insights into the ongoing disenfranchisement of former felons even after their sentences have been served. The disenfranchisement is all the more disturbing for its strong correlation with race. Behrens, Uggen, and Manza (2003).

[76] "Without norms of reciprocity and networks of civic engagement, the Hobbesian outcome of the Mezzogiorno—amoral familism, clientelism, lawlessness, ineffective government, and economic stagnation—seems likelier than successful democratization and economic development." Putnam, Leonardi, and Nanetti (1993: 183). Thus Putnam associates very low levels of social and political engagement with moral disengagement, as well as with economic and governmental inefficiency.

[77] "Insofar as important classes or groups of citizens are considerably less active and influential than others—and especially when this is itself a consequence of the design of the political system—then the reality of collective self rule is doubtful, and the political order's legitimacy is compromised." Macedo et al. (2005). Regarding similar concerns for the European Union's legitimacy, see Hayward (1996); Andersen and Eliassen (1996); Pharr and Putnam (2000).

[78] Barber (1984); Sandel (1996).

[79] Putnam, Leonardi, and Nanetti (1993); Putnam (1995 and 2000).

the undesirable conditions correlated with political disengagement. For example, the pervasive discontent expressed by disaffected citizens might owe more to the scope and complexity of modern societies—enough to make any individual feel inconsequential and ineffectual—than to a frustrated desire for intense political engagement. Nonetheless, very low political engagement could not conceivably bolster political legitimacy or citizens' perceived efficacy or contentment, so avoiding it seems a reasonable strategy.

Tocqueville develops one further line of reasoning. Reflecting on the French Revolution he worries that sustained, widespread, political disengagement may undermine citizens' perspective on the connection between individual and public interests and corrode their political judgment as well. As I note in chapter 4, Tocqueville abhors those French intellectuals whose disengagement from public life and "contempt for existing facts" culminated in a dangerously unrealistic approach to practical politics.[80] He pities the mass of citizens who, completely removed from political processes and institutions, followed the intellectuals' advice without reserve. According to Tocqueville's logic, which Arendt applies to pretotalitarian Germany, extreme political disengagement can encourage politically irresponsible action should the disengaged citizens suddenly mobilize. We lack the evidence to establish the Tocqueville/Arendt point conclusively, but the logic seems plausible, further recommending the avoidance of radical political disengagement.

The cautionary defense's most persuasive point may be that very low levels of political engagement tend disproportionately to harm the least privileged citizens. Poor, marginalized, and less well educated citizens are far less likely to be politically engaged than those higher up the socioeconomic and educational ladders, yet those citizens are precisely the ones most urgently in need of political voice and collective action.[81] Citizens' needs, demands, interests, and values gain public recognition and expression primarily through the legislative process, but legislators and advocates tend either to ignore the voices of nonparticipators or to misrepresent—even if unintentionally—the interests and values that disadvantaged citizens express when asked directly.[82] Further, at least in the United States political contributions have become such a common means of advancing an individual's or group's interests and values that those who lack such resources lose a vital means of making themselves heard.[83] Working to avoid political disengagement specifically among the poor

---

[80] Tocqueville, *ORR*, book 3, chap. 1, 195–202.
[81] Lijphart (1997: 1).
[82] Verba, Schlozman, and Brady (1995).
[83] Macedo et al. (2005)

and marginalized—and to decrease the role that monetary contributions play in political processes and decisions—might enhance a polity's claims to be representative, fair, and democratically legitimate.

Earlier I wrote that the most common arguments for political engagement's worth amount to circumstantial evidence. Each one marshals claims that might apply in some circumstances but not in all. None, by itself, could convince most citizens that even if political engagement seems undesirable to many and would be costly to promote, we should turn our attention and resources to promoting it. But the case for political engagement begins rather than ends with that broad assemblage of circumstantial evidence. Many people hear *circumstantial evidence* with suspicion, often adding the modifier *just*—as in, "there was no decisive proof, *just* circumstantial evidence."[84] Novels and movies may portray it as the obstacle to clearing a wrongly accused defendant.[85] But in fact circumstantial evidence "can be, and often is much more powerful than direct evidence," and most civil and criminal cases are decided on its basis.[86] One or two pieces of circumstantial evidence might be dismissed as coincidence, but in sufficient quantity it can carry great weight. Political engagement's best defense relies on that formula. The most influential arguments for its value lack conclusiveness individually, but assembled coherently they gain force.

The case proceeds thusly: political engagement deserves our esteem and care rather than our indifference. Very low political engagement is the worst; it cannot help, and might badly undermine, a democracy's claims to political legitimacy. In the absence of strong and responsive political institutions, very low political engagement could conceivably threaten instability or even despotic overthrow. Very low political engagement harms the least privileged citizens most. And forced political disengagement, whether legal disenfranchisement or informal exclusion (resulting from systematic lack of access to basic educational, economic, and political resources), threatens individuals with painful invisibility and the polity with a mark of shame.[87] For all of these reasons, democracies should avoid radically low political engagement and especially forced disengagement. But the evidence also carries us beyond that bare mini-

[84] Billy Dean's popular song, "Innocent Bystander," expresses a common attitude: "Now I have to say in my defense / I ain't done nothin' wrong / Just circumstantial evidence / Is all you got me on."

[85] For example, in the movie *Circumstantial Evidence* (1935), a newspaper reporter stages a murder for the sake of a story and becomes the prime suspect when his partner is found dead. See also Erle Stanley Gardner (1947), *The Case of the Perjured Parrot*.

[86] The New Jersey court system instructs potential jurors that "in many cases, circumstantial evidence may be more certain, satisfying and persuasive than direct evidence." See http://www.judiciary.state.nj.us/criminal/charges/non2c002.doc.

[87] Arendt, *MDT*; Dovi (2002).

mum. As I noted earlier, political engagement correlates with economic and governmental efficiency across countries, although the relationship does not hold in every country and correlation does not equal causation. Political engagement correlates with perceptions of political legitimacy as well, although, as discussed earlier, that relationship does not hold in every case. Further, insofar as higher political engagement is achieved by increasing the participation of the least well off as well as more privileged citizens, it seems likely to enhance the quality of representation and the polity's claims to fairness. Finally, political engagement may prove to be intrinsically rewarding to some people, and while that does not justify coerced engagement it should command our respect in the same way that we respect artistic expression and appreciation. Often, schools offer music and arts appreciation courses out of respect for the arts' intrinsic value, although few would claim they affect everyone equally. The point is to impart the ability to appreciate and participate in various arts; when children reach adulthood they can make their own, informed decision about further appreciation and participation. Political engagement deserves at least that much consideration.

These disparate arguments, taken together, support the case that we should care about avoiding very low political engagement and care about the increased, voluntary political engagement that might ensue were political institutions more responsive, political education more effective, and if our attention deficit democracy could be treated through liberal means (some of which I will discuss in chapter 6). But from the available evidence, we cannot conclude that democracies should promote very high and widespread political engagement unless citizens demonstrate that they want that intensity; the benefits elude precise demonstration while the costs are readily apparent. Promoting very high political engagement in the face of citizens' enduringly wandering attention would probably require either coercion or untenably high expense or both. Compulsory engagement with the threat of sanction would most likely penalize the least well off citizens. It would treat adult citizens with undue paternalism as well. Educating citizens about the benefits and pathways of political engagement, making political resources more available, and giving more power to local governments where citizens can reasonably feel more efficacious: these are more liberal means of promoting political engagement, although the long historical record of limited political attention gives us scant reason to expect liberal means to produce voluntary, high and widespread political engagement. That limitation need not worry us, as I argue throughout this chapter. Political engagement matters, and we can and should do more with our current resources, but high and widespread political engagement is neither forthcoming nor necessary. Just as important, to promote it through coercion and compulsion would be to introduce, in Madison's phrase, "a remedy . . . worse than the disease."[88]

Not only would it be unwise because illiberal, an invitation for further coercion by any plan to advance human flourishing that persuades a temporary majority, but it would also demonstrate misplaced priorities. Democracies can clearly survive and even flourish with a range of political engagement levels, as we can see from the widely divergent examples in the United States, Western Europe, and Asia. Political engagement should not be severely low but can be dispersed and intermittent, with some people paying attention all of the time—politicians, journalists, lobbyists, government watchdogs, and political junkies, for example, all of whom we might call attention monitors—alongside pockets of citizens that Philip Converse calls "issue publics," who may pay attention only to certain issues of special interest, accompanied by wide swaths of mostly inattentive citizens whose attention and energy can be mobilized when necessary.[89] But mobilization depends upon many nonpolitical factors, especially the citizens' levels of social and moral engagement. Membership in diverse social networks facilitates political mobilization efforts; mobilizers often concentrate their efforts on reaching citizens who are "centrally placed in social networks," and who in turn can reach out to fellow members.[90] Not only social engagement but certain kinds of moral engagement—trust, for example—also comprise a critical tool for mobilizing the previously disengaged. Unless disengaged citizens trust the political system enough to believe that their energies might bear fruit they are not likely to join in organized efforts.[91] And without sufficient trust in others—not necessarily all citizens, but those with whose values and experiences they can relate—they are not likely to take cues from the politically engaged attention monitors around them.

Widespread social and moral engagement are essential not only for their role in helping to mobilize citizens politically but also for their role in making any given society a desirable place to live. Putnam and many other social capital scholars have chronicled the meaningful, positive impact that widespread social engagement can have on citizens' quality of life. We still await the definitive project on moral engagement—attention to and activity in support of moral reasoning or principles—and the va-

[88] Hamilton, Madison, and Jay (1999, Paper 10).

[89] Converse (1964).

[90] Rosenstone and Hansen (1993: 210).

[91] A range of democratic theorists recommend that citizens trust one another but retain a healthy mistrust of government, often called "civic vigilance." See, for example, both the *Federalist Papers* and *Antifederalist Papers*, as well as Tocqueville's *Democracy in America*. But vigilant citizens, who would pay attention to the government so as to prevent corruption or usurpation, can still trust the system sufficiently that they believe in their own efficacy to prevent corruption or usurpation or to accomplish goals of importance.

rieties most important for making democracy work. Political theorists disagree about which moral standards, principles, or virtues require all citizens' attention and energy. But as Andrew Sabl notes, underneath that disagreement lies a broad consensus on several core virtues that liberal democracy cannot do without: toleration, nonviolence, and democratic sportsmanship.[92] In other words, a range of prominent theorists agree that liberal democratic citizens must attend to and act in accordance with norms of toleration, norms of nonviolence, and norms of political sportsmanship—norms that dictate how to be a good loser.[93] Different theorists might hope for still more—might hope that citizens will also to attend to and act in accordance with more rigorous moral standards and principles. But it would be difficult not to admire a democracy in which citizens met difference with toleration, met disagreements without violence, and met political losses with grace. If that democracy, where citizens could live without serious fear of strangers or rivals, were also to feature widespread, voluntary social engagement, with associations that admit of unrestrained entry and exit, it would contain the ingredients for a wide range of good lives. Earlier I wrote that only the most ardent participatory democrat would rank political engagement higher than sex. Only the same, rare bird would lament the democracy that I have just sketched simply because it happened to lack high and widespread political engagement.[94] Most people know a good thing when they see it.

[92] Sabl (2005b: 216–17). Some theorists contest whether toleration must actually be a "virtue" or simply a practice, but that distinction remains relatively unimportant here. Cf. Williams (1996).

[93] As Sabl puts it, "democratic citizens must be good losers, willing to accept with good grace and no loss of commitment to the polity that the democratic game will not always go their way." Sabl (2005b: 216).

[94] One could lament any number of societal problems and advocate increased political engagement if it were a proven means of addressing them, for example, advocate increased voting rates among the poor as a means of achieving greater representation for their interests, but in that case one would be lamenting the societal problem and not the absence of political engagement for its own sake.

Chapter 6

CONCLUSION

TOCQUEVILLE VS. THE FULL MONTY

> It is the political theorist's business to trace out that pattern . . . of thought
> and feeling which will enable the citizen to approach a new problem in
> some useful fashion. In that task he must not assume that the mass has
> political genius, but that men, even if they had genius, would give only a
> little time and attention to public affairs.
> —Walter Lippmann, *The Phantom Public*

THUS FAR I HAVE BLOWN the whistle on the hopelessly confusing uses of civic engagement that fail to distinguish between
political, social, and moral attention and energy. Civic engagement should cede the stage to its political, social, and moral cousins. I
have also chided idealistic conceptions of participatory democracy for
insisting that citizens invest much or most of their limited attention and
energy in politics. Idealistic conceptions of participatory democracy concern themselves not with how citizens act now, nor with the choices
that citizens express at present, but with how citizens might act and
choose under thoroughly altered conditions. They glimpse one kind of
good—political engagement—that seems inadequately supplied, and instead of attempting to fill the most distressing gaps, they aim for what I
call the Full Monty: high and widespread political engagement among
all citizens, all (or much) of the time, in spite of citizens' long-standing
inclinations toward the opposite.[1] The Full Monty approach can play
a valuable role in certain scholarly disquisitions but not in this book. I
have considered democracy as it appears today with hopes of making it
work better rather than ideally. I have taken seriously citizens' commitments, capabilities, and limitations as expressed by citizens themselves.
The goal has been to diagnose our political pitfalls and potential in a
manner that most citizens can recognize and endorse. But if the diagno-

---

[1] The "Full Monty," a British expression that gained currency in the 1990s, means "complete, the whole thing," or "everything included." It came to international attention with the
eponymous movie, released in 1997. In that context "the Full Monty" meant a burlesque
show with full frontal male nudity.

sis is attention deficit democracy, what is the prescription? I turn now to that difficult question.

When some readers see realistic models of politics championed over allegedly idealistic participatory models (or vice versa) they envision yet another round of the Dewey-Lippmann debate, which has recurred with astonishing regularity over the past eighty years. In this familiar repartee, one side insists that we become omnicompetent citizens and spend much of our time on self-governance; the other insists that because we cannot know much about the complex business of national politics we should leave those affairs to experts (or to the market). But even Lippmann and Dewey were working old ground, tilled by Hobbes and Rousseau centuries earlier. Hobbes, favoring stability and order above all, defended personal liberty and privacy but not political participation, as if the people's collective energies could only lead to disaster. Hobbes proposed to leave the people alone as long as they left the business of governing to the sovereign. Rousseau, favoring unity and transparency, promoted direct political participation achieved through governmental control of culture, the economy, and private life. Left to their own devices the people might pursue courses opposed to communal solidarity and equality; bound together in the social contract with a centrally controlled economy and strictly dictated cultural norms they could be "forced" to be free.

After Lippmann and Dewey reanimated the debate in the early twentieth century, the nonparticipatory side held sway for a generation. The specter of fascist and communist revolutions led scholars such as Joseph Schumpeter, William Kornhauser, and E. E. Schattschneider to caution readers against unrealistic expectations of high participation. In the 1960s and early 1970s, though, the resurgence of participatory democracy saw Arnold Kaufman resuscitate Dewey, coining the term *participatory democracy*, while Carole Pateman reasserted Rousseau's transformational aspiration.[2] Pateman took aim at the previous generation's theorists of elite democracy and championed, along with Kaufman, Dewey, and Rousseau, the intrinsic benefits of political engagement.[3] In *Participation and Democratic Theory* Pateman reasoned that if political engagement produces intrinsically valuable benefits, then all spheres of life must be politicized: "the democratic principle . . . must be applied not only or mainly to some special sphere of social action known as 'politics,' but to any and every form of social action."[4] Participation must be elicited not

[2] Kaufman (1968).

[3] Pateman focuses her attack on Schumpeter, Berelson, Dahl, Sartori, and Eckstein, with the last four being "descended directly from Schumpeter's attack on the 'classical' theory of democracy." Pateman (1970: 5).

[4] Ibid., 37. In the quoted passage Pateman is approvingly citing G.D.H. Cole (1920). With regard to Rousseau, Pateman simply shrugs off the criticism that his willingness to

only everywhere but from everyone, because "the experience of participation itself will develop and foster the 'democratic' personality . . . for all individuals."[5]

Neither Hobbes nor Rousseau, Lippmann nor Dewey, Schumpeter nor Pateman presents an attractive form of democracy for most contemporary citizens. I strive to break from their recurring cycle in which critics reacting to one another are, in Tocqueville's words, "generally reduced to choosing between two excesses."[6] Being realistic about democracy does not mean abandoning our hopes of achieving more participation, fairer representation, greater citizen vigilance, or improvements in the lot of the worst-off. Rather it means abandoning the idea that those goals should be achieved by the Rousseauian ambitions of changing human nature or coercing adult citizens for their own good. It also means realizing that many citizens hold reasonable, competing commitments—commitments to personal autonomy and the freedom to do without politics, for example—that might limit our ability to promote the first set of goals.[7] And it means identifying those resources (tastes, attention, and energy) whose presence, when directed toward politics, make political engagement possible yet whose limitations make fully participatory democracy unlikely. Some idealistic theories of democracy, the Full Monty versions, have asked too much of citizens' tastes, attention, and energy. They have asked more than citizens have been willing to give, either now or during any sustained period in the history of democracy.[8] But other theories, under the guise of realism, have asked for too little—for less political engagement than many citizens want and are capable of contributing.[9] Such theories have aspired for no Monty at all. I explore the territory between these two extremes, attempting to get more (and more meaningful) political engagement out of our tastes, attention, and energy without undue coercion and without obliterating privacy or citizens' freedom to do without politics.

It seems fitting that we turn to Tocqueville in closing, since his spirit has animated every page of this book.[10] Tocqueville himself would find

---

"force" citizens to be free could have "totalitarian" overtones or should worry democrats who are concerned with individual freedom. Ibid., 26n2.

[5] Ibid., 64.

[6] Tocqueville, *DA*: 43.

[7] Kaufman and Pateman joined Dewey in assuming that while citizens might at present evince little taste or drive for sustained political engagement, radical economic and institutional transformation would reshape their tastes and release untapped "human energy for pursuit of higher values." Kaufman (1968); Dewey (1935: 90).

[8] I refer to highly participatory models that have skimped on details of enactment, beginning with Dewey's and continuing through Pateman, Barber, and a host of "deliberative democrats."

[9] Here I have in mind the elite theories of democracy, including Lippmann's and Schumpeter's, as well as the recent, market-oriented update as espoused by Somin.

[10] Zunz and Kahan (2002: 219–20).

elements of contemporary American democracy repellant, but the ethic with which he embraced his task entails adaptation to changing contexts and acceptance of conditions that one finds personally distasteful. Tocqueville, for example, confessed a deep aversion to many elements of French democracy, some of which he found in parts of America as well—"the action of the masses, their violent and uneducated participation in affairs, the lower classes' envious passions, the irreligious tendencies"—but determined to make democracy work in spite of those factors.[11] His ethic of adaptation and innovation, finding functional equivalents for societal and political structures that might have changed or been lost over time, is an ethic appropriate to our changing times as well.

Tocqueville occupies the rich ground that lies between Hobbes and Rousseau, Lippmann and Dewey, and all of their intellectual heirs. I emphasize the role that tastes, attention, and energy (as well as self-efficacy) play in Tocqueville's democratic politics and civil society. Democracy requires an energetic government but also an energetic citizenry to counterbalance the former; representative democracy requires institutions that pool, channel, and limit citizens' energies effectively. But energy generally follows attention and attention often follows citizens' tastes, which seem unlikely to focus on any one subject enduringly. That is one reason why "habitual inattention must be reckoned the great vice of the democratic spirit."[12] Given the diagnosis of attention deficit democracy, a Tocquevillean response will focus on accomplishing more with our limited resources of energy, attention, and tastes than we have done in recent years, while trying to avoid paternalism and coercion.

In that spirit, I propose three approaches to improving democracy that accord with Tocqueville's premises and insights: (1) changing our approach to politics and political mobilization, (2) changing ourselves, and (3) changing our institutions. To elaborate: First, we citizens can attempt to attract more attention and energy toward political affairs, processes, and institutions by making politics seem more attractive—in other words, by appealing to citizens' existing tastes. Second, we can attempt to attract more of our attention and energy toward politics by making our tastes more political through education and habituation. Third, we citizens can economize on existing political attention and political energy, making them more efficacious by channeling them through more responsive institutions. (Making our institutions more responsive, and thus increasing citizens' expectations of efficacy, also fits within the institutional approach.) I also consider a fourth approach, derived not from Tocqueville but from my own reflections on contemporary political

[11] Tocqueville (2002: 219–20).
[12] *DA*: 611.

science scholarship. If we care about political equality and fair representation we can shift some of our resources from promoting political engagement among college students, who are already among the most likely to be politically engaged as adults, and instead target the attention and energy of specific demographic groups (including the poor and poorly educated) whose members are most prone to political disengagement and most likely to be misrepresented when inactive.

To be clear, I do not portray the following prescriptions as uncharted territory. Many of the initiatives have been considered by scholars and some have been implemented by practitioners. The originality stems from the union of such a diverse set of initiatives behind a single diagnosis—attention deficit democracy—drawn from Tocqueville's perspective and spirit. Further, because the combined initiatives entail achievable rather than revolutionary means, and stem from a diagnosis that a wide range of citizens already seem to endorse, the diagnosis plus ensuing prescriptions might reasonably be expected to win widespread backing and form the core of an emergent public philosophy.

Appeal to Existing Tastes

The first prescription for treating attention deficit democracy suggests that we elicit more attention and energy for politics by appealing to existing tastes or preferences. In other words, we might accept citizens' tastes as given and then subtly shape politics and political information to suit them, thus attracting citizens' attention and hopefully galvanizing their energy as well. For all of its faults, John F. Kennedy Jr.'s short-lived political magazine, *George*, modeled itself on those principles. Kennedy hoped to capture widespread attention with splashy covers featuring national celebrities dressed in George Washington costumes. Perhaps by looking like *Rolling Stone* the magazine might attract readers who did not ordinarily consume political news.[13] But *George*'s rapid descent into beltway gossip sans serious political analysis shows a danger of courting popular tastes to promote serious political content, lest the latter be lost in the packaging.[14]

The Daily Show, hosted by Jon Stewart on the Comedy Central cable network, much more successfully captures widespread political attention

---

[13] "When *George* magazine started up [in 1995], the ad copy sent out to prospective subscribers proclaimed that '*George* is to politics what *Rolling Stone* is to music.'" Bowman (1999: 310).

[14] The *National Journal* reported in January of 1998 that "the folks at *George* magazine are so busy not covering politics as usual, they can't tell the difference between House Budget Committee chairman John Kasich and Andrew Schiff, the Veep's new son-in-law." "By George! They Really Blew It," *National Journal*, January 24, 1998, vol. 30, no. 4: 143.

by appealing to consumers' tastes. David Mindich attributes the show's success not to its political content or ideological content but to its being "very, very funny . . . [it] drips with the kind of irony that many young people tell me they appreciate."[15] Although the program mocks current events and political leaders it also presents substantive news in the process, a reassuring fact considering that "nearly half of people under the age of 30 use late night comedians as a major source of news."[16] I cite *The Daily Show* not as an example of concerned citizens intentionally combating attention deficit democracy by making political news palatable, but as an instance of political attention attracted and sustained through an appeal to popular tastes. Whether Stewart could mobilize citizens' energies is another question altogether.

Rock the Vote aims to accomplish that very feat. The nonprofit organization uses music and music celebrities to appeal to young citizens' tastes, to attract their attention, and to mobilize the energy politically. Initially formed in 1990 by music industry executives to marshal support for free speech issues, the organization has gradually moved toward nonpartisan voter registration. One former Rock the Vote director candidly explains that "we target young people using pop culture." The organization's connections with music celebrities "helps us get in the face of young people who might not otherwise be interested in politics."[17] In exactly the language I use to describe engagement, "the design is to attract [young people's] attention" to political issues and then mobilize their energies at the polls.[18] Rock the Vote claims to have registered more than three million young adults since its inception, in part by aligning political engagement with celebrity hipness.

The 1940s witnessed an earlier, successful attempt to use celebrities and mass media to capture citizen attention and mobilize political activity. Radio shows during World War II voluntarily added patriotic messages, often with appeals for specific civil or political activities. Many of the most popular shows—programs such as *Fibber McGee and Molly*, *The Jack Benny Show*, and *The Aldrich Family*, that had already attracted citizens' attention by appealing to their tastes—incorporated the messages into their storylines and their humor, thus undertaking advocacy without lecturing.[19] Of course, the radio shows' capacity for

[15] Mindich (2005: 125).

[16] Ibid., 57, reporting on Pew Research Center for the People and the Press poll, "Audiences Fragmented and Skeptical: The Tough Job of Communicating with Voters," January 2000.

[17] Donna Frisby, quoted in Siegler (1997: 12).

[18] Buckley (1996: 94).

[19] For example, in the 1941–42 season the *Fibber McGee and Molly* show, then the most popular evening radio program (according to the Hooper Rating system), promoted episode titles such as "Collecting for the Armed Forces" (May 6, 1941), "Scrap Drive" (April 7, 1942), and "Mileage Rationing" (December 1, 1941). In 1943 *The Aldrich Family*, sixth in the national

advocacy could not be separated from their larger, historical context: a national war effort widely viewed as vital and just. Such mobilizing moments remain rare.

But entertainment programming, dealing in the business of attracting attention, retains the ability to promote desirable citizen engagements. Many observers credited the popular 1980s television program *L.A. Law* with increasing the number of law school applications nationwide. Medical dramas such as *E.R.* receive similar credit regarding medical school applications.[20] On the political front, the long-running program *The West Wing* made politics and political machinations more engaging for most people than news reports could effect, and may have increased the appeal of political careers. As Joe Lockhart, White House press secretary for President Clinton, argued:

> You know, when "LA Law" was a popular program, there was a study that showed law school applications going up. When "ER" was the big program, there was a big surge in interest, I think, in becoming a doctor . . . [*The West Wing*] shows people getting involved in government, in politics is actually a positive thing, and you can do good things, and it can be an honorable profession.[21]

On the negative side, to achieve and maintain popular interest, shows such as these must often appeal to viewers' interest in "sex, violence and youth," or glamorize their subjects unduly.[22] But as their successes demonstrate, entertainment programming that can appeal to viewers' tastes and hold their attention might also direct their energies. Willing producers could harness the medium to raise the profile of civil or political engagement undertaken by ordinary citizens as opposed to career politicians. Of course, such a program could only reach its aims if it were to entertain first and foremost, and even widely popular shows such as *L.A. Law* only influence viewers' energies for a limited time.[23]

Among all of the recent attempts to merge popular content with politics, conservative talk radio has enjoyed the most widespread influence.

Hooper Ratings, featured an episode in which the main characters went to great lengths and encountered humorous obstacles while trying to sell war bonds to their neighbors. For episode information, see Dunning (1998). For Hooper Rating information, see Summers (1971).

[20] "Best & Brightest: Education and Career Paths of Top Science and Engineering Students," Commission on Professionals in Science and Technology, 1996. See http://www.cpst.org/web/site/pages/pubs/bbrpt.htm.

[21] Joe Lockhart on PBS *NewsHour*, September 13, 2000. See http://www.pbs.org/newshour/media/west_wing/lockhart.html.

[22] The quote comes from medical ethicist George Annas discussing *E.R.*'s popularity. Annas (1995: 40).

[23] Torry (1996).

Rush Limbaugh, king of the conservative airwaves, infuriates some observers who charge him with hypocrisy, sophistry, and demagoguery.[24] But even Limbaugh's critics must admit to his mastery over the art of engagement.[25] Unfortunately, Limbaugh's and similar programs can provide like-minded citizens with an insular, self-reinforcing political world, or echo chamber, that negates political dissent and demonizes opponents.[26] Tocqueville laments the political balkanization that characterized pre-revolutionary France, but that ideological uniformity required geographical isolation. Modern technology allows individuals to shield themselves from dissenting views without changing locations. That worrisome prospect only underscores my earlier insistence that political engagement's value depends upon its context.

A closing thought on tastes and attention: we should expect to see celebrities increasingly involved with political advocacy and even political candidacy, because celebrities attract the precious resource of attention. It remains a separate question whether celebrity advocates can hold citizens' attention once they attract it or galvanize their attentive public into action. But political groups have long tried to woo whichever citizens they perceived to provide an attention-getting advantage, with military heroes and offspring of famous families traditionally heading the list.[27] Citizens might have different reasons for paying attention to military heroes and famous offspring; they might be impressed by the former's past service, virtue, and discipline and only be piqued by the latter's wealth and station. In the late eighteenth century some anti-Federalists opposed the new Union's larger sphere of government because citizens would likely "elect those persons you know only by common fame" instead of valuing virtue or public service.[28] Indeed, there is no reason to suppose that celebrity status translates into political insight. Former rock-and-roll star Alice Cooper ridicules the trend toward celebrities undertaking political advocacy: "If you are listening to a rock star in order to get your information on who to vote for . . . you are a bigger moron than they are. Why are we rock stars? Because we're morons."[29] Morons or savants, celebrities attract the scarce resource of attention and so will probably loom large in the world of political advocacy.

[24] Franken (1999); Brock (2004).

[25] Some critics allege that Limbaugh owes some of his popularity to his captive audience on Armed Services Radio, whose listeners hear Limbaugh every day and no other political commentators. That argument carries some force, but even without his Armed Services Radio audience Limbaugh would be one of the most popular radio personalities in America. Boehlert (2004).

[26] Jamieson and Capella (2008).

[27] Somit (1948).

[28] John DeWitt III (November 5, 1787: 315), in *The Anti-Federalist Papers*, Ketcham (2003).

[29] Leiby (2004).

Shape Tastes and Habits Politically

The second Tocquevillean strategy for treating attention deficit democracy involves eliciting more political attention and energy by making our tastes more political. To Tocqueville, the tastes that often steer our attention may themselves be shaped by education and habituation. In this regard he agrees with Aristotle, who insists that education must cultivate not only good habits but also good tastes: "enjoying and hating the right things seems to be most important for virtue of character."[30] That seems to be the impulse behind some of the proposals for mandatory public service.

But attempting to engineer adult citizens' tastes risks paternalism or coercion unacceptable to liberal democrats. Indeed, Tocqueville stops far short of condoning the strong "formative impulse" that Michael Sandel locates in certain early American thinkers, an impulse to transform adults' thoughts, tastes, feelings, and character.[31] In *The Old Regime* Tocqueville savagely criticizes the French physiocrats who aimed "to form the citizen's mind according to a particular model set out in advance . . . to fill the citizen's head with certain ideas and to furnish his heart with certain feelings that it judged necessary," and for whom the state "not only reformed men, it transformed them."[32] In *Democracy in America* Tocqueville describes as a "tyranny" any government that extends its grasp beyond "the political world which is properly its domain" and "penetrates into private life," any government that "aspires to regiment [adults'] tastes" as well as actions.[33] And if a government commits to transforming adult citizens' tastes and actions in order to promote virtue, a coercive method threatens to undermine the goal. To recall Tocqueville's insistence, "one will never encounter . . . genuine power among men except in the free concurrence of their wills."[34]

But children are a different story. Most liberals recognize the state's legitimate interest in shaping children's characters so as to socialize them for effective and law-abiding citizenship, with the understanding that once children reach adulthood they may think, choose, and act as they please. Education cannot work miracles but it represents one means of shaping nascent tastes that may later attract adults' attention and en-

---

[30] Aristotle (1985: 1172a25).

[31] As noted earlier in this work, Sandel cites without endorsing Benjamin Rush's alarming aspiration, through use of public education, to "convert men into republican machines." Sandel (1996: 129, citing Rush, "Thoughts Upon the Mode of Education Proper in a Republic").

[32] Tocqueville, ORR: 212.

[33] Tocqueville, DA: 159.

[34] DA: 89.

ergy to self-government. How might schools help to accomplish this goal? One possibility lies in the partial democratization of classrooms. John Dewey envisioned the school as an embryonic society and a microcosm of participatory democracy. Similarly, Amy Gutmann argues that "the cultivation of participatory virtues should become more prominent among the purposes of primary schooling, especially as children mature intellectually and emotionally, and become more capable of engaging in free and equal discussion with teachers and their peers."[35] Dewey's and Gutmann's goal is less to teach a body of information concerning politics than to inculcate the habit of (and taste for) solving common problems politically. Dewey stipulates that simply "going through the motions" of political practice will not do: "The formation of habits is a purely mechanical thing unless habits are also *tastes*—habitual modes of preference and esteem, an effective sense of excellence."[36] Dewey hoped that students might learn to like discussing shared concerns with their peers, speaking confidently to those in authority, and taking responsibility for problems within their reach. Toward that end, classmates might consider and debate proposals for trivial matters such as a class mascot or for more meaningful matters relating to curricula. Teachers might encourage students to voice complaints or suggestions about class dynamics, class procedures, or even educational content, and to strive collectively to devise reasonable responses. Dewey wisely stopped short of according students equal authority or jurisdiction with teachers, because trained specialists must oversee the educational process. But he aspired to familiarize students with political processes and, by making those processes rewarding and even fun, to build a taste for future engagements.

The aspiration to shape students' tastes is nothing new. Consider art and music appreciation courses: rather than simply imparting information, they aim at inculcating a taste for the relevant arts.[37] As an American educator wrote ninety years ago: "This, then, is the purpose of a course in Music Appreciation; not to teach us facts about composers, but to help us to love their works."[38] But music and art are imperfect analogies for political engagement. The rationale for teaching them tends to focus on art's intrinsic value, whereas I claim that political engagement is much easier to defend on instrumental grounds. Further, for all of their

[35] Gutmann (1987: 92). Dewey's and Gutmann's attention to habituation accords with Aristotle's pedagogical strategy as well: "it is very important, indeed all-important . . . to acquire one sort of habit or another, right from our youth." Aristotle (1985: 1104a25e).

[36] Dewey (1921: 276).

[37] Literally, to *appreciate* means to *value* or *esteem*. However, educators generally hope to achieve more than that. One could esteem a subject and yet not give it any attention or time, whereas most educators hope that their students, as adults, will actually engage with music or art and thus keep it alive. They hope that their students will develop a taste for their subject.

[38] Kent (1917: 18).

merit, arts appreciation courses probably exert only minor influence on students' tastes once they reach maturity. One author of music appreciation books reports that "the majority of [my] buyers are not teenagers, but those in their middle years" who "did not develop a taste for classical music until their forties."[39] Another wonders whether "dubiously titled 'music appreciation' courses don't create an outright aversion to classical music" by foisting it heavy-handedly on unreceptive ears.[40]

Physical education represents a closer analogy to political education and a more promising model for politicizing students' tastes. The primary rationale for investing in both physical and political education stems from demonstrable, instrumental benefits. Athletic involvement correlates with a range of short-term advantages for middle and high school students, but educators also hope to inculcate life-long tastes and habits for physical fitness and athleticism—and for good reasons.[41] Adults who exercise regularly evince a decreased risk for many physical disorders, depression and anxiety, and better results with self-confidence and weight control.[42] But, just as with American civics curricula, physical education is not in good shape. Significantly fewer students attend daily physical education classes now than at the beginning of the 1990s, and many schools have dropped a gym requirement altogether.[43] Budgetary pressures and governmental directives such as No Child Left Behind account for some of the curricular cuts but not for the students' own lack of interest. Adolescent girls in particular show distressing signs of disengagement from physical education and physical activity, a disengagement that increases with age. In response, educators have begun to question traditional pedagogical approaches to physical education that emphasize only a few, competitive sports and joyless, Spartan calisthenics. Newer approaches aim to make physical exercise more appealing, sociable, and fun. They also employ different pedagogical strategies with different groups of students; for example, adolescent girls respond especially well to games involving benefi-

---

[39] Kavanaugh (2003: 53).

[40] Cynthia Joyce, "For Those about to Bach—We Salute You," *Salon* August 26, 1996. See http://www.salon.com/weekly/exile960826.html.

[41] As one study puts it, "the most important objective of quality physical education is long-term health." Shephard and Trudeau (2000: 35). See also "Guidelines for School and Community Programs to Promote Lifelong Physical Activity among Young People," *Morbidity and Mortality Weekly Report*, March 07, 1997. See http://www.cdc.gov/mmwR/preview/mmwrhtml/00046823.htm.

[42] For a range of short-term instrumental benefits, see Marsh and Kleitman (2003). For longer-term benefits, see Shephard and Trudeau (2000).

[43] "Overall, the prevalence of attending PE class daily declined significantly from 1991 (41.6%) to 1995 (25.4%) and did not change significantly from 1995 (25.4%) to 2003 (28.4%)." "Participation in High School Physical Education—United States, 1991–2003," *Morbidity and Mortality Weekly Report* (Center for Disease Control), September 17, 2004, vol. 53, no. 36: 844–47.

cial exercise but which are relatively easy to master and thus promote a sense of self-efficacy.[44]

We might employ a similar set of approaches in teaching politics and political engagement; indeed, Tocqueville implicitly recommends that strategy. As with physical education, political education once occupied a much more prominent place in many schools but has fallen on hard times. Civics classes, which once covered not only basic information on the three branches of government but also the role that citizens can play in local and state politics, have waned markedly in elementary and high schools over the past forty years.[45] But simply teaching information about government and citizenship seems unlikely to make students' tastes more political. As with physical education, we should strive to make political engagement more engaging and fun. In physical education classes students learn useful information but they also learn by doing, participating in team and individual sports that hopefully will be fun on their own merits.[46] By the same token, students might form a greater taste for political engagement by not only learning about what citizens can do but also by undertaking some of those functions in their schools. One of the more appealing recent initiatives comes from Project Citizen, designed by the Center for Civic Education and funded by the U.S. Department of Education.[47] Project Citizen invites middle and secondary school students cooperatively to identify a local public policy problem, compare a variety of existing policy responses, and formulate their own recommendations involving various political actors and institutions. Students learn by doing (as well as by reading and writing), and they see their proposals taken seriously by adults. In essence, Project Citizen invites students to play the role of Tocqueville's township citizens, attentive to and active in the operation of local governance. As such, it stands between traditional civics courses, which primarily imparted information about government and politics, and certain service learning courses that involve compulsory community service undertaken outside the classroom.[48] According

[44] Prochaska et al. (2003).

[45] Kahne and Middaugh (2008: 27). Also, "Does a Downturn in Civic Education Signal a Disconnect to Democracy?" *Carnegie Reporter*, vol. 2 (Fall 2003). See http://carnegie.org/publications/carnegie-reporter/single/view/article/item/97.

[46] Political education that aspires only to impart information about the political system has shown only minor and indirect effects on citizens' later political engagement. Verba, Schlozman, and Brady (1995).

[47] See http://www.civiced.org/index.php?page=introduction.

[48] Service learning can introduce students to valuable experiences of voluntarism and social service, and may play a positive role in political socialization, but some worry that by making social and civil engagement compulsory such programs run a risk of triggering resistance. Stukas, Snyder, and Clary (1999) support that concern. But more empirical research seems to suggest that mandatory engagement for the young may increase future

to preliminary studies, Project Citizen's benefits include significantly increased knowledge of public affairs and policy processes among participants, an increased sense of political efficacy, and—most significantly for my purposes—increased desire for further political engagement.[49]

The preceding strategies considered only children and adolescents. Trying to shape adults' tastes and attention can be a much more tenuous project for liberals, who wish to avoid coercion and paternalism. Yet Tocqueville, who shares that concern, enthusiastically endorses America's jury system because it focuses adult citizens' attention on communal interests and hence enlarges their social and political perspective:

> Juries invest each citizen with a sort of magisterial office; they make all men feel that they have duties toward society and that they take a share in its government. By making men pay attention to things other than their own affairs, they combat that individual selfishness which is like rust in society.[50]

Elsewhere Tocqueville warns us that coerced attention and energy are rarely efficacious. Why should the jury system's means of "making men pay attention to things other than their own affairs" be different? One reason might be its long-standing legitimacy: citizen juries comprised an extant system that enjoyed wide acceptance. Citizens expected to serve and, during the late colonial period, were even willing to fight for that right.[51] Thus American juries seemed to meet Tocqueville's standard of "the free concurrence of men's wills." John Gastil finds evidence that juries still serve the purposes Tocqueville observes, changing citizens' perception of their relationship to their government and perhaps boosting political engagement.[52] But modern-day proposals to demand adult citizens' attention and energy should proceed with more caution. Consider the numerous proposals for mandatory public service, such as the Universal Service Act of 2003 (introduced into the House of Representatives by Charles Rangel [D-NY], John Conyers [D-MI], and Senator Fritz Hollings [D-SC]), which would require all Americans to complete two years of national service between the ages of eighteen and twenty-six. Mandatory service plans owe their intellectual roots to William James's famous essay, "The Moral Equivalent of War," which proposes to inculcate young adults with "conceptions of order and discipline, the tradition of service and devotion, of physical fitness, unstinted exertion, and universal responsibility" through service to public works instead of mili-

---

engagement and at least will not diminish it. Metz and Youniss (2003) support the first contention; Henderson et al. (2007) support the second.

[49] Johanek and Puckett (2005: 144).

[50] *DA*: 274; stress added.

[51] Pole (1993).

[52] Gastil et al. (2010).

tary conquest. James and his modern-day heirs express admirable sentiments. From a Tocquevillean perspective, though, admiration gives way
to doubt. On one hand, liberalism rejects coercion and paternalism unless the community's survival absolutely requires them. But beyond any
normative objections, a practical one remains: adults' coerced attention
and energy are rarely efficacious. On numerous occasions Tocqueville
warns that "humanity is so constituted that it prefers to stay still rather
than march forward without independence toward an unknown goal."[53]
Under dire circumstances, when a war has "brought all their petty undertakings to ruin," democratic citizens can show great fighting energy
and spirit.[54] On the other hand, under grave duress, when real emergency
has "destroyed every industry," awakened citizens act from necessity and
self-preservation rather than serve an end imposed by fellow citizens or
government. True, Tocqueville worries about democratic citizens' tendency to dedicate themselves exclusively to business and petty pleasures,
which can undermine their commitment to collective action and the public interest.[55] For that reason, he might endorse a public service program
that could attract sufficient numbers relying on incentives and persuasion
rather than coercion and force. Otherwise, shaping tastes and future attention through compulsory learning or service remains a strategy best
employed on the young.

Channel Existing Energies More Effectively

The third approach to treating attention deficit democracy, rather than
trying to elicit more political attention or energy immediately, recognizes
present-day democracy as energy inefficient and seeks to get more out of
citizens' existing political energies. It follows Tocqueville's insistence that
political energies should be pooled and channeled by networked institutions that link energies at the local, state, and national levels. In Tocqueville's era of decentralized government and localized political engagement,
channeling institutions included participatory municipal governments
with connections to state and national governments and a robust system

[53] *DA*: 92. One might wonder why compulsory jury duty could escape the problem of
coerced attention and energy. The answer probably lies in its longstanding acceptance and
legitimacy with the population, with American roots that date to colonial times. In fact,
with England's attempt to limit or purge the colonists' right to jury trials, "the preservation
of jury trials became one of the symbols fueling the Revolution." Jonakait (2006: 21).

[54] *DA*: 657.

[55] "Intent only on getting rich, they do not notice the close connection between private fortunes and general prosperity. . . . They find it a tiresome inconvenience to exercise political rights
which distract them from industry. When required to elect representatives, to support authority
by personal service, or to discuss public business together, they find they have no time." *DA*: 540.

of networked political associations. For better or worse, thoroughly decentralized government probably no longer presents a feasible option. The complexities of twenty-first-century governance involving a diverse population and shifting, global alliances demand a fair amount of government centralization. At any rate, entrenched bureaucracies have always been very difficult to shrink or dislodge. Nonetheless, municipal institutions can do a better job of eliciting and focusing citizens' political energies and channeling them occasionally toward state and national issues, and even ostensibly nonpolitical associations can help to render citizens' collected energies more politically efficacious.

Political parties can do a better job as well. Modern political parties have become bloodless corporations primarily directed toward fund-raising and advertising, but they were not always so. Scholars wistfully recall earlier eras of party politics in which "torchlight parades illuminated the night and the faithful endorsed national tickets with the passion sports fans feel for playoff teams."[56] Mid-nineteenth-century political parties were also "rooted in the local experiences and, often, the daily life of citizens, or at least far more than the parties of today."[57] Now "our political parties, once intimately coupled to the capillaries of community life, have become evanescent confections of pollsters and media consultants and independent political entrepreneurs—the very antithesis of social capital."[58] Some scholars contest the extent of ordinary citizens' involvement with political parties and political issues even during the thriving period of party development from 1840 to 1900, but earlier political parties indisputably had a much greater connection with citizens' daily lives and social networks than they do at present.[59]

Some participatory democrats might envision rank-and-file membership actively steering party governance and developing party platforms, but that level of participation could undermine parties' efficacy.[60] Leaving aside the desirability of hands-on governance by rank-and-file members, I focus on a different angle altogether: making parties more sociable, or putting the "party" back in political parties. The goal would be for political parties to reclaim their former role as sites for socializing and networking among friends and neighbors in addition to their role as political institutions. That transformation might only boost social capital and generalized trust among like-minded people, generating bonding rather than

---

[56] Kerbel (2002: 189).

[57] Aldrich (1995: 168).

[58] As Putnam puts it: "Our political parties, once intimately coupled to the capillaries of community life, have become evanescent confections of pollsters and media consultants and independent political entrepreneurs—the very antithesis of social capital." Putnam (1993).

[59] Cf. Altschuler and Blumin (2000) and Uslaner (2005).

[60] Uslaner (2005, citing Michels and Schattschneider).

bridging social capital.[61] But the goal of making parties more sociable would be to give citizens a reason for continual, rather than occasional, connection to political institutions.

Socializing among local chapter members could focus on political talk or other nonpolitical, shared interests. In San Francisco progressive groups have formed "weekly chapter meetings" of drinking groups for like-minded citizens, "trying to brew a politics-and-fun mix," but "underneath the fun is movement-building."[62] As a further example, one could easily envision political party membership gelling around popular, local sports teams. Given that citizens already convene to view and cheer local sports teams, political parties could follow the wisdom of community organizers and take their messages where the action is. Republican and Democratic chapters of sports team fan clubs would allow those who want to engage socially on a regular basis, and who share political affiliations, to combine the energy of the former (more regular) association with the shared beliefs of the latter. People might come together for the shared sports experience but also value the opportunity to bond with politically like-minded fans.

Nonetheless, national parties will not commit to social networks and local engagement over mass-marketed fund-raising and advertising—will not commit to social over financial capital—unless that path promises better electoral outcomes. Barack Obama's successful campaigns in the 2008 primary and general elections channeled citizens' political energies using social networking technologies such as the Internet and e-mail and cell phone parties (in which supporters would get together to call undecided voters in contested states). Obama organizers implored supporters to invite friends and colleagues personally to join the process. Obama's campaign success may prompt both political parties to experiment with similar networking and organizing tactics, using social engagement to generate political engagement more than parties have done in recent years.

We have no magical blueprint for revitalizing political parties, but Tocqueville's work contains an insight relevant not only to parties but also to nonpolitical associations that can channel citizens' energies, occasionally focusing them on politics. The insight is that institutional linkages, federations, and networks matter.[63] When citizens interact with political parties as discrete consumers—contributing money as individuals, consuming political advertising as individuals, voting as individuals—they become

---

[61] Ibid.

[62] Joe Garofoli, "Putting the Party Back into Politics," *San Francisco Chronicle*, March 9, 2006, A-1.

[63] Theda Skocpol stands out as the contemporary scholar most in tune with Tocqueville on this issue. See Skocpol (1999, 2003).

private patrons, in effect "isolated and then dropped one by one into the common mass."[64] But an association of associations, which links either political or apolitical groups into a larger federation, can give individuals a variety of means through which to pool their resources and raise their voices on issues of importance. If local chapters of the Democratic and Republican parties comprised vibrant social groups on their own, and kept members socially active during nonelection years, voters' collected energies would be much easier to mobilize for electoral politics.

In describing nineteenth-century political associations Tocqueville depicts three developmental stages, beginning with localized collective action and ending in vast, networked groups that can channel their energies into political power. The first stage of association "unites the energies of divergent minds and vigorously directs them toward a clearly indicated goal." This occurs when previously isolated individuals discover others who share not only opinions, values, or tastes but also some sort of collective goal. The second stage spreads attention and energy to "centers of action at certain important places in the country," and the "final stage" involves miniature "electoral colleges" where members of associations "appoint mandatories to represent them in a central assembly."[65] As Tocqueville explains,

> In the first of these cases, men sharing one opinion are held together by a purely intellectual tie; in the second case, they meet together in small assemblies representing only a fraction of the party; finally, in the third case, they form something like a separate nation within the nation and a government within the government.[66]

Although Tocqueville had political associations in mind, his developmental account matches Theda Skocpol's depiction of late nineteenth-century American voluntary associations.[67] Skocpol chronicles the ways in which large voluntary associations, such as the Knights of Columbus or Daughters of the American Revolution, used federated structures to forge ties between local membership and state and national leaders. Local chapters annually sent representatives to regional or national conventions and generated "bridging" social capital. And while members joined

---

[64] Tocqueville, *DA*: 87.

[65] Ibid., 190.

[66] Ibid.

[67] A further difference: while Tocqueville's "first stage" of association can involve localized group membership, it is consistent with nonsocial associating—in Tocqueville's words, "a purely intellectual tie." That is why he identifies the "first stage" with "freedom to write" and the second stage with "freedom of assembly." All three of Skocpol's federated levels, conversely, involve face-to-face assemblies of voluntarily associating individuals. Still, Tocqueville's three stages and Skocpol's three tiers both differentiate between associations grouped at the local, more dispersed (i.e., state), and national levels.

ostensibly for nonpolitical purposes, when a sufficient number were moved by a common principle or interest they could pool their considerable energies and lobby state and national government to great effect. Thus social engagement organized in networked institutions generated occasional political power that members could not have achieved on their own.[68]

The Tocquevillean point is that channeling institutions, especially those linked by a federated structure, take attention and energy wherever they present themselves—sometimes in purely social organizations—and increase their political potential and efficacy. Grassroots community organizers have long emulated that model. In the 1930s and 1940s Saul Alinsky, legendary innovator behind the Industrial Areas Foundation (IAF), helped Chicago's local leaders to organize community-oriented People's Organizations in a wide range of low-income neighborhoods. Rather than build political organizations right away, however, he sought to work with the "multiple agencies and organizations" already present in the communities, "ranging from churches, athletic groups, nationality associations, benevolent orders, religious societies, women's clubs, labor unions, businessmen's groups, service organizations, recreation groups," and others.[69] Many of those groups would initially view a politicized People's Organization warily, a potential competitor for scarce community resources, but the successful organizer eventually could "work with all of the agencies of the community to build . . . an organization of organizations . . . of which they were the very foundation."[70] Alinsky employs Tocquevillean terminology in describing his ultimate goal: "an organization of all of the People's Organizations, institutions, and the people themselves" across many municipalities and states, which would "secure the invincible strength that flows from the pooling of the popular pressures inherent within the people and their organizations."[71] The model was simple: reach people in the organizations where their tastes, habits, and interests have taken them; organize those organizations into a larger structure that can channel its members' energies into local political engagement; and link those larger structures or People's Organizations across many cities and states in order to pool the collected energies with even more political clout.

[68] "Membership federations certainly helped to create a democratic civil society in which large numbers of ordinary people could participate, forge recurrent ties to one another, and engage in two-way relationships with powerful leaders. They institutionalized remarkable balances between intimate face-to-face activities and leverage in state, regional, and national affairs." Skocpol, "How Americans Became Civic," in Skocpol and Fiorina (1999: 70). Also Skocpol (2003).

[69] Alinsky (1969: 84).

[70] Ibid., 86.

[71] Ibid., 199. For Alinsky's Tocquevilleanism, see Sabl (2002a).

In subsequent years the IAF has continued to seek ways of linking municipal institutions such as schools, where people are bound to congregate already, with People's Organizations and also formal government. In the early 1990s, Ernesto Cortes and the Southwestern IAF's network of People's Organizations partnered with the Texas Education Agency (TEA) and "a network of schools in low-income areas that were willing to innovate and to engage parents to enhance students' academic achievement."[72] The goal was to elicit and pool attention and energy at a variety of levels toward the shared goal of improving scholastic performance, with the side goal of enhancing political efficacy among low-income parents. While "school change can easily be blocked on many levels when it is undertaken in isolation from broader movements and coalitions which support reform," the Alliance School network bolstered innovative teachers and administrators with a reservoir of pooled resources and connections.[73] It also welcomed parents from low-income families, many of them poorly educated themselves, who gathered in living room meetings to discuss goals for their children's education. The Alliance School network, organized by professionals as opposed to bubbling up from grass roots, nonetheless gave local residents their first taste of collective action and a budding sense of political efficacy.

The Alliance School example speaks to ideals commonly espoused among progressives: empowerment of low-income, immigrant families to make public schools more effective and responsive. But the political right can also use networked institutions as tools of collective energy and political efficacy, as the home schooling movement has ably shown. Parents who have chosen to home-school their children tend to be more religiously and culturally conservative than the mainstream population. In the past twenty years they have effectively pooled their attention, energies, and intellectual resources—their human and social capital—in organizations "set up for essentially non-political purposes" that can yet "become a central resource in a grassroots lobbying effort."[74] Rather than remaining isolated units and thus politically powerless, home-schooling parents have united in grassroots organizations and "lobbying groups locally, regionally, and nationally . . . ready to act when their rights are threatened and their needs are unmet."[75]

[72] Shirley (1997: 200).

[73] "The individual parent, teacher or even principal who attempts to bring about change faces a battery of bureaucratic restraints concerning innocuous issues . . . and the vital educational matters which relate to instruction, curricula and assessment. With the formalization of the relationship between the Texas IAF and the TEA, Texas IAF schools had new credibility in their districts." Shirley (1997: 203).

[74] Bates (1991: 11–12).

[75] Cooper and Sureau (2007: 124).

The preceding examples demonstrate the ways in which associations—often organized for ostensibly apolitical purposes such as improving children's educational performance—can join with like-minded groups and channel members' energies toward collective problem solving, occasionally generating political pressure on issues of shared concern. Archon Fung advocates for a different approach that similarly evokes a Tocquevillean resonance. Fung's empowered participation describes a model of municipal participation and deliberation, already showing positive results in Chicago, in which people's existing attention and energy might be more effectively utilized for cooperative problem solving. In Fung's narrative Chicago's public schools and community policing, formerly dominated by a central authority, "were reorganized to create new channels through which residents could exercise their collective voice and influence."[76] When a broad range of community members realized that their contributions could actually make a difference they gained a sense of efficacy and participated in steering the public school and community policing agendas in a way that few political scientists would have predicted. The reforms incorporated "citizen participation, pragmatic deliberation, and centralized coordination and accountability"—in other words, citizens met together and with officials from the school boards and police departments, established methods of respectful deliberation, and worked with those in the central authority to implement the best suggestions while preventing factional domination of one group over another. Results were mixed, in part because some neighborhoods began the democratic experiments with very poor socioeconomic resources, a condition that correlates negatively with social and political engagement. But "while it is true that the most advantaged neighborhood . . . was also the one in which deliberations were most fair and effective, all of the other cases gained much more from accountable autonomy relative to what insular bureaucratic arrangements had given them."[77] The citizens whom Fung observed were invited but not compelled to participate, which accords with Tocqueville's liberal spirit. Invitations arrived in the form of local advertising and community organizers' outreach; motivation derived from pent-up frustration at the municipal institutions' poor performance and opacity. As with Tocqueville's engaged New England townships, many of Fung's Chicago residents approached the participatory opportunities for self-interested reasons, but some left with a greater feeling of efficacy and civil engagement.

While I might be warier than Fung about the potential for empowered participation to reshape a wide swath of American democracy, I share his

[76] Fung (2006: 2).
[77] Ibid., 225.

admiration for the few inspiring successes and his hope for further experiments in the Chicago mold. Obstacles remain, most likely from urban bureaucracies reluctant to share their power with citizen participants, but political pressure could overcome their resistance. The prospect for Tocquevillean citizen participation in municipal affairs, with citizens able to influence outcomes that affect their daily experience, deserves our support and merits a political fight. All the more so because the deliberative environments in Fung's study achieved a fair degree of participant satisfaction in the presence of great diversity, attracting participants from a wide range of income levels, educational backgrounds, and ethnic and racial groups without certain participants feeling systematically unheard or invisible.[78]

If liberal democrats value the idea of promoting political efficacy among marginalized citizens, difficult choices lie ahead. Our limited resources might yield greater results when invested in community organizing associations and further experiments with "empowered participation" than when invested in expensive experiments such as a paid national holiday for citizen deliberation, as Bruce Ackerman and James Fishkin propose, or even in mainstream voter mobilization efforts.[79] Community organizing seems unlikely to draw government funding because organizers often approach local governments from an adversarial stance. But private foundations and donors interested in channeling citizens' attention and energy more efficaciously, especially among poor and marginalized populations, should give community organizing associations serious consideration. Fung's empowered participation also deserves further investigation and resources in order to test its effectiveness in other municipalities. While political scientists often treat voting as the holy grail of political engagement, and political theorists may lionize grueling deliberation, democracy depends upon citizens investing attention and energy cooperatively in a wide variety of associations, both political and nonpolitical, in the process achieving a sense of efficacy to influence political outcomes through collective action. Citizens whose voices are not often heard at the national level—especially the poor and poorly educated—stand to gain more control over their daily environments, and to develop an attendant sense of political efficacy, by participating in local community organizing movements or helping to direct municipal institutions than by casting a vote in the national election. I do not mean to denigrate or dismiss the act of voting; "public officials know who is paying attention to what

[78] Mansbridge (1980) presents a classic account of town hall meetings, dominated by opinionated individuals, many of whom do not welcome participation or openness. Lupia and McCubbins (1998: 227) also find that "the mere construction of a deliberative setting does not guarantee that the cream of the collective's knowledge will rise to the top."

[79] Ackerman and Fishkin (2004).

they do," so citizens who have "identifiable, politically relevant attributes become visible through political activity"; they can make public officials pay attention to them.[80] But community organizing and participation in municipal institutions allow citizens to take a more active role in influencing issues close to their lives, and in the process to develop the kind of "self-esteem" or efficacy that Tocqueville associates with localized political engagement.[81]

But as I note in chapter 2, strictly localized engagement—participation in social and political associations that address only local issues—risks becoming what Tocqueville called "collective individualism," a kind of balkanized engagement that lacks broader linkages and bridges. Without institutional linkages, local associations lose the opportunity to pool their members' energies and to influence decisions and policies made at a nonlocal level. Armed with the knowledge that associational linkages matter, we might also try to promote what Skocpol calls "governing in partnership with membership associations." By "membership associations" she means associations that boast active memberships—perhaps associations such as the PTA or labor unions that feature federated structures at the local, state, and national levels—as opposed to simply "mailing list associations" or lobbying groups that represent money rather than masses. Rather than being advised by experts, professional advocates, and pollsters, public officials could give "institutions, movements, and associations with large memberships . . . more prominent roles in congressional hearings and consultations by congressional staffs."[82] Skocpol suggests that the associations' leaders could play a mediating role, querying their constituencies at the local level and bringing their findings back to policymakers. The point would be for public officials to rely upon, and partner with, associational members whose primary purposes might not be political but whose attention and energies could be focused occasionally on policy debates involving their core interests or values.

Of the three preceding approaches to treating attention deficit democracy—appealing to citizens' existing tastes, shaping their tastes and habits politically, and channeling their existing energies more effectively—I am least sanguine about the first and most sanguine about the third. Tocqueville offers unqualified praise for networked institutions that can pool and channel members' energies into cooperative pursuits and occasionally convert them into political engagement and pressure. But tastes and attention are a trickier matter. Tocqueville acknowledges that for politics

---

[80] Verba, Schlozman, and Brady (1995: 45).

[81] Tocqueville refers specifically to those who assume local, public office or serve in a municipal administration: "A man of the people, when asked to share the task of governing society, acquires a certain self-esteem." *DA*: 244.

[82] Skocpol (2003: 288–89).

to attract the latter it will probably have to appeal to the former, but he remains wary about cheapening politics for an easy sale because self-government is not a commodity. We would do well to share Tocqueville's attitude. No friend of democracy could wish to see local or national elections transformed into a version of *American Idol*. Thus we should strive to raise political issues from invisibility while taking care not to lower them into triviality.

Target the Attention and Energy of Marginalized Citizens

A fourth prescription for treating attention deficit democracy, targeting the attention and energy of politically marginalized citizens, follows not from Tocqueville but from a reflection on recent trends. To be clear, I do not claim to be discovering the problem of politically marginalized citizens or a range of new solutions for empowering them. But citizens interested in prescriptive suggestions for treating the diagnosis of attention deficit democracy (which, together with the prescriptive suggestions, comprise the public philosophy of attention deficit democracy) should focus their own attention on the challenge of marginalized voices. Throughout this book I stress that we should avoid the worst of democracy's problems before attempting to pursue idealistic goals such as high and widespread political engagement. From the perspective of fairness and equality, the political marginalization of citizens in the lowest socioeconomic strata comprises one combatable aspect of democracy's worst.[83] Ample research agrees that political engagement correlates with economic and educational attainment. Citizens with the least income and education are least likely to pay attention to and invest energy in politics, and when they do engage—lacking financial resources—they are the least well equipped to amplify their voices through monetary donations.[84] Even more worrisome from the perspective of representative fairness, not only are the poor "less likely to be [politically] active," but also "the activists drawn from among them do not accurately represent their level of need or their preferences for governmental help."[85] Thus political disengagement hits the poor and poorly educated doubly hard: they are least likely to engage and most likely to be poorly represented when disengaged. Increasing political engagement among poor and marginalized citizens—increasing

---

[83]Dahl (1989: 322) acknowledges that attempting to reduce political inequalities (as opposed to trying to ensure complete political equality) "would facilitate the maximal achievement of democracy and its values" given "feasible human limits."

[84]Bartels (2009: 167).

[85]Verba, Schlozman, and Brady (1995: 215); Strolovitch (2007).

their sense of efficacy and bolstering their political voice—seems a plausible priority for advocates of participatory democracy.

But while the citizenry's most marginalized segments are certainly not ignored by participatory reformers (individuals or institutions dedicated to revitalizing participatory democracy), neither do they tend to receive top billing.[86] When political parties and activists recruit citizens for political engagement they are much less likely to target those low on the socioeconomic ladder than to approach more affluent and educated citizens.[87] At present, government agencies and political parties have little incentive to mobilize the disadvantaged. Thanks to advances in market research, government agencies and political parties know which groups are paying attention to their performance (and on which issues), which groups are most likely to donate time and money, and which groups are most likely to vote. Thanks to advances in political marketing and consultancy they also know how to target those groups.[88] From the perspective of costly political outreach, poor and poorly educated citizens do not seem to offer government agencies and political parties the same return on investment as their more privileged counterparts. One way of changing the existing calculus would be to implement thoroughgoing electoral changes—for example, limiting the role that donations can play in campaign finance, or making political parties more reliant on social than on financial capital.[89] But many analysts have cautioned that campaign finance reforms, while well intentioned, are no panacea and could even have the unintended effect of limiting political outreach to working-class and lower-income citizens.[90] Further, if citizens in the lower socioeconomic strata are generally less inclined to invest attention and energy politically, as the data suggest, why should limitations on campaign contributions increase their inclination to attend? One hope for making government agencies and political parties more receptive to, and solicitous of, marginalized citizens' attention and energies would be through Skocpol's model of "governing through associations"—specifically, associations in which those in lower socioeconomic brackets are most likely to engage (such as religious institutions and community organizing groups). But that kind of model is much easier to propose than to implement. Through which

---

[86] Among those who do prioritize the problem, one set of responses aims to protect marginalized citizens' interests more fully even if they themselves disengage. See Williams (2000). See also Brady Schlozman, and Verba (1999). Further, campaign finance reform is sometimes advocated as a means of tempering the unequal influence wielded by wealthy political donors. Gross and Goidel (2003).

[87] Brady, Schlozman, and Verba (1999).

[88] Ganz (1994).

[89] Ibid.

[90] Judis (1997); Skocpol (2003: 280–85).

other pathways might we target the attention and energies of those least likely to engage?

I have already described some ways in which community organizing associations empower marginalized citizens directly by helping them to speak in their own, amplified voices. Yet community organizers seldom receive a lion's share of governmental or foundational funding.[91] That snub owes partly to the nature of community organizing: organizers prioritize marginalized citizens' voices over governmental or foundational directives, which makes them difficult to control, and they may take adversarial stances against government policies. Organizers face the prospect of co-optation, should they court funding from bureaucratic sources, or penury should they forgo it.[92] Organizers depend upon support from rank-and-file members and supportive citizens generally. At any rate, they cannot work alone. In the 1960s and 1970s Frances Fox Piven and Richard A. Cloward advocated a poor people's movement powered only by constituents; shunning organization or networks, the poor would advocate for their interests by overloading the welfare system, precipitating a crisis, and thus forcing elites to meet their needs more completely.[93] But leaving aside the controversial nature of such quasi-revolutionary methods, strong evidence suggests that disadvantaged citizens can best express their interests and achieve their goals through cross-class partnerships and institutional linkages.[94] The partnerships can involve community organizing groups, organized labor, and religious associations such as churches, among others.[95] Indeed, the IAF and other community organizing groups have worked extensively with religious associations because low-income citizens' attention and energies are more likely to be focused there than on other kinds of voluntary associations.[96] Community organizers have also partnered with administrators and parents connected to middle schools and high schools, as the IAF did in its Texas Alliance School intervention.[97]

Colleges and universities can partner with the poor as well. But too many institutions of higher education, while possessing the resources to play this role, may unintentionally favor the favored instead. Educators and educational funders—private and public—spend vast resources pro-

[91] By "foundational" I mean "relating to foundations," in this case charitable nonprofit foundations.

[92] Incite! Women of Color Against Violence (2007).

[93] Piven and Cloward (1966, 1977).

[94] Roach and Roach (1978, 1980).

[95] For partnerships with organized labor, see Roach and Roach (1978); for religious associations see Mark E. Warren (2001).

[96] Verba, Schlozman, and Brady (1995) detail low-income citizens' strong participation in religious associations relative to political and other kinds of civil associations.

[97] Shirley (1997).

moting civic engagement at colleges and universities, although the target populations are statistically much more likely to become politically and socially engaged than those lacking college degrees or affluent parents.[98] The point here is not that colleges and universities should refrain from encouraging engagement among their students, but that they should do so in ways that engage the less fortunate equally. To be sure, educational institutions have been trying to serve disadvantaged communities over the past several decades. But frequently their efforts are more geared toward "doing for" than "doing with": solving problems for communities in need, or simply studying those communities, rather than prioritizing community members' voices and helping to actualize their expressed concerns.[99] The goals are often noble; some educators wish to inculcate empathy and to prompt their privileged students to anticipate and address other citizens' needs.[100] But the more democratic, and Tocquevillean, approach would be to focus more resources on helping politically marginalized citizens to articulate their own needs and utilize the political institutions that others take for granted. Of course, many higher educational programs already have adopted that approach.[101] Many more should emulate its aims and practice.[102] I offer this critique in the friendliest possible spirit, because I share with many public-spirited foundations, and most educators who practice service learning or community-based learning, the goal of promoting greater political responsiveness and equity. Involving students in projects to enhance the voice of politically marginalized citizens promotes education about American democracy's promises and pitfalls while also promoting Tocquevillean ends.

The prescription of targeting marginalized citizens' attention and energies entails all three of the approaches sketched earlier: appealing to those citizens' tastes (for example, by arranging political outreach by celebrities popular among the groups to be engaged), shaping those citizens' tastes and habits politically (for example, through an increased focus on fun

---

[98] Kahne and Middaugh (2008). Robert Rhoads (2003: 25) eulogizes university-level "civic engagement" because "a democracy depends upon the willingness of learned citizens to engage in the public realm for the betterment of the larger social good." That sentiment rings true as a general ideal but not as a justification for concentrating the lion's share of our money, time, and expertise on affluent and well-educated young adults.

[99] Ward and Wolf-Wendel (2000).

[100] Robert Rhodes (2003) suggests that educators inculcate in privileged students a "caring self" and an appreciation of "otherness," which might prompt those privileged students to "act to eliminate the intolerable, to reduce the pain, to fill the need, to actualize the dream" (Noddings 1984, cited in Rhoads 2003: 27).

[101] Stanton, Giles, and Cruz (1999: 144–77).

[102] Hayes (2006: 27) notes that scholarship focuses almost exclusively on demonstrating positive effects of "service learning" courses on college and university students, while "there is little related research on how service learning impacts community organizations or the community at large."

political education in underprivileged schools), and channeling their existing attention and energy more efficiently toward political ends (as per Skocpol's model of governing with associations). Myriad scholars and practitioners will offer more concrete proposals. The main point of this short section has been to establish the priority, not the exact means, of making political engagement more accessible and meaningful for those citizens in the lower socioeconomic strata.

Earlier I located the public philosophy of attention deficit democracy between the two extremes of John Dewey's excessive optimism and Walter Lippmann's excessive pessimism about the extent of citizen engagement that we might and must achieve. But a middle ground need not be bland or uninspiring. The first three prescriptions for treating attention deficit democracy, drawn from Tocqueville's spirit and logic, proffer achievable platforms (employing creative and sometimes entertaining methods) that could revitalize rather than revolutionize political engagement among those who desire it. The fourth prescription, drawn from contemporary research, underscores an unfortunate reality—that those who need political engagement most are the least likely to undertake it and most likely to be poorly represented when disengaged—and specifies a priority for deploying the first three prescriptions, even if success is far from assured. Thus the public philosophy of attention deficit democracy combines elements both achievable and aspirational.

This book has been spurred by a liberal (and Tocquevillean) concern: we citizens are the best available judges of our individual interests, but we err nonetheless. Our own free choices may bring undesired consequences. We freely choosing citizens may opt out of broader social networks and political participation, in spite of a need for collective action, preferring the familiarity of family, friends, and colleagues. We may turn our attention from political issues and processes and invest our energies in the myriad nonpolitical pursuits of modern life. By disengaging from face-to-face social engagement we might unintentionally affect forms of moral engagement, including norms of generalized trust and civility.[103] But if "making democracy work" requires widespread social and moral engagement and at least moderate and episodic political engagement, how should we cope with wandering attention and freely chosen disengagement? Unlike some civic republicans or collectivists, liberals refuse to compel attention and energy unless the community faces clear-cut, imminent harm, preferring instead to educate the young and persuade the mature about engage-

---

[103] Of course, some types of personal technology facilitate social networking across great distances. But others, such as television, video games, and personal music players help users to hive themselves off from the diverse communities around them.

ments that might better satisfy citizens' own long-term preferences and interests (which are often tied to the public welfare).[104]

Dropping the umbrella term "*civic* engagement" allows us to see engagement itself, in its many varieties, as a defining anxiety of the modern age. We worry about engagement because we worry about attention and energy, its constituent parts. These have always been scarce resources but may seem, in recent years, to have been painfully stretched. As in earlier generations, many commitments demand our limited attention and energy: work, play, entertainment, family, school, politics, social life, hobbies, and reflection, among others.[105] But the mixed blessing of communication technology lets them now intrude en masse instead of single file, inviting us to spread our attention and energy even more thinly via multitasking. In such a milieu it seems difficult to believe that anyone would give political engagement front billing continuously, except perhaps political experts or junkies. Many of us find politics confrontational and distasteful; some of us wish that we could participate more meaningfully; and yet none of that jibes with the occasional dressing-down delivered by participatory democrats who insist that if the system were reformed we would and should flock to the agora.[106] Our common experiences indicate the diagnosis of attention deficit democracy.

I characterize the diagnosis, and attendant prescriptions, of attention deficit democracy as an accessible public philosophy: a public philosophy, insofar as it can "specify general directions for public policy within a basic understanding of how the world works"; an accessible one, insofar as its "basic understanding of how the world works" resonates with many citizens' lived experiences and reasonable antinomies.[107] I have culled that diagnosis, or basic understanding, not only from others' empirical research into citizens' attitudes and actions but also from Tocqueville's enduring insights into the same. Tocqueville speaks to our contemporary situation not because he anticipates all of democracy's changes but because he understands its constancies. He foresees that in future democracies, attention and energy will still form the lifeblood of politics or any intensive engagement; attention and energy will still be limited resources; politics will still compete—often unsuccessfully—with the myriad rewarding engagements that a free society offers (as well as the less

---

[104] To restate a point made several times already, the civic republican tradition encompasses several strands, and not all of them countenance coerced participation. The "institutional" civic republican tradition, deriving from ancient Rome and finding contemporary outlet in the works of Philip Pettit and Quentin Skinner, does not emphasize active citizenship any more than many liberal political theories.

[105] Schor (1991).

[106] Hibbing and Theiss-Morse (2002); Mutz (2006).

[107] Galston (1998: 64).

rewarding obligations that demand our daily focus). That is the baseline from which we must begin when discussing participatory democracy and the prospects for political engagement. To ignore contemporary citizens' considered misgivings about continual political engagement, or the long historical record of citizens' political inattention, would be to approach democratic theory undemocratically. We who have dedicated our careers to studying or practicing politics should not project our tastes onto the general population.

We should also resist elevating political over other kinds of engagements. Perhaps some political scientists and political theorists defend political engagement vociferously because they see its prestige as being tied to their own. That would be an unfortunate view. Nor should we expand the rubric of *the political* so that it encompasses all engagements, a move that might make politics seem more important but also makes it more difficult to study, measure, compare, and discuss. Political science and theory will not suffer if political engagement proves somewhat less essential than some have assumed. Political scientists and theorists should be studying all kinds of engagement that contribute to "making democracy work," including social, moral, and the social-moral combination of civil engagement. Aristotle called political science the "architectonic" or "highest ruling" science for its ability to unite and employ data and insights from many different fields. In that spirit, contemporary political scientists and theorists can weave nonpolitical engagements into a theory of democratic flourishing without needing to call them political in the process.[108] The goal should be to discern which types of engagement serve which kinds of societal and personal goals in a variety of settings, and how they might best be cultivated without coercion.

In closing this book on attention deficit democracy and its associated prescriptions, I do not close the book on idealistic political theory. If I am correct in asserting that attention deficit democracy comprises an accessible public philosophy, likely to appeal to many citizens once articulated, then it offers a foundation for further discussion and aspiration. Some like-minded scholars might innovate on the Tocquevillean principles that I have sketched, proposing more effective means for eliciting new political attention and energies, channeling our existing political energies more effectively, and making our existing tastes more political. Some participatory enthusiasts might still lobby for much more political engagement than I have deemed necessary, but not without providing a better defense of its importance than they have done thus far. Political and social scientists might focus on the essential building blocks of attention and energy,

---

[108] Aristotle (1985: I.2 1094a26-8).

seeking better ways to measure and understand them, better means of attracting and harnessing them.

Earlier I rejected the romantic definition according to which "democracy means paying attention."[109] In practice democracy means, and has always meant, citizens struggling to pay attention and invest energy in the business of self-government. But that realization leads us to another one: studying democracy means paying attention to attention.[110] With civic engagement gracefully retired we are free to see more clearly the multiple ways and subjects in which people invest and divest their attention and energy. Following Tocqueville, we can stop attributing inattention to vice or corruption and better understand the factors that affect citizens' choices. Following Tocqueville further, we can investigate the kinds of institutions that most effectively channel citizens' limited attention and energy toward collective action. And following Tocqueville one last time, we can undertake these inquiries with the goal of making democracy work better rather than ideally.

[109] Bellah et al. (1992: 255).

[110] This insight itself is certainly not new. As I note in chapter 1, many political scientists—although not so many political theorists—have studied the limitations of citizens' political attention and the implications for democratic politics. Cf. Popkin (1994), and Lupia and McCubbins (1998). My purpose has been to underscore to political theorists the importance of limited attention, and to political scientists the many ways beyond voting behavior that attention affects political, social, and moral engagement.

BIBLIOGRAPHY

Ackerman, Bruce A., and James S. Fishkin. 2004. *Deliberation Day*. New Haven, CT: Yale University Press.

Aldrich, John H. 1995. *Why Parties? The Origin and Transformation of Political Parties in America*. Chicago: University of Chicago Press.

Alinsky, Saul. 1969. *Reveille for Radicals*. New York: Random House.

Allen, Danielle. 2004. *Talking to Strangers: Anxieties of Citizenship since* Brown v. Board of Education. Chicago: University of Chicago Press.

Almond, Gabriel A., and Sidney Verba. 1963. *The Civic Culture: Political Attitudes and Democracy in Five Nations*. Princeton, NJ: Princeton University Press.

———. 1989. *The Civic Culture: Political Attitudes and Democracy in Five Nations*. New ed. Newbury Park, CA: Sage Publications.

Altschuler, Glenn C., and Stuart M. Blumin. 2000. *Rude Republic: Americans and Their Politics in the Nineteenth Century*. Princeton, NJ: Princeton University Press.

Andersen, Svein, and Kjell A. Eliassen. 1996. *The European Union: How Democratic Is It?* London: Sage Publications.

Annas, George J. 1995. "Sex, Money, and Bioethics: Watching *E.R.* and *Chicago Hope*." *Hastings Center Report* 25 (September–October): 40–43.

Apter, David Ernest. 1964. *Ideology and Discontent*. International Yearbook of Political Behavior Research. London: Free Press of Glencoe.

Arendt, Hannah. 1959. *The Human Condition*. Garden City, NY: Doubleday.

———. 1961. *Between Past and Future: Six Exercises in Political Thought*. New York: Viking Press.

———. 1963. *On Revolution*. New York: Viking Press.

———. 1964. *Eichmann in Jerusalem: A Report on the Banality of Evil*. Rev. and enl. ed. New York: Viking Press.

———. 1972. *Crises of the Republic: Lying in Politics; Civil Disobedience; On Violence; Thoughts on Politics and Revolution*. 1st ed. New York: Harcourt Brace Jovanovich.

———. 1973. *The Origins of Totalitarianism*. New ed. New York: Harcourt Brace Jovanovich.

———. 1978. *The Life of the Mind*. 1st ed. 2 vols. New York: Harcourt Brace Jovanovich.

———. 1993. *Men in Dark Times*. New York: Harcourt Brace.

Aristophanes. 1927. *Aristophanes' Works*. Trans. Arthur S. Way. London: Macmillan.

Aristotle. 1926. *The Art of Rhetoric*. Trans. J. H. Freese. Loeb Classical Library. Cambridge, MA: Harvard University Press.

———. 1935. *The Athenian Constitution; the Eudemian Ethics; On Virtues and Vices*. Trans. H. Rackham. Loeb Classical Library. Cambridge, MA: Harvard University Press.

Aristotle. 1966. *Metaphysics*. Trans. Hippocrates George Apostle. Bloomington: Indiana University Press.

———. 1984. *The Politics*. Trans. Carnes Lord. Chicago: University of Chicago Press.

———. 1985. *Nicomachean Ethics*. Trans. Terence Irwin. Indianapolis: Hackett.

———. 1988. *De Anima*. Trans. Robert Drew Hicks. Reprint ed. History of Ideas in Ancient Greece. Salem, NH: Ayer.

Armony, Ariel. 2004. *The Dubious Link: Civic Engagement and Democratization*. Palo Alto, CA: Stanford University Press.

Ascheim, Steven E, ed. 2001. *Hannah Arendt in Jerusalem*. Berkeley: University of California Press.

Austin, J. L. 1961. *Philosophical Papers*. Ed. J. O. Urmson and G. J. Warnock. Oxford: Clarendon Press.

Bachrach, Peter. 1967. *The Theory of Democratic Elitism: A Critique*. Basic Studies in Politics. Boston: Little, Brown.

Bacon, Francis. 1856. *The Physical and Metaphysical Works of Lord Bacon: Including His Dignity and Advancement of Learning, in Nine Books, and His Novum Organum, or, Precepts for the Interpretation of Nature*. Ed. Joseph Devey. London: H. G. Bohn.

Bandura, Albert. 1977. "Self-Efficacy: Toward a Unifying Theory of Behavioral Change." *Psychological Review* 84 (March): 191–215.

———. 1996. "Mechanisms of Moral Disengagement in the Exercise of Moral Agency." *Journal of Personality and Social Psychology* 71: 11.

Banfield, Edward. 1991. "The Illiberal Tocqueville." In *Interpreting Tocqueville's Democracy in America*. Ed. Ken Masugi. Maryland: Rowman and Littlefield.

Barber, Benjamin R. 1984. *Strong Democracy: Participatory Politics for a New Age*. Berkeley: University of California Press.

———. 1996. *Jihad vs. McWorld*. 1st Ballantine Books ed. New York: Ballantine Books.

———. 1998. *A Place for Us: How to Make Society Civil and Democracy Strong*. 1st ed. New York: Hill and Wang.

———. 2000. "The Crack in the Picture Window." *The Nation*, August 7–14.

Bartels, Larry M. 2009. "Economic Inequality and Political Representation." In *The Unsustainable American State*. Ed. Lawrence R. Jacobs and Desmond S. King. Oxford: Oxford University Press.

Bates, Vernon L. 1991. "Lobbying for the Lord: The New Christian Right Home-Schooling Movement and Grassroots Lobbying." *Review of Religious Research* 33 (September): 3–17.

Baudrillard, Jean. 1998. *The Consumer Society: Myths and Structures*. Thousand Oaks, CA: Sage Publications.

Behrens, Angela, Christopher Uggen, and Jeff Manza. 2003. "Ballot Manipulation and the 'Menace of Negro Domination': Racial Threat and Felon Disenfranchisement in the United States, 1850–2002." *American Journal of Sociology* 109: 559–605.

Bell, Daniel A. 1993. *Communitarianism and Its Critics*. Oxford: Clarendon Press.

Bellah, Robert N., Richard Madsen, William M. Sullivan, Ann Swidler, and Steven M. Tipton. 1985. *Habits of the Heart: Individualism and Commitment in American Life*. Berkeley: University of California Press.

———. 1992. *The Good Society*. New York: Vintage Press.

Benhabib, Seyla. 1990. "Hannah Arendt and the Redemptive Power of Narrative." *Social Research* 57, no. 1: 30.

———. 1994. "Hannah Arendt and the Redemptive Power of Narrative." In *Hannah Arendt: Critical Essays*. Ed. Lewis and Sandra Hinchman. Albany: State University of New York Press.

Berger, Benjamin. 2010. "Neorepublicanism." *Encyclopedia of Political Theory*. Thousand Oaks, CA: Sage Publications.

Berkowitz, Peter. 1999. *Virtue and the Making of Modern Liberalism*. New Forum Books. Princeton, NJ: Princeton University Press.

Berman, Sheri. 1997. "Civil Society and the Collapse of the Weimar Republic." *World Politics* 47 (April): 30.

Bermeo, Nancy. 2003. *Ordinary People in Extraordinary Times: The Citizenry and the Breakdown of Democracy*. Princeton, NJ: Princeton University Press.

Billig, Michael. 1995. "Imagining Nationhood." In *Social Movements and Culture*. Ed. Hank Johnston and Bert Klandermans. Minneapolis: University of Minneapolis Press.

———. 1996. *Arguing and Thinking: A Rhetorical Approach to Social Psychology*. Cambridge: Cambridge University Press.

Blondel, Jean, R. Sinnott, and Palle Svensson. 1998. *People and Parliament in the European Union: Participation, Democracy, and Legitimacy*. Oxford: Clarendon Press; New York: Oxford University Press.

Boehlert, Eric. 2004. "Rush's Forced Conscripts," Salon.com, May 26, http://dir.salon.com/story/news/feature/2004/05/26/rush_limbaugh/.

Bohman, James. 1996. *Public Deliberation: Pluralism, Complexity, and Democracy*. Studies in Contemporary German Social Thought. Cambridge, MA: MIT Press.

Bowler, Shaun, Todd Donovan, and Robert Hanneman. 2003. "Art for Democracy's Sake? Group Membership and Political Engagement in Europe." *Journal of Politics* 65 (November): 19.

Bowman, James. 1999. "Postmodern Journalism." *World and I* 14 (May): 310.

Brady, Henry E., Kay Lehman Schlozman, and Sidney Verba. 1999. "Prospecting for Participants: Rational Expectations and the Recruitment of Political Activists." *American Political Science Review* 93 (March): 153–68.

Bratton, Michael. 1999. "Political Participation in a New Democracy." *Comparative Political Studies* (August): 42.

Brock, David. 2004. *The Republican Noise Machine: Right Wing Media and How It Corrupts Democracy*. New York: Random House.

Brooks, Arthur C. 2005. "Does Social Capital Make You Generous?" *Social Science Quarterly* 86 (March): 15.

Buber, Martin. 1970. *Paths in Utopia*. Boston: Beacon Press.

Buckley, William F. 1996. "Get Out the Hip-Hop Vote." *National Review* (October 14).

Callan, Eamonn. 1997. *Creating Citizens: Political Education and Liberal Democracy*. Oxford Political Theory. Oxford: Clarendon Press; New York: Oxford University Press.

Canovan, Margaret. 1992. *Hannah Arendt: A Reinterpretation of Her Political Thought*. New York: Cambridge University Press.

———. 1994. "Politics as High Culture." In *Hannah Arendt: Critical Essays*. Ed. Lewis and Sandra Hinchman. Albany: State University of New York Press.

Caplan, Bryan. 2007. *The Myth of the Rational Voter: Why Democracies Choose Bad Policies*. Princeton, NJ: Princeton University Press.

Chambers, Simone, and Jeffrey Kopstein. 2001. "Bad Civil Society." *Political Theory* 29, no. 6: 29.

Chesterton, G. K. 1909. *Orthodoxy*. New York: John Lane.

Chrislip, David D. 1994. "American Renewal: Reconnecting Citizens with Public Life." *National Civic Review* 83 (Winter): 25–31.

Christiano, Thomas. 1996. "Is the Participation Argument Self-Defeating?" *Philosophical Studies* 82 (April): 1–12.

———. 1997. "The Significance of Public Deliberation." In *Deliberative Democracy: Essays on Reason and Politics*. Ed. James Bohman and William Rehg, 243–78. Cambridge, MA: MIT Press.

Cohen, Asher, and Hagit Magen. 2005. "Hierarchical Systems of Attention and Action." In *Attention in Action: Advances from Cognitive Neuroscience*. Ed. Glyn W. Humphreys and M. Jane Riddoch. New York: Psychology Press.

Cohen, Jean L., and Andrew Arato. 1992. *Civil Society and Political Theory*. Studies in Contemporary German Social Thought. Cambridge, MA: MIT Press.

Cohen, Joshua. 1989. "Deliberation and Democratic Legitimacy." In *The Good Polity*. Ed. Alan Hamlin and Philip Pettit. Oxford: Basil Blackwell.

Coleman, James Samuel. 1990. *Foundations of Social Theory*. Cambridge, MA: Belknap Press of Harvard University Press.

Coleman, James Samuel, and Thomas J. Fararo, eds. 1992. *Rational Choice Theory: Advocacy and Critique*. Key Issues in Sociological Theory. Newbury Park, CA: Sage Publications.

Collier, David, and James E. Mahon Jr. 1993. "Conceptual Stretching Revisited: Adapting Categories in Comparative Analysis." *American Political Science Review* 87 (December): 11.

Connolly, Gerald E. 2006. "Many Residents and One Book: An Invitation to Share." *Washington Post*, June 8.

Converse, Philip. 1964. "The Nature of Belief Systems in Mass Publics." In *Ideology and Discontent*. Ed. David E. Apter, 206–61. London: Free Press of Glencoe.

Cooper, Mary H. 2000. "Low Voter Turnout: Is America's Democracy in Trouble?" *CQ Researcher*: 10–36.

Cooper, Bruce S., and John Sureau. 2007. "The Politics of Homeschooling: New Developments, New Challenges." *Education Policy* 21 (January): 110–31.

Craiutu, Aurelian. 2005. "Tocqueville's Paradoxical Moderation." *Review of Politics* 67 (Autumn): 599–629.

Craiutu, Aurelian, and Jeremy Jennings. 2004. "The Third Democracy: Tocqueville's Views of America after 1840." *American Political Science Review* 98 (August): 391–404.

Csikszentmihalyi, Mihaly. 1991. *Flow: The Psychology of Optimal Experience.* New York: HarperPerennial.

Dagger, Richard. 1997. *Civic Virtues: Rights, Citizenship, and Republican Liberalism.* New York: Oxford University Press.

Dahl, Robert Alan. 1961. *Who Governs? Democracy and Power in an American City.* Yale Studies in Political Science. New Haven, CT: Yale University Press.

———. 1989. *Democracy and Its Critics.* New Haven, CT: Yale University Press.

Damon, William. 1988. "Political Development for a Democratic Future: A Commentary." *Journal of Social Issues* 54, no. 3: 621–27.

Day, Nancy. 1995. "Our Separate Ways." *People,* September 25, 125–27.

Derrida, Jacques. *Dissemination.* 1983. Trans. Barbara Johnson. Chicago: University of Chicago Press.

Descartes, René. 1970. *Descartes: Philosophical Letters.* Trans. Anthony Kenny. Oxford: Oxford University Press.

Dewey, John. 1921. *Democracy and Education: An Introduction to the Philosophy of Education.* New York: Macmillan.

———. 1927. *The Public and Its Problems.* New York: H. Holt.

———. 1935. *Liberalism and Social Action.* New York: Putnam.

Dietz, Mary. 2000. "Arendt and the Holocaust." In *The Cambridge Companion to Hannah Arendt.* Ed. Dana Villa. Cambridge: Cambridge University Press.

Domínguez, Jorge I. 1997. *Technopols: Freeing Politics and Markets in Latin America in the 1990s.* University Park: Pennsylvania State University Press.

Dossa, Shiraz. 1989. *Public Realm and the Public Self: The Political Theory of Hannah Arendt.* Waterloo, ON: Wilfrid Laurier University Press.

Dovi, Suzanne. 2002. "Preferable Descriptive Representatives: Will Just Any Woman, Black, or Latino Do?" *American Political Science Review* 96 (December): 729–43.

Dunning, John. 1998. *On the Air: The Encyclopedia of Old-Time Radio.* New York: Oxford University Press.

Durkheim, Émile. 1951. *Suicide: A Study in Sociology.* Glencoe, IL: Free Press.

Dworkin, Ronald. 1977. *Taking Rights Seriously.* Cambridge, MA: Harvard University Press.

Ehrenhalt, Alan. 1995. *The Lost City: Discovering the Forgotten Virtues of Community in the Chicago of the 1950s.* New York: Basic Books.

Elazar, Daniel. "Tocqueville and the Cultural Basis of American Democracy." *Political Science and Politics* (June 1): 4.

Elshtain, Jean Bethke. 1999. "A Call to Civil Society." *Society* 36 (July/August): 9.

Elster, Jon. 1983. *Sour Grapes: Studies in the Subversion of Rationality.* Cambridge: Cambridge University Press.

———. 2009. *Alexis de Tocqueville, the First Social Scientist.* Cambridge: Cambridge University Press.

Etzioni, Amitai. 1993. *The Spirit of Community: Rights, Responsibilities, and the Communitarian Agenda.* 1st ed. New York: Crown.

Fallows, James. 2010. "How America Can Rise Again." *Atlantic* (January/February), http://www.theatlantic.com/doc/201001/american-decline.

Feinberg, Joel. 1990. *Harmless Wrongdoing*. The Moral Limits of the Criminal Law, vol. 4. New York: Oxford University Press.

Finkel, Steven E. 1985. "Reciprocal Effects of Participation and Political Efficacy: A Panel Analysis." *American Journal of Political Science* 29 (November): 891–913.

———. 1987. "The Effects of Participation on Political Efficacy and Political Support: Evidence from a West German Panel." *Journal of Politics* 49: 441–64.

Fishkin, James S. 1991. *Democracy and Deliberation: New Directions for Democratic Reform*. New Haven, CT: Yale University Press.

———. 1997. *The Voice of the People: Public Opinion and Democracy*. New Haven, CT: Yale University Press.

Fishkin, James S., and Robert Luskin. 2005. "Experimenting with a Democratic Ideal: Deliberative Polling and Public Opinion." *Acta Politica* 40: 284–98.

Foley, Michael W., and Bob Edwards. 1996. "The Paradox of Civil Society." *Journal of Democracy* 7 (July 7): 15.

Foot, Kirsten A., Steven M. Schneider, Michael Xenos, and Meghan Dougherty. 2003. "Opportunities for Civic Engagement on Campaign Sites." *Political Web. Info*. Ed. Kirsten A. Foot and Steven M. Schneider, March 4, http://politicalweb.info/reports/engagement.html.

Foucault, Michel. 1977. *Discipline and Punish: The Birth of the Prison*. 1st U.S. ed. New York: Pantheon Books.

Franken, Al. 1999. *Rush Limbaugh Is a Big Fat Idiot*. New York: Dell.

Frankena, William K. 1973. *Ethics*. 2nd ed. Englewood Cliffs, NJ: Prentice-Hall.

Franklin, Benjamin. 1996. *The Autobiography of Benjamin Franklin*. Mineola, NY: Dover Publications.

Freie, John F. 1998. *Counterfeit Community: The Exploitation of Our Longings for Connectedness*. Lanham, MD: Rowman and Littlefield.

Frey, B. S., and A. Stutzer. 2000. "Happiness Prospers in Democracy." *Journal of Happiness Studies* 1: 79–102.

———. 2005. "Beyond Outcomes: Measuring Procedural Utility." *Oxford Economic Papers* 57: 90–111.

Fukuyama, Francis. 1995. *Trust: Social Virtues and the Creation of Prosperity*. New York: Free Press.

Fung, Archon. 2006. *Empowered Participation: Reinventing Urban Democracy*. Princeton, NJ: Princeton University Press.

Gabardi, Wayne. 2001. "Contemporary Models of Democracy." *Polity* 33, no. 1: 17.

Galston, William. 1991. *Liberal Purposes: Goods, Virtues, and Diversity in the Liberal State*. Cambridge Studies in Philosophy and Public Policy. Cambridge; New York: Cambridge University Press.

———. 1997. "America's Civic Condition: A Glance at the Evidence." *Brookings Review* (Fall): 4.

———. 1998. "Political Economy and the Politics of Virtue: U.S. Public Philosophy at Century's End." In *Debating Democracy's Discontent: Essays on Ameri-*

can Politics, Law, and Public Philosophy. Ed. Anita L. Allen and Milton C. Regan. Oxford: Oxford University Press.

Gamm, Gerald, and Robert Putnam. 1999. "The Growth of Voluntary Associations in America." *Journal of Interdisciplinary History* 29 (Spring): 511–58.

Gans, Curtis. 1992. "Turnout Tribulations." *Journal of State Government* 65, no. 1: 3.

Ganz, Marshall. 1994. "Voters in the Crosshairs: How Technology and the Market Are Destroying Politics." *American Prospect* (Winter): 10.

Gastil, John, E. Pierre Deess, Philip J. Weiser, and Cindy Simmons. 2010. *The Jury and Democracy: How Jury Deliberation Promotes Civic Engagement and Political Participation*. New York: Oxford University Press.

Gastil, John, and Peter Levine, eds. 2005. *The Deliberative Democracy Handbook: Strategies for Effective Civic Engagement in the Twenty-First Century*. San Francisco: Jossey-Bass.

Geertz, Clifford. 1973. *The Interpretation of Cultures*. New York: Basic Books.

Geis, Karlyn, and Catherine E. Ross. 1997. "A New Look at Urban Alienation: The Effect of Neighborhood Disorder on Perceived Powerlessness." *Communication Theory* 7, no. 4: 232–46.

Gerring, John. 1999. "What Makes a Concept Good?" *Polity* 31 (Spring): 37.

Glazer, Nathan. 2000. "Tocqueville and Riesman." *Society* (May–June): 7.

Gottsegen, Michael C. 1994. *The Political Thought of Hannah Arendt*. Albany: State University of New York Press.

Gough, Austin. 1994. "Democracy's Undoing: Centralism and Separatism." *IPA Review* 47, no. 1: 35–36.

Greene, Graham. 1956. *The Quiet American*. New York: Viking Press.

Gross, Donald August, and Robert K. Goidel. *The States of Campaign Finance Reform*. Columbus: Ohio State University Press, 2003.

Guest, Stephen. 2002. "The Value of Art." *Art, Antiquity, and Law* 7, no. 4: 305–16.

Gutmann, Amy. 1987. *Democratic Education*. Princeton, NJ: Princeton University Press.

———. 1998. *Freedom of Association*. The University Center for Human Values Series. Princeton, NJ: Princeton University Press.

Gutmann, Amy, and Dennis F. Thompson. 1996. *Democracy and Disagreement*. Cambridge, MA: Belknap Press of Harvard University Press.

———. 2004. *Why Deliberative Democracy?* Princeton, NJ: Princeton University Press.

Habermas, Jürgen. 1984a. *The Theory of Communicative Action*. Trans. Thomas McCarthy. Vol. 1. Boston: Beacon Press.

———. 1984b. *The Theory of Communicative Action*. Trans. Thomas McCarthy. Vol. 2. Boston: Beacon Press.

———. 1988. *Legitimation Crisis*. Trans. Thomas McCarthy. Cambridge: Polity Press.

Hamilton, Alexander, James Madison, and John Jay. 1999. *The Federalist Papers*. Ed. Clinton L. Rossiter. New York: Mentor.

Hansen, Mogens Herman. 1987. *The Athenian Assembly in the Age of Demosthenes*. Oxford: Blackwell.

Hartog, Joseph, J. Ralph Audy, and Yehudi A. Cohen. 1980. *The Anatomy of Loneliness*. New York: International Universities Press.

Havel, Václav. 1991. *Open Letters: Selected Prose, 1965–1990*. London: Faber.

Havel, Václav, et al. 1990. *The Power of the Powerless: Citizens against the State in Central-Eastern Europe*: Armonk, NY: M. E. Sharpe.

Hayes, Emilie. 2006. *Community Service Learning: Annotated Bibliography*. Ed. Christa King. Calgary, AB: Max Bell Foundation.

Hayward, Jack. 1996. *The Crisis of Representation in Europe*. New York: Routledge.

Held, David. 1980. *Introduction to Critical Theory: Horkheimer to Habermas*. Berkeley: University of California Press.

Henderson, Alisa, Steven D. Brown, S. Mark Pancer, and Kimberly Ellis-Hale. 2007. "Mandated Community Service in High School and Subsequent Civic Engagement: The Case of the 'Double Cohort' in Ontario, Canada." *Journal of Youth and Adolescence* 36 (October).

Hertz, Joseph H. 1945. *Sayings of the Fathers, or, Pirke Aboth*. New York: Behrman House.

Hibbing, John R., and Elizabeth Thiess-Morse. 2002. *Stealth Democracy: Americans' Beliefs about How Democracy Should Work*. Cambridge: Cambridge University Press.

Hobbes, Thomas. 1996. *Leviathan*. Trans. Richard Tuck. Cambridge: Cambridge University Press.

Holliday, Ian. 1994. "Democracy and Democratization in Great Britain." In *Democracy and Democratization*. Ed. Geraint Parry and Michael Moran. New York: Routledge.

Honohan, Iseult. 2002. *Civic Republicanism*. The Problems of Philosophy. London; New York: Routledge.

Hont, Istvan, and Michael Ignatieff. 1983. *Wealth and Virtue: The Shaping of Political Economy in the Scottish Enlightenment*. Cambridge; New York: Cambridge University Press.

Hortulanus, R. P., Anja Machielse, and Ludwien Meeuwesen. 2006. *Social Isolation in Modern Society*. Routledge Advances in Sociology. London; New York: Routledge.

House, J. S., K. R. Landis, and D. Umberson. 1988. "Social Relationships and Health." *Science* 241: 540–45.

Huntington, Samuel P. 1981. *American Politics: The Promise of Disharmony*. Cambridge, MA: Harvard University Press.

Incite! Women of Color Against Violence, ed. 2007. *The Revolution Will Not Be Funded: Beyond the Non-Profit Industrial Complex*. Cambridge, MA: South End Press.

Isaac, Jeffrey. 1992. *Arendt, Camus, and Modern Rebellion*. New Haven, CT: Yale University Press.

James, William. 1890. *The Principles of Psychology*. 2 vols. New York: H. Holt.

———. 1899. *Talks to Teachers on Psychology: And to Students on Some of Life's Ideals*. New York: H. Holt.

Jamieson, Kathleen Hall, and Joseph N. Capella. 2008. *Echo Chamber: Rush Limbaugh and the Conservative Media Establishment*. Oxford: Oxford University Press.

Jefferson, Thomas. 1903. *The Writings of Thomas Jefferson*. Ed. Andrew Adgate Lipscomb, Albert Ellery Bergh, and Richard Holland Johnston. Comp. Thomas Jefferson Memorial Association of the United States. Washington, DC: Issued under the auspices of the Thomas Jefferson Memorial Association of the United States.

Johanek, Michael C., and John Puckett. 2005. "The State of Civic Education: Preparing Students in an Era of Accountability." In *The Public Schools*. Ed. Susan Fuhrman and Marvin Lazerson. Oxford: Oxford University Press.

Johnston, Hank, and Bert Klandermans. 1995. *Social Movements and Culture*. Minneapolis: University of Minnesota Press.

Jonakait, Randolph. 2006. *The American Jury System*. New Haven, CT: Yale University Press.

Jones, Jeffrey P. 2005. *Entertaining Politics: New Political Television and Civic Culture*. Communication, Media, and Politics. Lanham, MD: Rowman and Littlefield.

Judis, John B. 1997. "Below the Beltway: Goo-Goos vs. Populists." *American Prospect* 30 (January/February): 12–14.

Kahan, Alan S. 1992. *Aristocratic Liberalism: The Social and Political Thought of Jacob Burckhardt, John Stuart Mill, and Alexis de Tocqueville*. New York: Oxford University Press.

Kahne, Joseph, and Ellen Middaugh. 2008. CIRCLE Working Paper 59: "Democracy for Some—The Civic Opportunity Gap in High School." February.

Kant, Immanuel. 1952. *Critique of Judgment*. Ed. James Creed Meredith. Oxford: Oxford University Press.

———. 1991. *Kant: Political Writings*. Ed. Hans Siegbert Reiss. 2nd enl. ed. Cambridge Texts in the History of Political Thought. Cambridge; New York: Cambridge University Press.

———. 1993. *Grounding for the Metaphysics of Morals; with, on a Supposed Right to Lie Because of Philanthropic Concerns*. Ed. James W. Ellington. 3rd ed. Indianapolis: Hackett.

Kateb, George. 1983. *Hannah Arendt, Politics, Conscience, Evil*. Totowa, NJ: Rowman and Allanheld.

———. 1992. *The Inner Ocean: Individualism and Democratic Culture*. Contestations. Ithaca, NY: Cornell University Press.

———. 2000. "Political Action: Its Nature and Advantages." In *The Cambridge Companion to Hannah Arendt*. Ed. Dana Villa. Cambridge: Cambridge University Press.

Katz, Jon. 1997. "The Digital Citizen." *Wired* 5 (December).

Kaufman, Arnold S. 1968. *The Radical Liberal, New Man in American Politics*. New York: Atherton Press.

———. 1969. "Human Nature and Participatory Democracy." In *The Bias of Pluralism*. Ed. William Connolly. New York: Atherton Press.

Kavanaugh, Patrick. 2003. "Rumors Greatly Exaggerated." *National Review* 55, June 30.

Kennedy-Shaffer, Alan. 2009. *The Obama Revolution*. Beverly Hills: Phoenix Books.

Kent, Willys P. 1917. "Why Study Music Appreciation? A Talk to High School Pupils." *Music Supervisors' Journal* 4, no. 1.

Kerbel, Matthew Robert. 2002. "Political Parties in the Media: Where Elephants and Donkeys Are Pigs." In *The Parties Respond: Changes in American Parties and Campaigns*. Ed. Louis Sandy Maisel. Boulder, CO: Westview Press.

Kessler, Sanford. 1994. *Tocqueville's Civil Religion: American Christianity and the Prospects for Freedom*. Albany: State University of New York Press.

Ketcham, Ralph Louis. 2003. *The Anti-Federalist Papers and the Constitutional Convention Debates*. New York: Signet Classic.

Keyes, Ralph. 1973. *We, the Lonely People; Searching for Community*. 1st ed. New York: Harper and Row.

King, Martin Luther, Jr. 1963. *Letter from a Birmingham City Jail*. Philadelphia: American Friends Service Committee.

———. 1967. *Where Do We Go from Here: Chaos or Community?* 1st ed. New York: Harper and Row.

Kohli, Atul. 1990. *Democracy and Discontent: India's Growing Crisis of Governability*. Cambridge; New York: Cambridge University Press.

Kornhauser, William. 1959. *The Politics of Mass Society*. Glencoe, IL: Free Press.

Korsgaard, Christine M. 1996. *Creating the Kingdom of Ends*. Cambridge: Cambridge University Press.

Krygier, Martin. 2005. *Civil Passions: Selected Writings*. Melbourne: Schwartz Publishing.

Kuklinski, James H., and Paul J. Quirk. 2000. "Reconsidering the Rational Public: Cognition, Heuristics, and Mass Opinion." In *Elements of Reason*. Ed. Arthur Lupia, Mathew McCubbins, and Samuel Popkin. Cambridge: Cambridge University Press.

Ladd, Carl Everett. 1999a. "The American Way: Civic Engagement Thrives." *Christian Science Monitor*, March 1.

———. 1999b. *The Ladd Report*. New York: Free Press.

Lasch, Christopher. 1977. *Haven in a Heartless World: The Family Besieged*. New York: Basic Books.

Leib, Ethan J. 2005. *Deliberative Democracy in America: A Proposal for a Popular Branch of Government*. University Park: Pennsylvania State University Press.

Leiby, Richard. 2004. "Alice Cooper's Political Makeup." *Washington Post*, August 24, C03.

Leighninger, Matt. 2002. "Enlisting Citizens: Building Political Legitimacy." *National Civic Review*, 91: 137–48.

Levine, Peter. 2007. *The Future of Democracy: Developing the Next Generation of American Citizens*. Medford, MA: Tufts University Press.

Levinger, Beryl, and Jean Mulroy. 2003. "Making a Little Go a Long Way: How the World Bank's Small Grants Program Promotes Civic Engagement." In *So-

cial Development Papers: Participation and Civic Engagement. World Bank (September).

Levinson, Arlene. 2000. "High School Seniors Bored, Worry about Loans." *AP Online* (January).

Li, Hongyi, Lyn Squire, and Heng-fu Zou. 1998. "Explaining International and Intertemporal Variations in Income Inequality." *Review of Development Economics* 2 (October): 318–34.

Lijphart, Arend. 1997. "Unequal Participation: Democracy's Unresolved Dilemma." *American Political Science Review* 91, no. 1: 1–14.

Linnenbrink, E. A., and P. R. Pintrich. 2003. "The Role of Self-Efficacy Beliefs in Student Engagement and Learning in the Classroom." *Reading and Writing Quarterly* 19 (April): 119–37.

Lippmann, Walter. 1925. *The Phantom Public.* New York: Harcourt, Brace.

———. 1929. *Public Opinion.* New York: Macmillan.

Lloyd, Margie. 1995. "In Tocqueville's Shadow: Hannah Arendt's Liberal Republicanism." *Review of Politics* 57 (Winter).

Lukes, Steven. 1977. *Essays in Social Theory.* New York: Columbia University Press.

———. 1998. "The Responsive Community." *Dissent* (Spring): 87–89.

Lupia, Arthur, and Mathew D. McCubbins. 1998. *The Democratic Dilemma: Can Citizens Learn What They Really Need to Know?* Political Economy of Institutions and Decisions. Cambridge; New York: Cambridge University Press.

Lyon, David. 1994. *The Electronic Eye: The Rise of Surveillance Society.* Minneapolis: University of Minneapolis Press.

Macedo, Stephen. 1990. *Liberal Virtues: Citizenship, Virtue, and Community in Liberal Constitutionalism.* Oxford: Oxford University Press.

Macedo, Stephen, et al. 2005. *Democracy at Risk: How Political Choices Undermine Citizen Participation and What We Can Do about It.* Washington, DC: Brookings Institution Press.

Machiavelli, Niccolo. 1984. *The Discourses.* Trans. Leslie J. Walker and Bernard Crick. New York: Penguin Classics.

Madison, James. 1962. *Papers.* Ed. William Thomas Hutchinson and William M. E. Rachal. Chicago: University of Chicago Press.

Maiello, Carmine, Fritz Oser, and Horst Biedermann. 2003. "Civic Knowledge, Civic Skills, and Civic Engagement." *European Educational Research Journal* 2, no. 3: 384–95.

Maimonides, Moses, Moses Hyamson, and Bodleian Library. 1962. *Mishneh Torah: The Book of Knowledge.* Jerusalem; New York: Feldheim Publishers.

Manent, Pierre. 1998. "Democratic Man, Aristocratic Man, and Man: Simply Some Remarks on an Equivocation in Tocqueville's Thought." Trans. Daniel J. Mahoney and Paul Seaton. *Perspectives on Political Science* 27, no. 2.

Mansbridge, Jane J. 1980. *Beyond Adversary Democracy.* New York: Basic Books.

———. 1999. "On the Idea That Participation Makes Better Citizens." In *Citizen Competence and Democratic Institutions.* Ed. Stephen L. Elkin and Karol Soltan. University Park: Pennsylvania State University Press.

Mansfield, Harvey Claflin. 1991. *America's Constitutional Soul*. The Johns Hopkins Series in Constitutional Thought. Baltimore: Johns Hopkins University Press.

Manza, Jeff, and Christopher Uggen. 2004. "Punishment and Democracy: The Disenfranchisement of Nonincarcerated Felons in the United States." *Perspectives on Politics* 2: 491–505.

———. 2006. *Locked Out: Felon Disenfranchisement and American Democracy*. New York: Oxford University Press.

Marcus, George E., and Michael B. MacKuen. 1993. "Anxiety, Enthusiasm, and the Vote: The Emotional Underpinnings of Learning and Involvement during Presidential Campaigns." *American Political Science Review* 87 (September): 672–85.

Marsh, H. W., and S. Kleitman. 2003. "School Athletic Participation: Mostly Gain with Little Pain." *Journal of Sport and Exercise Psychology* 25: 205–28.

Martin, Thomas R. 2000. *Ancient Greece: From Prehistoric to Hellenistic Times*. New Haven, CT: Yale University Press.

Marx, Karl, and Friedrich Engels. 1978. *The Marx-Engels Reader*. Trans. Robert C. Tucker. 2nd ed. New York: Norton.

Masugi, Ken, ed. 1991. *Interpreting Tocqueville's* Democracy in America. Lanham, MD: Rowman and Littlefield.

Maynor, John. 2002. "Another Instrumental Republican Approach?" *European Journal of Political Theory* 1, no. 1: 71–89.

McAllister, Ian. 1998. "Civic Education and Political Education in Australia." *Australian Journal of Political Science* 33, no. 7.

McEachern, William A. 1996. "Economist as Movie Hero?" *Teaching Economist* 12 (Fall).

McGann, James, and Mary Johnstone. 2006. "The Power Shift and the NGO Credibility Crisis." *International Journal of Not-for-Profit Law* 6 (January).

McLuhan, Eric, and Frank Zingrone. 1995. *The Essential McLuhan*. Ed. Marshall McLuhan. New York: Basic Books.

McLuhan, Marshall. 1962. *The Gutenberg Galaxy: The Making of Typographic Man*. Toronto: University of Toronto Press.

McLuhan, Marshall, and Eric McLuhan. 1988. *Laws of Media: The New Science*. Toronto; Buffalo, NY: University of Toronto.

Melvin, Ann. 1996. "Television Brought Civic Disengagement." *Dallas Morning Star*, March 9.

Menant, Pierre. 1998. "Democratic Man, Aristocratic Man, and Man Simply." *Perspectives on Political Science* 27 (Spring): 6.

Merton, Robert King. 1957. *Social Theory and Social Structure*. Rev. and enl. ed. Glencoe, IL: Free Press.

Metz, E., and J. Youniss,. 2003. "A Demonstration That School-Based Required Service Does Not Deter—but Heightens—Volunteerism." *PS: Political Science and Politics* 36: 281–86.

Meyers, Peter Alexander. 2008. *Civic War and the Corruption of the Citizen*. Chicago: University of Chicago Press.

Meyrowitz, Joshua. 1985. *No Sense of Place: The Impact of Electronic Media on Social Behavior*. New York: Oxford University Press.

Mill, John Stuart. 1978. *On Liberty*. Ed. Elizabeth Rapaport. Indianapolis: Hackett.

Miller, David. 1995. *On Nationality*. Oxford Political Theory. Oxford: Clarendon Press.

Miller, Jeffrey. 1979. "The Pathos of Novelty: Hannah Arendt's Image of Freedom in the Modern World." In *Hannah Arendt: The Recovery of the Public World*. Ed. Melvyn A. Hill. New York: St. Martin's Press.

Mindich, David T. Z. 2005. *Tuned Out: Why Americans under 40 Don't Follow the News*. Oxford: Oxford University Press.

Mishnayot. 1963. Vol. 4. Ed. Philip Blackman. New York: Judaica Press.

Mitchell, Joshua. 1995. *The Fragility of Freedom: Tocqueville on Religion, Democracy, and the American Future*. Chicago: University of Chicago Press.

Moeller, Susan D. 1999. *Compassion Fatigue: How the Media Sell Disease, Famine, War, and Death*. New York: Routledge.

Mutz, Diana. 2002. "The Consequences of Cross-Cutting Networks for Political Participation." *American Journal of Political Science* 46 (October).

———. 2006. *Hearing the Other Side: Deliberative versus Participatory Democracy*. Cambridge: Cambridge University Press.

Nagle, D. Brendan. 2006. *The Household as the Foundation of Aristotle's Polis*. Cambridge: Cambridge University Press.

National Commission on Civic Renewal. 1997. "Final Report." Edited by executive director William Galston. College Park, MD.

National Commission on Philanthropy and Civic Renewal. 1998. Washington DC: Hudson Institute.

"The Nation's Index of Civic Engagement." 1998. National Commission on Philanthropy and Civic Renewal. Washington DC: Hudson Institute.

Neale, Robert E. 1984. *Loneliness, Solitude, and Companionship*. Philadelphia: Westminster Press.

Nicholson, Stephen P. 2003. "The Political Environment and Ballot Proposition Awareness." *American Journal of Political Science* 47 (July): 8.

Norris, Pippa. 2005. Democracy Indicators Cross-National Time-Series Dataset. Cambridge, MA: Harvard's Kennedy School of Government.

Nozick, Robert. 1974. *Anarchy, State, and Utopia*. New York: Basic Books.

Nussbaum, Martha. 1992. "Human Functioning and Social Justice: In Defense of Aristotelian Essentialism." *Political Theory* 20 (May): 45.

Ober, Josiah. 1991. *Mass and Elite in Democratic Athens: Rhetoric, Ideology, and the Power of the People*. Princeton, NJ: Princeton University Press.

Oldenburg, Ray. 2001. *Celebrating the Third Place: Inspiring Stories about The "Great Good Places" at the Heart of Our Communities*. New York: Marlowe.

Oldenquist, Andrew, and Menahem Rosner. 1991. *Alienation, Community, and Work*. New York: Greenwood Press.

Ossewaarde, M.R.R. 2004. *Tocqueville's Political and Moral Thought: New Liberalism*. New York: Routledge.

Parfit, Derek. 1997. "Equality and Priority." *Ratio* 10 (December).

Partridge, D. 1985. "After the First 100 Days." *Queensland Courier Mail*, July 23.

Passerin d'Entrèves, Maurizio. 1993. *The Political Philosophy of Hannah Arendt.* New York: Routledge.

Pateman, Carole. 1970. *Participation and Democratic Theory.* Cambridge: University Press.

———. 1988. *The Sexual Contract.* Stanford, CA: Stanford University Press.

Pettit, Philip. 1997. *Republicanism: A Theory of Freedom and Government.* Oxford Political Theory. Oxford: Clarendon Press.

Pharr, Susan J., and Robert D. Putnam. 2000. *Disaffected Democracies: What's Troubling the Trilateral Countries?* Princeton, NJ: Princeton University Press.

Pierce, Neal. 2007. "The 'Humane Metropolis': Are We Ready?" *Nation's Cities Weekly,* April 2, 2.

Pilley, Kevin. 1992. "First Night of the Prom, Prom, Proms." *The Guardian,* May 25.

Pitkin, Hanna Fenichel. 1967. *The Concept of Representation.* Berkeley: University of California Press.

———. 1981. "Justice: On Relating Private and Public." *Political Theory* 9, no. 3: 26.

———. 1998. *The Attack of the Blob: Hannah Arendt's Concept of the Social.* Chicago: University of Chicago Press.

Piven, Frances Fox, and Richard A. Clowerd. 1966. "The Weight of the Poor: A Strategy to End Poverty." *The Nation* (May 2): 510.

———. 1977. *Poor People's Movements: Why They Succeed, How They Fail.* New York: Pantheon Books.

Plato. 1991. *The Republic of Plato.* Trans. Allan Bloom. 2nd ed. New York: Basic Books.

Pocock, J.G.A. 1975. *The Machiavellian Moment.* Princeton, NJ: Princeton University Press.

Pole, J. R. 1993. "Reflections on American Law and the American Revolution." *William and Mary Quarterly,* Law and Society in Early America, 3rd series, 50, no. 1, 123–59.

Popkin, Samuel. 1994. *The Reasoning Voter: Communication and Persuasion in Presidential Campaigns.* 2nd ed. Chicago: University of Chicago Press.

Posner, Richard A. 2003. *Law, Pragmatism, and Democracy.* Cambridge, MA: Harvard University Press.

Prochaska, J. J., J. F. Sallis, D. J. Slymen, and T. L. McKenzie. 2003. "A Longitudinal Study of Children's Enjoyment of Physical Education." *Pediatric Exercise Science* 15: 170–78.

Przeworski, Adam, Michael E. Alvarez, Jose Antonio Cheibub, and Fernando Limongi. 2000. *Democracy and Development: Political Institutions and Well-Being in the World, 1950–1990.* Cambridge: Cambridge University Press.

Putnam, Robert. 1993. "The Prosperous Community: Social Capital and Public Life." *American Prospect* 13 (Spring): 35–42.

———. 1995. "Bowling Alone: America's Declining Social Capital." *Journal of Democracy* 6: 65–78.

———. 1996. "The Strange Disappearance of Civic America." *American Prospect* (Winter).

———. 2000. *Bowling Alone: The Collapse and Revival of American Community*. New York: Simon and Schuster.

Putnam, Robert, with Robert Leonardi and Raffaella Nanetti. 1993. *Making Democracy Work: Civic Traditions in Modern Italy*. Princeton, NJ: Princeton University Press.

Ravitch, Diane, and Joseph P. Vitteri, eds. 2001. *Making Good Citizens: Education and Civil Society*. New Haven, CT: Yale University Press.

Rawls, John. 1971. *A Theory of Justice*. Cambridge, MA: Belknap Press of Harvard University Press.

Reinhart, Mark. 1997. *The Art of Being Free: Taking Liberties with Marx, Tocqueville, and Arendt*. Ithaca, NY: Cornell University Press.

Rhoads, Robert. 1997. *Community Service and Higher Learning: Explorations of the Caring Self*. Albany: State University of New York Press.

———. 2003. "How Civic Engagement Is Reframing Liberal Education." *Peer Review* (Spring): 25–28.

Riesman, David. 1950. *The Lonely Crowd: A Study of the Changing American Character*. New Haven, CT: Yale University Press.

Roach, Jack L., and Janet K. Roach. 1978. "Mobilizing the Poor: Road to a Dead End." *Social Problems* 26 (December): 160–71.

———. 1980. "Turmoil in Command of Politics: Organizing the Poor." *Sociological Quarterly* 21, no. 2: 259–70.

Roark, Eric. 2004. "Tocqueville's Fix: Solving the Problem of Democracy with Enlightened Self-Interest." *Studies in Social and Political Thought* 10: 19–38.

Rosenblatt, Susannah. 2004. "Lend an Ear to Q-Tip: Hip-Hopper Works Crowds for Rock the Vote." *Los Angeles Times*, February 8.

Rosenblum, Nancy. 1998a. "Compelled Associations." In *Freedom of Association*. Ed. Amy Gutmann. Princeton, NJ: Princeton University Press.

———. 1998b. *Membership and Morals: The Personal Uses of Pluralism in America*. Princeton, NJ: Princeton University Press.

Rosenstone, Steven J., and John Mark Hansen. 1993. *Mobilization, Participation, and Democracy in America*. New Topics in Politics. New York: Macmillan.

Rousseau, Jean-Jacques. 1960. *Politics and the Arts, Letter to M. D'Alembert on the Theatre*. Trans. Allan Bloom. Glencoe, IL: Free Press.

———. 1968. *The Social Contract*. Trans. Maurice William Cranston. Penguin Classics. London; New York: Penguin Books.

———. 1992. *The Reveries of the Solitary Walker*. Trans. Charles Butterworth. Indianapolis: Hackett.

Sabl, Andrew. 2002a. "Community Organizing as Tocquevillean Politics: The Art, Practice and Ethos of Association." *American Journal of Political Science* 46 (January): 1–19.

———. 2002b. *Ruling Passions: Political Offices and Democratic Ethics*. Princeton, NJ: Princeton University Press.

———. 2005a. "Deliberation in Its Place." *Election Law Journal* 4 (April): 147–52.

———. 2005b. "Virtue for Pluralists." *Journal of Moral Philosophy* 2, no. 2: 207–35.

Salkever, Stephen G. 2005. "Aristotle's Social Science." In *Aristotle's Politics: Critical Essays*. Ed. Richard Kraut and Steven Skultety, 27–64. New York: Rowman and Littlefield.

Sandel, Michael J. 1996. *Democracy's Discontent: America in Search of a Public Philosophy*. Cambridge, MA: Belknap Press of Harvard University Press.

———. 2004. "Introduction." In *Liberalism and Its Critics*. Ed. Michael J. Sandel. New York: New York University Press.

Sartori, Giovanni. 1970. "Concept Misinformation in Comparative Politics." *American Political Science Review* 64, no. 4.

Schattschneider, E. E. 1960. *The Semisovereign People: A Realist's View of Democracy in America*. New York: Holt, Rinehart and Winston.

Schmitter, Philippe. 1995. "More Liberal, Preliberal, or Postliberal?" *Journal of Democracy* 6, no. 1: 15–22.

Schonfeld, William R. 1975. "The Meaning of Democratic Participation." *World Politics* 28 (October): 134–58.

Schor, Juliet. 1991. *The Overworked American: The Unexpected Decline of Leisure*. New York: Basic Books.

Schudson, Michael. 1996. "What If Civic Life Didn't Die?" *American Prospect* (Winter): 18–27.

———. 1998. *The Good Citizen: A History of American Civic Life*. New York: Martin Kessler Books.

Schumpeter, Joseph Alois. 1942. *Capitalism, Socialism, and Democracy*. New York: Harper.

Schwartz, Barry. 2004. *The Paradox of Choice: Why More Is Less*. New York: HarperCollins.

Sennett, Richard. 1977. *The Fall of Public Man*. 1st ed. New York: Knopf.

Shaftesbury, Anthony Ashley Cooper, with Philip Ayres. 1999. *Characteristics of Men, Manners, Opinions, Times*. 2 vols. New York: Oxford University Press.

Shakespeare, William. 1970. *King Lear*. Trans. Alfred Harbage. Rev. ed. Baltimore: Penguin Books.

———. 2006. *As You Like It*. Trans. Juliet Dusinberre. London: Arden Shakespeare.

Shephard, R. J., and F. Trudeau. 2000. "The Legacy of Physical Education: Influences on Adult Lifestyle." *Pediatric Exercise Science* 12.

Shirley, Dennis. 1997. *Community Organizing for Urban School Reform*. Austin: University of Texas Press.

Shklar, Judith N. 1984. *Ordinary Vices*. Cambridge, MA: Belknap Press of Harvard University Press.

Shklar, Judith N., and Stanley Hoffmann. 1998. *Political Thought and Political Thinkers*. Chicago: University of Chicago Press.

Shumer, Robert. 1997. "What Research Tells Us about Designing Service Learning Programs." *National Association of Secondary School Principals Bulletin* 81 (October).

Siegler, Dylan. 1997. "Rock the Vote Still Rolling." *Billboard*, December 6.

Silver, Nate. 2010. "Understanding and Misunderstanding the 'Enthusiasm Gap.'" *New York Times*, October 6.

Sirianni, Carmen, and Lewis Friedland. 2001. *Civic Innovation in America: Community Empowerment, Public Policy, and the Movement for Civic Renewal.* Berkeley: University of California Press.

Skocpol, Theda. 1997a. "America's Voluntary Groups Thrive in a Civic Network." *Brookings Review* 15 (Fall).

———. 1997b. "The Tocqueville Problem: Civic Engagement in American Democracy." *Social Science History* 21 (Winter): 25.

———. 1999. "How Americans Became Civic." In *Civic Engagement in American Democracy.* Ed. Theda Skocpol and Morris P. Fiorina. Washington, DC; New York: Brookings Institution Press.

———. 2003. *Diminished Democracy.* Norman: University of Oklahoma Press.

Skocpol, Theda, and Morris P. Fiorina. 1999. *Civic Engagement in American Democracy.* Washington, DC; New York: Brookings Institution Press.

Smith, Aaron. 2009. "Civic Engagement Online: Politics as Usual." Pew Internet and American Life Project, September 1, http://pewresearch.org/pubs/1328/online-political-civic-engagement-activity.

Smith, Jackie. 1998. "Global Civil Society?" *American Behavioral Scientist* 42 (September): 15.

Somin, Ilya. 1998. "Voter Ignorance and the Democratic Ideal." *Critical Review* 12 (Autumn): 46.

Somit, Albert. 1948. "The Military Hero as Presidential Candidate." *Public Opinion Quarterly* 12 (Summer): 192–200.

Staff. 1988. "Dog Ears." *Melbourne Herald Sun*, 1.

Stanton, Timothy K., Dwight E. Giles Jr., and Nadine Cruz. 1999. *Service Learning: A Movement's Pioneers Reflect on Its Origins, Practice, and Future.* Indianapolis: Jossey-Bass.

Stolle, Dietland, and Thomas R. Rochon. 1998. "Are All Associations Alike?" *American Behavioral Scientist* (September): 19.

Strolovitch, Dara Z. 2007. *Affirmative Advocacy: Race, Class, and Gender in Interest Group Politics.* Chicago: University of Chicago Press.

Stukas, A. A., M. Snyder, and E. G. Clary. 1999. "The Effects of 'Mandatory Volunteerism' on Intentions to Volunteer." *Psychological Science* 10, no. 1: 59–64.

Summers, Harrison Boyd. 1971. *A Thirty-Year History of Programs Carried on National Radio Networks in the United States, 1926–1956.* New York: Arno Press.

Tamir, Yael. 1998. "Revisiting the Civic Sphere." In *Freedom of Association.* Ed. Amy Gutmann. Princeton, NJ: Princeton University Press.

Taylor, Charles. 1989. *Sources of the Self: The Making of the Modern Identity.* Cambridge, MA: Harvard University Press.

Thompson, Dennis. 1970. *The Democratic Citizen: Social Science and Democratic Theory in the Twentieth Century.* London: Cambridge University Press.

Tillotson, Kristin. 2006. "Beyond Brokeback: Gay-Cinema Fests Can Now Reach around the Globe, but They Face New Challenges." *Minneapolis Star-Tribune*, June 18.

Tocqueville, Alexis de. 1969. *Democracy in America.* Trans. George Lawrence. Ed. J. P. Mayer. New York: HarperPerennial Modern Classics.

——. 1997. *Memoir on Pauperism*. Trans. Seymour Drescher. Chicago: Ivan R. Dee.

——. 1998. *The Old Regime and the Revolution*. Trans. Alan S. Kahan. Ed. François Furet and Françoise Mélonio. Chicago: University of Chicago Press.

——. 2002. *The Tocqueville Reader*. Ed. Olivier Zunz and Alan S. Kahan. Oxford: Blackwell.

Tönnies, Ferdinand. 2002. *Community and Society*: Mineola, NY: Dover Publications.

Torry, Saundra. 1996. "The Paper Chase Slows Down, Here and Nationally." *Washington Post*, June 10.

Tsao, Roy. 2002. "Arendt against Athens." *Political Theory* 30, no. 1.

Turkle, Sherry. 1995. *Life on the Screen: Identity in the Age of the Internet*. New York: Simon and Schuster.

Uslaner, Eric. 1999. "Trust but Verify: Social Capital and Moral Behavior." *Social Science Information* 38, no. 1: 29–55.

——. 2005. "Political Parties *and* Social Capital, Political Parties *or* Social Capital." In *Handbook of Political Parties*. Ed. Richard S. Katz and Willam Crotty. London: Sage Publications.

——. 2006. "Political Parties *and* Social Capital, Political Parties *or* Social Capital?" In *Handbook of Party Politics*. Ed. Richard S. Katz and William Crotty. Thousand Oaks, CA: Sage Publications.

Valelly, Richard M. 1996. "Couch Potato Democracy?" *American Prospect* (Winter): 17–27.

Van Deth, Jan, ed. 1999. *Social Capital and European Democracy*. New York: Routledge.

Verba, Sidney, Kay Lehman Schlozman, and Henry E. Brady. 1995. *Voice and Equality: Civic Voluntarism in American Politics*. Cambridge, MA: Harvard University Press.

Villa, Dana Richard. 1996. *Arendt and Heidegger: The Fate of the Political*. Princeton, NJ: Princeton University Press.

——. 2001. *Socratic Citizenship*. Princeton, NJ: Princeton University Press.

——. 2008. *Public Freedom*. Princeton, NJ: Princeton University Press.

Viroli, Maurizio. 1995. *For Love of Country: An Essay on Patriotism and Nationalism*. New York: Clarendon Press.

Walzer, Michael. 1983. *Spheres of Justice: A Defense of Pluralism and Equality*. New York: Basic Books.

——. 1992. "The Civil Society Argument." In *Dimensions of Radical Democracy: Pluralism, Citizenship, Community*. Ed. Chantal Mouffe. London; New York: Verso.

Ward, Kelly, and Lisa Wolf-Wendel. 2000. "Community-Centered Service Learning: Moving From Doing For to Doing With." *American Behavioral Scientist* 43 (February): 767–80.

Warren, Mark E. 2001. *Democracy and Association*. Princeton, NJ: Princeton University Press.

Warren, Mark R. 2001. *Dry Bones Rattling*. Princeton, NJ: Princeton University Press.

Wattenberg, Martin P. 2007. *Is Voting for Young People?* London: Longman.

Weaver, James H., Michael T. Rock, and Kenneth Kusterer. 1997. *Achieving Broad-Based Sustainable Development: Governance, Environment, and Growth with Equity*. West Hartford, CT: Kumarian Press.

Weber, Max. 2007. *From Max Weber: Essays in Sociology*. Ed. H. H. Gerth. New York: Routledge.

Weeks, Edward. 2000. "The Practice of Deliberative Democracy: Results from Four Large-Scale Trials." *Public Administration Review* 60 (July/August): 13.

Weitz-Shapiro, Rebecca, and Matthew S. Winters. 2008. "Political Participation and Quality of Life." Inter-American Development Bank, Working Paper #638.

Wellhofer, E. Spencer. 2005. "Democracy, Fascism, and Civil Society." In *Democracy and the Role of Associations: Political, Organizational, and Social Contexts*. Ed. Sigrid Rossteutscher. New York: Routledge.

Williams, Bernard. 1996. "Toleration: An Impossible Virtue?" In *Toleration: An Elusive Virtue*. Ed. David Heyd. Princeton, NJ: Princeton University Press.

Williams, Melissa S. 2000. *Voice, Trust, and Memory: Marginalized Groups and the Failings of Liberal Representation*. Princeton, NJ: Princeton University Press.

Wittgenstein, Ludwig. 1968. *Philosophical Investigations*. Trans. G.E.M. Anscombe. Oxford: Basil Blackwell.

Wolfe, Alan. 1998. *One Nation after All: What Middle Class Americans Really Think about God, Country, Family, Racism, Welfare, Immigration, Homosexuality, Work, the Right, the Left, and Each Other*. New York: Viking.

Wolin, Sheldon. 1983. "Hannah Arendt: Democracy and the Political." *Salmagundi* 60: 17. Reprinted in *Hannah Arendt: Critical Essays*. Ed. Lewis and Sandra Hinchman. Albany: State University of New York Press, 1994.

———. 2004. *Politics and Vision: Continuity and Innovation in Western Political Thought*. Expanded ed. Princeton, NJ: Princeton University Press.

———. 2008. *Democracy Incorporated: Managed Democracy and the Specter of Inverted Totalitarianism*. Princeton, NJ: Princeton University Press.

Wuthnow, Robert. 1996. *Sharing the Journey: Support Groups and America's New Quest for Community*. 1st Free Press paperback ed. New York: Free Press. Distributed by Simon and Schuster.

Yack, Bernard. 1993. *The Problems of a Political Animal: Community, Justice, and Conflict in Aristotelian Political Thought*. Berkeley: University of California Press.

Yates, Heather. 2008. "Comparing Political Participation in Compulsory and Non-Compulsory Voting Systems." Paper presented at the annual meeting of the Southern Political Science Association, January 9, New Orleans, LA.

Young-Bruehl, Elisabeth. 1982. *For Love of the World: A Biography of Hannah Arendt*. New Haven, CT: Yale University Press.

Zaller, John. 1992. *The Nature and Origins of Mass Opinion*. Cambridge; New York: Cambridge University Press.

Zaretsky, Eli. 1997. "Hannah Arendt and the Meaning of the Public/Private Distinction." In *Hannah Arendt and the Meaning of Politics*. Ed. Craig Calhoun and John McGowan. Minneapolis: University of Minnesota Press.

Zukin, Cliff, Scott Keeter, Molly Andolina, Krista Jenkins, and Michael X. Delli Carpini. 2006. *A New Engagement? Political Participation, Civic Life, and the Changing American Citizen*. New York: Oxford University Press.

Zunz, Olivier, and Alan S. Kahan, eds. 2002. *The Tocqueville Reader*. Oxford: Blackwell.

INDEX

Note: Page numbers in *italics* indicate figures; those with a *t* indicate tables.